NEVER

SAY

SELL

NEVER SAY SELL

How the World's Best Consulting and Professional Services Firms Expand Client Relationships

TOM McMAKIN

JACOB PARKS

WILEY

Copyright © 2021 by Tom McMakin and Jacob Parks. All rights reserved.

Published by John Wiley & Sons, Inc., Hoboken, New Jersey.
Published simultaneously in Canada.

For general information on our other products and services or for technical support, please contact our Customer Care Department within the United States at (800) 762-2974, outside the United States at (317) 572-3993 or fax (317) 572-4002.

Wiley publishes in a variety of print and electronic formats and by print-on-demand. Some material included with standard print versions of this book may not be included in e-books or in print-on-demand. If this book refers to media such as a CD or DVD that is not included in the version you purchased, you may download this material at http://booksupport.wiley.com. For more information about Wiley products, visit www.wiley.com.

Library of Congress Cataloging-in-Publication Data is Available

ISBN 9781119683780 (Hardcover)

ISBN 9781119684169 (ePDF)

ISBN 9781119683803 (ePub)

Cover Design: Wiley
Author Photos: Carlie Auger

Printed in the United States of America

SKY10021286_091720

*Tom dedicates this book to his parents, Dave and Jackie.
Thank you for everything.
Jacob dedicates this book to his wife, Amy, who displays courage,
grace, and kindness in the face of arduous challenges.*

Contents

Foreword   *ix*

Why We Never Say Sell

Section 1: Who We Are and the Problems We Want to Solve   3

1   From Foothold to Footprint   5

Section 2: The Imperative and the Opportunity   15

2   Learning to Farm   17
3   The Diamond of Opportunity   26

Section 3: The Challenges   41

4   The Challenge of Knowing Too Much about the Wrong Thing   43
5   The Challenge of Complex Organizations   52
6   The Challenge of Serving Complex Networks   57
7   The Challenge of Introducing Your Colleagues   66
8   The Challenge of Scale   71

How We Can Help

Section 4: Farming for Knowledge   85

9   Know Thyself   87

10   Know Thy Client   101

11   The Secrets of Diamond Account Planning   111

Section 5: The Seven Disciplines of Successful Farming   119

12   Discipline 1: Do Good Work   121

13   Discipline 2: Be a Good Friend   138

14   Discipline 3: Leverage Your Team   150

15   Discipline 4: Incent Good Work   157

16   Discipline 5: Listen   165

17   Discipline 6: Tell Great Stories   169

18   Discipline 7: Master the Art of the Ask   176

Section 6: Seeds of Change   185

19   The Power of Peers   187

20   The Power of Routers   197

21   The Power of Technology   207

22   The Power of Experience and Insight   217

Further Reading   223

Acknowledgments   225

About the Authors   227

Index   229

Foreword

A Place in Time

Outside, a new day dawns in the east, the sky daubed with great washes of purple and orange. It is May 1st, and today is the day our manuscript is due. We are just putting our final touches on the draft, numbering pages, and adding in the endnotes as puffed-up robins strut through the newly green grass.

Yet on what should be a day of celebration, we feel somewhat melancholy; the moment is stained by the COVID-19 pandemic that hangs over the world like a shroud.

We don't have to tell you – the news washes over us every day in unrelenting waves from all corners. Healthcare workers are overtaxed. There's not enough personal protective equipment. There's more death. It is a sobering time – a time when all of us have our heads down and are just a little more focused on our work, if we are lucky enough to be decamped at our kitchen tables taking Zoom calls.

It is against this backdrop that this project has taken on a fresh urgency for us. During a time when our institutions and mores are being stressed, we need the help of smart people to navigate through and beyond our current raft of challenges. To us, this is the essence of why we have written this book – to help all of us build more durable bridges between our experience and insight and the challenges that this expertise can help.

Although we're not on the front lines with the nurses in Queens or the ER doctors in Kirkland, we should still be asking ourselves each day, "How can we help?" As experts of all different stripes, there is a need for the solutions we offer; the world needs all of us to lean in more.

We hope you find this book useful – not only to help build back any prosperity you may have lost in this crisis, but, more importantly, to think anew about how your unique background, skillset, and wisdom can help your clients architect a brighter future for their communities and their customers.

Thanks for picking up this book. Stay safe.

Tom and Jacob

NEVER SAY SELL

Why We Never Say Sell

Walt Shill looked around the room at his client team. He had gathered them from far reaches of the globe to review Accenture's previous year's work with a major client with an eye for how they might increase their mandate over the next year. As they reviewed the different elements of the business that could benefit from Accenture's skillset, a handful of suggestions were made by team members with a deep understanding of this client's business model (supply chain optimization, back-office centralization, and a new technology for budgeting, to name a few) when, abruptly, the brainstorming was interrupted by one member of the team who said, "What are we doing here? We don't want to be ambulance chasers!"

Shill, a passionate man, erupted.

> "What are you talking about? We *are* the fucking ambulance! If you don't think we can help people and that we can add value, then you need to look for another job. We have a moral obligation to use our skills to solve their problems."

Our observation, after a collective 50-plus years in expert services, is that there is a strong correlation between expert services and aversion to what is perceived as selling. Interestingly, it seems to grow stronger as you move into job descriptions that require unique degrees or certifications, such as the legal or accounting professions. A photo on a bus bench might be effective for a realtor, but it would be unimaginable for a top-tier attorney. Somehow, we think if we are good, the world should beat a path to our door. But the truth is that experts should feel a moral obligation to assist clients in need: We should *be* the ambulance when our clients need help.

1

Section 1: Who We Are and the Problems We Want to Solve

1

From Foothold to Footprint

We're jetting back and forth across the country visiting clients. It's Friday afternoon, and we are looking forward to finally spending a weekend at home. Jacob, the younger of us, is thinking about the prospect of winning Spokane's Hoopfest for the third year in a row with his in-laws. Tom is dreaming about scouting for elk in southwestern Montana in preparation for hunting season.

We are coming off a two-day string of meetings in Manhattan with clients and prospects. It's been a fast-paced and satisfying trip, but as we contemplate our travel home, with the long layover and dozens of follow-up emails from our last two days, we both let out a sigh.

Tom's wearing a blue suit, print tie, and black lace-up shoes. Jacob's sporting a natty charcoal suit, no tie, and brown shoes with green argyle socks. Two business-people, each with varying degrees of gray hair, pushing our way through LaGuardia on our way home.

We duck into the bathroom at the east end of the terminal, and change from our suits into jeans, comfortable shoes, and sweaters for flight back home. Tom is headed to Bozeman while Jacob will part ways with him in Salt Lake City and head home to Spokane.

There are certain rules to changing at the airport. Don't pick a stall without a hook, don't take off your socks, and don't put the roller board on the toilet seat or it won't stop flushing.

Like you, we're road warriors, crisscrossing the country in service of our clients. Our particular expertise is helping expert services firms drive business development, but we could equally be accountants, human resources specialists, attorneys, software integrators, engineers, strategy consultants, or cybersecurity wizards.

We all share one thing in common: We are fellow travelers in the land of building trust and credibility in an effort to sell our expertise. We recognize problems in client companies and help them meet those challenges. This work looks different across the spectrum of professional services, but the work all aims to accomplish the same outcome for clients: to innovate, to solve, to create, and to build.

The Economist recently wrote that consultants "scare companies by laying bare where they are failing, then soothe them with counsel on how to improve." We don't agree with the "scaring" part – that sounds like the kind of sales manipulation we hate – but we do know that expert services providers work to help improve their clients. As experts, we offer our experience, our point of view, our intelligence, our training, and the bitter lessons we have learned from doing what we do for many years.

The Question

This book is a sequel of sorts to a book Tom wrote with Doug Fletcher called *How Clients Buy: A Practical Guide to Business Development for Consulting and Professional Services*. In that book, we asked the question,

What's the secret to winning new work in professional services?

We interviewed rainmakers at leading legal, consulting, engineering, and financial services firms to learn more about the process of how clients engage with expert services providers. We learned a lot, but the book wasn't out long before many of you wrote us to say: What we're *really* interested in is expanding our relationships with our *current* clients. How do we do that?

This feedback isn't surprising. When we ask expert services providers how much of their year-over-year growth in revenues comes from new logos versus expanded assignments, they report new work with existing clients represents an astonishing 80% to 90% of new revenues. We see those same numbers at our company, Profitable Ideas Exchange (PIE™). In the short run, at least, expanding current relationships represents a much larger opportunity than cold calling new prospects.

Sometimes we hear rainmakers talk about how they work to "land and expand" a client. If *How Clients Buy* gave us landing lessons, *Never Say Sell* describes how to *expand*, asking a simple question,

What's the secret to growing your work within clients?

Expert Services Are Different

In *How Clients Buy*, we learned that expert services are bought differently than, say, a laptop. Tom and his wife, Mary, just bought a new family computer and landed on a Lenovo X1 (on sale at Costco with 16 GB of RAM!). They did the research, comparing processor speed, reliability tests, weight, size, color, storage capacity, and price. They relied on *PC Magazine*'s side-by-side descriptions, building out a matrix that laid out various laptops' key qualities. Then they compared the qualities that were most important to each of them. Mary wanted something light and fast; Tom wanted something that would last for years. Both agreed they would mostly use it for email and the Internet.

Tom and Mary ranked several machines they identified against their priorities, narrowing the choices and easily making the final decision. This approach to buying, call it the "Excel-driven comparative shopping method," is the way we buy cars, phones, and air travel as we seek to balance features and attributes in the search for a good fit with our needs and budget.

That's *not* how we buy expert services, however. Expert services are bought on reputation, referral, and relationships, not features and attributes or even price.

As Michael McLaughlin has written, "What sets service providers apart from other sellers is that (we) are first and foremost idea merchants."

For example, imagine your parents have retired to the coral beaches of Naples, Florida. They are of an age where it doesn't make sense for them to do their taxes (they can't remember where they put their car keys, much less whether their K-1 income qualifies for a 20% deduction this year). They call you one day and say, "Can you help us find someone down here who can do our taxes?"

You don't have any idea whom you should use. There's no *PC Magazine* that ranks Floridian tax accountants and no online grid that balances services against price and quality. You fly down to see them at Thanksgiving, take a Lyft to the graduated assisted living facility, and spot a billboard on the side of the road that says, "McMakin and Parks: Collier County's Smartest CPAs." You chuckle because that is a bold and somewhat ridiculous claim.

You pick up a brochure in the lobby of their living facility. It proclaims, "Dewey, Cheatum, and Howe: Paradise Coast's Cheapest CPAs." You chuckle again.

That's not what you are looking for. You want a good tax accountant, not to take the last penny off the table. Indeed, you find yourself wondering if there might be an inverse relationship between the price an expert services provider charges and perceived quality. After all, a $1,500-per-hour San Francisco attorney is thought to be better than one that charges $150 per hour.

In the end, you call a friend from college who works at Ernst & Young out of the Miami office and ask if they could recommend a CPA in Naples?

They say something like, "I do cross-border work, so I'm not your guy, but I have a partner here whose little sister graduated a couple of years ago from the University of Texas in Austin at the top of her class. She's got a small firm in Fort Myers, and it has a great reputation. In fact, she is doing taxes for some of the partners who have retired. I'll introduce you."

Bam. You're done. No spreadsheet. No ranking of features or processor speed. Just reputation, referral, and relationship. That's how clients buy expertise.

Growing Your Work: How Hard Can It Be?

Doing more work for a client with whom we have already worked should be easy. Once we have completed a project for a client, opportunities should start pooling at our feet like puddles after a spring shower. We've built credibility by delivering good work and trust in our relationships. We think of *credibility* – delivering good work – and *trust* – building strong relationships – as the two bulwarks of a productive consulting relationship and we've now cemented both. Our client has other things they need help with and where our expertise would be useful. The phone should be ringing off the hook.

Maybe, but maybe not.

We'll use PIE as an example. When we joined forces 10 years ago as CEO and COO, the company had a single client that accounted for 95% of revenues. That worried us a lot, so we turned all our attention to winning new clients.

Today, our biggest client represents a fifth of the firm's revenues. The rest comes from the new accounts the team has brought on. Our theory was that if we could establish a meaningful presence in these new accounts – most of which are multibillion-dollar companies – future growth would be easy. In a kind of Ray Kinsella – inspired *Field of Dreams* strategy, we thought, "if we build it, they will come."

But that didn't always happen.

Add-on work didn't magically appear. We've had to fight for it. One of our oldest projects, for example – a $140,000 recurring annual program – with a client that is a $14 billion information services firm, failed to grow itself. The client was delighted with our work and asked us back to the dance every year, but not one of their 44,000 employees ever called us up and asked us to do this same work in other parts of the business.

Likewise, PIE has worked for a large IT integration firm for 15 years, aggregating groups of chief financial officers, chief information officers, and chief operating officers. Five years ago, the client pivoted and announced that it was focused on helping chief digital officers navigate disruption and transformation. Did it call PIE and ask us to pull together groups of chief digital officers? No. This, despite the fact they know we do good work, they trust us, and we have a long record of high ROI performance.

We began to suspect there were structural, systemic reasons that expanding one's work within a client is difficult. Our readers from *How Clients Buy* agreed:

> I took an early retirement package from a global energy company and decided to set up a consulting practice. I was one of the leading experts in negotiating sub-Saharan oil field exploration contracts and figured, with everyone I knew in the industry, it would be easy for me to do this work on a consulting basis with Exxon Mobil, BP, and the other big players. Soon I was hiring MBAs to help execute on the various projects I'd secured. Somewhere around 20 people, though, our growth plateaued. We're doing work with all the upstream majors, based largely on my network, but the nut we can't crack is doing more work inside a client company. I've talked to my friends at the big consulting firms, and they say most of their new revenues came from existing clients. What do they know that we don't?

> I was excited to take over the cybersecurity practice at my firm, one of the Big Four. We have a great brand name in an exploding space. My boss came in July and said, "I need your next year's revenue estimates. We have a firm-wide goal of 12%." I think I must have blanched. I'm just not sure I know how to expand our footprint in the client.

Do You Sell Pies?

Every month or two someone walks into our office and asks what types of fresh pie we have and, sadly, we have to turn them away empty-handed. We do in fact sell a service we internally refer to as a *PIE*, just not the type these buyers are looking for; ours are executive peer groups of our clients' likely buyers, whom we convene for ongoing, targeted discussions – not fresh rhubarb inside a buttery, layered crust.

We land squarely in the world of expert services. We *provide* our expertise – business development support, primarily via facilitated executive peer exchange – to clients who are *also* in the expert services business. As Tom's son, Wilson, likes to say, "My dad's a consultant to consultants – he's a meta-consultant." This typically gets a bit of a laugh from his college friends.

Because of this niche we have carved out for ourselves in assisting expert services firms in business development, we spend our professional and free time thinking not only about how we can grow our own business, but also about how we can help clients grow their businesses. Our collective experience, working on behalf of many of the largest consulting, technology, and accounting firms around the world, gives us a unique perspective. Between us, we have 50-plus years of experience in this industry, providing countless stories and relationships from which to draw.

The Promise of *Never Say Sell*

The world is full of thorny problems made worse by growing complexity. It can feel overwhelming. The good news, however, is that, increasingly, we are a planet populated by educated, strongly experienced experts able to address these challenges.

The trick is to learn how to connect challenges with those who can best help solve them – to make the world smarter and smaller. When we shrink the world by wiring us all together in collaboration and connection, we make the world stronger, safer, and more stable.

None of that happens, however, unless we speak up and learn not to "hide our light under a bushel," particularly with clients who already know we are good people and are able to create value. Our job must be to spot opportunities and build on our track record of delivering excellent work to do even more work, time and time again.

This book will unpack the question of how to do this. Our method was simple; we asked leading rainmakers how they deepen engagement with clients and scope more work in order to understand the approaches they used in finding success, assuming, of course, that the client has needs with which they could help. Like Gretel dropping crumbs of bread on the trail, we knew that achievement in business development would leave clues, and that if we followed those clues, we too could grow our clients two-, five-, and tenfold.

A Roadmap for the Book

This book is divided into two parts. In Part I, "Why We Never Say Sell," we begin with the opportunity and the challenge. We describe the space open to us as expert services providers to grow our footprint within a client and then the five challenges that explain why this kind of new work doesn't come to us more naturally. It is here that we introduce the Diamond of Opportunity, six distinct ways in which rainmakers describe increasing the amount of work they do with clients. We also review the seven elements that must be present before a client is prepared to buy: the elements of awareness, understanding, interest, credibility, trust, ability, and readiness. We explain why these elements apply differently to winning work with a new client versus growing work with an existing client.

In Part II, "How We Can Help," we dive into account planning and the sorts of questions you should be asking in preparation for making a plan. We also describe the seven disciplines of a master farmer, focusing on the practices as well as the tools for breaking beyond existing work to grow within a client. We break down each of the seven disciplines that underpin successful growth: Do good work, be a good friend, leverage your team, incent good work, listen, tell great stories, and master the art of the ask. Finally, we discuss some of the implications of what we have written for expert service firms' business development organizations and how technology will drive change and empower more effective engagement with clients.

A Word about Words

Walt Shill is the head of business development for the worldwide environmental and sustainability consulting firm, ERM. Previously, he managed the North American strategy practice for Accenture, and before that was a partner at McKinsey. Early in our process of writing this book, Jacob asked him, "How are expert services sold?" Walt was spending his Saturday afternoon relaxing in his flower garden at his home in Reston, Virginia.

"Jacob," he said, "never say *sell*. Consulting isn't sold. We're trusted advisors to our clients."

Walt explained that, as expert services providers, we're there to be of assistance as our clients work to achieve their business goals.

Scott Wallace, an attorney at Perkins Coie, agrees: "We never talk about sales at the firm. I don't think I have ever heard the words 'make a sale,' or 'sales.' You do hear the term 'business development,' but not 'sales.'"

Expert service providers don't sell. We work with people to solve problems.

We like words, so one of our first questions was, "Is 'business development' a euphemism for 'sales,' propagated by white-shoe consultants afraid of being lumped in with car salespeople? Or is it something different?"

We think the two terms are different. The definition of *sales*, to our mind, is the act of exchanging goods based on an agreed-upon price. Salespeople thrive in the world of transactions. After all, when we purchase a computer, a car, or a house, we are measuring the merits and relative comparisons on fixed attributes. A satisfying transaction can include transparency and civility, but it is not contingent on trust or long-term relationships. "Salespeople" often carry a negative association because they're thought of as those who jump at the chance to take advantage of information asymmetries. The car salesperson knows what they bought the car for and where there are opportunities to upsell you after the sale on extended warranties, low APR loans with high fees, and undercarriage protection. The buyer does not.

By contrast, we think business development is about establishing relationships and listening to clients. It is contingent upon a baseline of trust and credibility, both of which grow as you consistently deliver good work and add value in collaboration.

Economists talk about expert services as being a "credence good." *Credence* comes from the Latin word, *credere*, which means "to give trust to." A client gives you their trust before they engage with you. Why? Because you know more than they do.

When we hire a cybersecurity firm to protect us from intrusion, their experts know more about cyber-threats and defenses than we ever will. That puts them in a position of power in their relationship with us: They are both diagnosing the problem and making recommendations. Once they peek under the hood of our network, a cyber protection firm might say, we will need to erect a cloud-based firewall monitored by a 24/7 operations desk. Alternatively, they may simply say Windows Defender is fine. We wouldn't know the difference.

That's one of the signal differences concerning goods that are sold on features and attributes like Tom's family's computer and expert services. With goods, we can diagnose the problem. The old laptop is slow, has no battery life left, and weighs more than a three-year-old. When cash loosens up, Tom and Mary decide they need to fix that problem. But with expert services, it's different: We need to trust the provider to tell us the truth about the problem and then right-size a solution.

And so, goods are sold, but expert services are not. With goods, it's helpful to have someone (the salesperson) explain the features and attributes and make comparative claims against the competition. With services, the secret is not in telling but rather in listening. Only by listening do we uncover opportunities where our skills and the trust we have built with clients align and produce mutual opportunity.

To Sell or Not to Sell?

This is why we hate the word *upselling* in connection to expanding our engagement with a client. Saying "May I supersize that for you, Ma'am?" smacks of manipulation and the power of hidden suggestion.

Cross-selling, too, is a word often found in books written about how to more deeply engage with clients. The problem is we are not sure what *cross-selling* means, exactly. When we cross-sell, are we offering different capabilities to a client, or are we offering the same capabilities across the client organization to different buyers within that organization?

Rather than borrowing words from the world of product sales that are not a perfect fit with expert services, let's start over and actually describe what we are trying to do.

What if we flipped the questions "How should we upsell?" and "How can we cross-sell?" to the much simpler "How can we help?" Even that simple word change invites a mental shift away from a transaction and toward a relationship that looks more like a friendship, encouraging us to imagine what we would do if our client's well-being was our highest priority, which – returning to Walt – is exactly our job.

A couple of additional thoughts about language: We think about ourselves being part of a profession that includes consultants, accountants, lawyers, engineers, and strategists. Rather than repeat that long string, we will refer to those in our profession as "experts" or "expert services providers." These will serve as umbrella terms to describe those who, like us, offer services built on trust and credibility.

Finally, in addition to the interviews we conducted for this book, we've decided to tell some of our own stories. These stories reflect our collective experience, and they are based on real people and companies we have worked with over the past 25 years. Some names and identifying details of the individuals and companies involved have been changed.

Enough preamble, though, let's dig in.

Section 2: The Imperative and the Opportunity

2

Learning to Farm

Charlie Mercer was a Blue Devil from before he could remember:

I grew up in Raleigh, and it was a lifelong dream to go to Duke.

A natural athlete in high school, tall and broad-shouldered, Charlie played first baseman on the baseball team and forward on the basketball squad while getting good grades, being in band, and participating in student government – the picture of the well-rounded student.

"It's unbelievable what young people accomplish these days," Charlie says from his office in the Research Triangle. "They invent something or distinguish themselves in some big way before they even get to college. That wasn't me. I was good at a lot of things but not exceptional at any one thing."

At Duke, he served as vice president of his fraternity and played in a band called "The Facebook All Stars" while majoring in public policy.

"There's a common theme here," he says. "Public policy covered everything from economics and leadership to classes on nonprofits and political science. It was the ability to study all sorts of things that drew me into that major."

In other words, Charlie was ripe to be picked up by a consulting firm after graduation, where the ability to walk into any setting, see patterns, and make a connection with clients is highly prized, and where the ability to lead a team is an important rung on the career ladder.

His first job was with The Advisory Board, after which he joined Stockamp & Associates, a consulting firm that concentrated on healthcare consulting and, specifically, revenue cycle process improvements. Later, the firm was acquired by Huron Consulting.

His strong work at Stockamp earned him a place at North Carolina's Kenan-Flagler School of Business where he got his MBA, joining Deloitte after graduation.

Commenting on his move to Deloitte, Charlie explains,

At Stockamp, we often did the same thing over and over again. After my first year at business school, I interned at a private equity firm. I loved how every day was different. So, it's no surprise I ended up back in consulting, but at a firm where I could explore different industries and work on different projects. When I was at Deloitte, I joined the Strategy and Operations group where I worked on strategy, M&A, and process improvement projects. I was exposed to different types of business problems and saw how those problems compared across industries.

Like a duck in water, Charlie thrived at Deloitte:

Right out of undergraduate, they call you an analyst, but I was hired out of business school. If you do that, they call you a senior consultant. You aren't yet a project manager because you haven't proven yourself. We thought of it as a two-year apprenticeship, but maybe it was a two-year trial! Every project you work on is different. You might be doing analyst work on one project. On another, you might be managing an analyst and responsible for a workstream.

Grinders, Minders, and Finders

In consulting, there are grinders, minders, and finders: those who do the work, those who manage others doing the work, and those who land new work for others to manage. For two years, Charlie was a *grinder*, trundling from project to project – deep in the salt mines of large projects, *doing* the work.

But because of that work, and his ability to do it well, he was quickly promoted to manager. He says, "My job as manager was to lead projects. A partner would sell a project and define its scope. As a manager, I'd be responsible for corralling the team and getting them pointed in the right direction to make sure the scope was delivered and it was to the client's liking."

That's when Deloitte sent him to Deloitte University in Westlake, Texas, where he and his fellow newly minted project managers learned how to set expectations with those on their teams and how to manage them in a way that produced results. They learned how to be *minders*.

Charlie quickly learned it was important to build his brand within the firm. He says, "You need to become known for something. Be the go-to person for the firm on a specific subject and develop a track record of excellent delivery with a handful of partners. As they sell more, they will request you to run their projects, and, over time, they will begin to fold you into the business development process."

Charlie was being groomed to be a *finder*. He explains, "The partner's job on a project is to manage the project as a whole and to ensure the client's needs are met. As I worked with several partners, they began to trust me more, and I got more and more responsibility, including exposure to business development."

Partners would use Charlie to help prepare decks, do research on a proposed project, and join them in presenting to clients. He wasn't expected to drive business development, yet, so much as to absorb what he saw by osmosis.

Charlie recalls, "Working on a proposal with a partner led to me being staffed on that project. I was absolutely incentivized to do a good job on the proposal, but I was not incentivized or rewarded if that proposal turned into a sale. That went to the partner."

Charlie left Deloitte before taking the next step – a promotion to senior manager, deciding instead to co-found Capstone Event Group, a firm that manages running races (Capstone just added San Francisco's Bay to Breakers franchise to their growing stable). As Charlie describes it, his firm "has been able to give some really special community events a long-term home by acquiring them and managing them effectively."

If Charlie had stayed at Deloitte, he would have likely, over time, moved into a *finder* role. He expands,

As a senior manager, I would have begun to have goals that were tied directly to sales. A senior manager is, essentially, a partner-in-training. That's when it starts to shift, and Deloitte takes a person who has historically been rewarded and promoted based on analytics and then on their ability to manage, to a place where they are rewarded for new business. It is a slow ramp, but eventually you get to try and win new business, which is the road to being partner; and once you are a partner, of course, business development is what it's all about.

I think the core message Deloitte tried to send, culturally, was that partners want to help bring people along. You were never just given a sales goal. To the contrary, with fewer senior people, the message was do good work, establish strong relationships, and over time you will get pulled into the sales process.

Call this the "partner's imperative." If you want to drink from the cool, clear waters of profit participation in an expert services firm, you have to be prepared to make it rain. Both Deloitte and Charlie were clear about this from the start.

Next Generation Power

Firms often struggle with how to bring up junior partners. "I worry about where our next generation of rainmakers will come from," says a partner at a leading HR consultancy.

There are a variety of training programs and distinct steps that firms employ to prepare their newer hires to one day land and expand work on their own. Ashley Horne at Womble Bond Dickinson describes her law firm's learning and development program. "We provide a lot of training and upskilling for our attorneys. We have a *Leadership Womble* program that's directed at our partners. It allows them to get a kind of mini-MBA in which they really dig into a business development issue the firm is grappling with and help develop solutions. We also have a *Getting to Equity* program for counsel where they learn about relationship management, how to look for triggering issues that are good from a BD perspective, and how to drive the growth of their books of business. They meet with various sides of our firm (both operationally and Client Development – focused) to better inform their efforts."

That said, although some firms have a curriculum and "universities" focused on helping senior managers make this leap to becoming a "finder," the rule is still that most young professionals learn business development by osmosis with partners proactively deciding to bring someone along in apprenticeship – not by structured or systematic training.

They surely didn't learn it at their professional schools. Says Cole Silver, chief client officer at Blank Rome, "Law schools are missing the boat. You know, they teach us how to be really good lawyers and tacticians, but they don't really teach us anything about the business of law, about getting clients, about managing other lawyers, or about taking care of clients in a service-oriented way. I even, actually, approached the dean of the law school once to teach a class on marketing and business development for the law school, and they said, 'Well, we can't get accreditation through the ABA, so we can't do it.'"

Leading firms often try to combine the best of both worlds, creating structured programs that bring high potential professionals together in a peer-learning setting and rotate them between accomplished partners to give the future finders exposure to a variety of rainmaking styles, and a culture of best practices emerges, where these managers share their lessons and various approaches with one another.

Firms ignore this kind of intentional training at their peril. As Trey Cox, partner at Gibson, Dunn & Crutcher, says, "[We] went to law school. We spent our time there learning the law. No one taught us this stuff. It is neither natural nor instinctive."

The Opportunity

The partner's imperative takes two forms. You can bring in new work from companies with whom your firm has never worked before or you can increase the amount of work you are doing for a current client. In many ways this latter form of growth is the bigger opportunity even if it is a challenge.

It's a fall day. Crisp as hard cider. Reds, yellows, greens, and chocolate browns paint the oaks and elms. We walk up to the front entrance of one of America's most storied technology and business consulting firms. They put a man on the moon, invented the ATM, and designed an artificial intelligence program that rivals Ken Jennings at *Jeopardy!* A part of global business life for more than 100 years, no one in corporate America ever got in trouble for hiring them.

We have an appointment with the head of strategy for one of the company's business units.

"What's the secret to driving business development with current clients?" we ask over espressos in the ground floor café. We elaborate, "Your sales force is legendary, and you're known for your quality. Is that the magic combo?"

"You'd think so," our host says, the wind rustling the tops of the trees out past an expansive lawn, "but here's the thing: We ran an analysis on two of our business units. We found that the lion's share of the revenues and profits in each business came from a concentrated core of customers. It was the Pareto Principle at work. On either side of the house, 80% of our business came from 20% of our clients."

"We see that in a lot of firms." We say, "The relationship between client numbers and revenues is inversely related."

A slight man with a calm intelligence, our host continues,

We're not alone. A lot of firms segment their clients in this way. They'll call their most productive clients "Diamonds" or "Platinum Accounts" or something similar. Here's what's interesting: When we compared the 80/20 list in the two business units, we only found a 10% overlap in our biggest clients. Imagine! We do hundreds of millions of dollars in consulting work with a Silicon Valley software company and sell them no technology while we outfit a global pharmaceutical distribution company with technology but do no services work with them. It's like the practice leads on either side of the house live on different planets.

Our host describes one of the foundational challenges to growing work within a client: the disconnect between different practice areas or realms of expertise within a company – in his case technology services and business consulting services – between themselves and their client.

The left hand doesn't know what the right hand is doing.

Bloom Where You Are Planted

"(At Deloitte), we were encouraged to do good work," reports Charlie, "to build great relationships with clients, and to be there when a client has problems so we could offer to help."

Bill Burch is an accomplished expert services rainmaker, currently driving revenues at ECFx from his home base in Leesburg, Virginia. He says:

> There is a totally different way to sell to an existing customer than there is to a new customer. The person who brings in a new account is a sales hunter. They will be highly skilled. They'll know the competition and know how to compete against the competition. Someone who focuses on add-on sales to current clients has a different skillset. In the sales vernacular, they're called farmers.

Peter Bryant of Clareo agrees. "Farmers bring home world-class project delivery and are very good at developing relationships inside the client. It is the reason they get the follow-on work."

Deloitte knew reaching outside of a client to lasso a new logo is really hard, particularly for more junior people, but they also knew that *harvesting add-on opportunities with an existing client is a much higher percentage activity*. This is why Deloitte focused Charlie on farming first, urging him "to be there when a client has problems so we could help."

Our friend who said 80% of his firm's business comes from 20% of his clients described what statisticians call a power-law relationship or the phenomenon of two data sets relating to each other in predictable ways regardless of how the set grows or contracts. Power laws – in this case the inverse relationship between client numbers and revenues – emerge when there is reinforcing feedback. In expert services, that feedback is the hard-to-accumulate, easy-to-destroy twin propellers of trust and credibility. When both are pulling strongly through the wind, we gain institutional momentum: Good work begets more good work and the gigs roll in exponentially.

This book is about how to farm. Farming current clients for new business is attractive for a number of reasons.

Farming Has a Better ROI Than Hunting

Cold business development outreach costs money. Chasing leads from one end of the planet to the other burns jet fuel and exhausts our best people, often with very little to show for it. Writing thought leadership, going to conferences, or buying advertising is even less effective, because it is terribly expensive. It is far better to look closer to home. If you had $25,000 to spend on business development and had the choice between advertising in *CEO Magazine* for three months or having 50 dinners with clients, you would choose the salmon and Sauvignon Blanc every day of the week. That's because the chances of inking work are much greater when we talk to people who already respect our capabilities and trust us with their businesses.

Dr. Christopher Stevens, a professor at Gonzaga's Graduate School of Business Administration, says,

> It's at least six, maybe eight times as expensive to get a new client as it is to keep an existing one . . . This is especially true if you're doing engagement-based consulting where you go out and learn the client's business. You're building up all of this knowledge base about who they are and what they do. The absolute last thing you'd want to do is squander that by not capitalizing on that intimacy to find other value options for them.

Farming Alerts You to Opportunities Early

When we sit down with clients and have real conversations about where their business is going, we see opportunities to help – sometimes even before they do. The world of business is not mechanical. It's a world where people are busy and distracted, but a world where, every once in a while, we're able to step back with a friend and get some perspective on what we're doing.

"Allison, I love having lunch with you," your client may say to you as you brainstorm over egg salad sandwiches. "You always ask the best questions. It's helpful. You cause me to have new ideas."

Being on-site with our clients and getting to the level where we can be open, spill our unperfected thinking out on the table, and hash ideas back and forth, means we are present at the creation. The ideas that come out of this sort of brainstorming are what end up in a buyer's annual budget proposal. Not only are you collaborating pre-RFP (request for proposal), but, importantly, it can be the source of non-RFP work. That's how we get asked to expand our statements of work (SOWs) – to keep digging into the challenges for which we've shown an appetite to help.

Farming Keeps You Close

Most experts have a story that goes something like this: We were in Bentonville and shared with the team how we had strong capabilities designing customer experience at the point of transaction. We felt we had established rapport with the Walmart team, and they began to talk about how our work might help, particularly in their Mexico stores. But they were slow to follow up. Months turned into quarters and quarters into a year and half. Then we read in the trades that our biggest competitor out of Houston had won a transaction transformation project with them. It wasn't that we were bad. It was just that we weren't the last blue suits in the door.

Being proximate to opportunity matters, and nothing is more proximate than being on the job site. You hear of client challenges first, and you are still there four months later when they are looking to engage.

Reports Charlie,

> Deloitte recognized that projects led to new work. I was often involved in M&A [mergers and acquisitions] projects before there was a deal, researching an industry, evaluating a potential acquisition, or running analysis on what a client thought they could do with a company once they acquired it. If they ended up doing the deal, there becomes a host of follow-on work to integrate the two companies. Integration is very complex, and a company can lose a lot of value if anything goes wrong. As a project manager, we would go through a process of asking ourselves what we thought the biggest challenges would be for the client. Would their current technology work or would they need something different? If they were choosing between technologies, would they need help in evaluating which one to use? If there were departments that needed to be cut to drive synergies, which ones should be cut? We'd actively talk about what were the biggest opportunities for Deloitte to help the client with their next phase, and that's what we would talk about when the partner came to the project site, especially toward the end of a project.

Farming Is Less Time Intensive

John Nord, a managing director at PIE, grew up in the small Minnesota town of Owatonna, where his father sold hogs and worked at the grain elevator and his mother was an office manager.

> I played hockey day and night. In the winter, my dad and I would flood our machine shed that we had at our place and set up lights and a warming hut. You learn pretty quickly that hockey is a low percentage sport and goals are hard to come by. Scores are often 2 to 1 or even 0 to 0 and that's after an hour of hard play. The trick is to take high percentage shots. Shooting a slapshot from halfway down the rink isn't going to work. Even if you can get one on net, the chances of scoring a goal are slim.

Another way to think about business development in expert services companies is like hockey. It's a low percentage sport marked by long sell cycles. At PIE, if we bring on eight juicy new contracts a year, that can drive double-digit revenue growth. In that environment, it's important to pick our shots. For us, as with other expert services firms, that means working to expand our client mandates – the much higher percentage shots. Also, while winning a new client can take more than a year in some instances, add-on projects with existing clients can often get underway in a matter of weeks.

Farming Reduces Risk

Esther Veenhuizen, marketing director for Protiviti's Global Financial Services Industry Practice, says, "If we have just one buyer in a firm, that's a huge risk. What if the person leaves?" All it takes is for that buyer to leave – by choice or by force – and we're back in the position of needing to land a "new" client all over again. We're in a much better position if we have buyers and champions all across a client organization. Then, when one of our buyers leaves, we have others who can vouch for us. When our main buyer is pitching our services internally, there are others in the room who can speak to the quality of our work and echo our buyer's proposal to engage with us.

Account Planning

Setting down the bow and taking up the plow is attractive on many levels. It is why firms emphasize account planning – a fancy way of saying, "Let's sit down and talk about how we might be more helpful to a roster of current clients." So much has already been proven with a client, it is where the easiest harvest is found.

Sit in on those account planning sessions, though, and you will be surprised by how the conversation sounds muddled – a mishmash of industries, service sets, relationships, domain expertise, geographies, and respective appetites for risk.

"We should try and introduce our customer experience people to their ops team."
"Here or in Europe?"
"I was thinking here, but now that I think about it all your relationships are out of London."
"Have we ever done CX for a fintech company? I thought most of our case studies were in consumer products."
"Don't worry about that. If you can get the team in front of their global COO, they can make the pitch. Nothing ventured, nothing gained."
"Easy for you to say. They are our keystone client, and the truth is that all the work we have done to date is in continental baby care. I wouldn't know the global COO if he sat down next to me on the Tube."

Knowing that farming is such a compelling place to play, let's see if we can't bring some structure to how we think about various add-on opportunities with a client.

3

The Diamond of Opportunity

Sun gushes through an open window and pools on Susie Krueger's orange desk and lampshades. Susie loves orange; she says it puts her in a good mood. A quiet breeze spills in, rustling the leaves on her Spanish ivy.

Susie is a director at PIE and an accomplished facilitator. One of her projects is wrangling Am Law 100 chief financial officers (CFOs) and chief information officers (CIOs) for her client, Thomson Reuters, the nearly $6B information services company headquartered in Toronto. She says:

> I'm focused. For 10 years we've been delivering great value to the Thomson Reuters team, helping them create substantive relationships with their most-likely buyers. We know they're happy, because they renew our contract every year and tell us how much they love working with PIE.

Susie has been able to grow the relationship little by little, but she's keenly aware that PIE hasn't yet been able to open the floodgates to the full breadth of potential work with them. She continues,

> There is so much more we could be doing to help other parts of Thomson Reuters. We've managed to put them in a place where they are talking to CFOs and CIOs of the largest law firms – their exact target. They know our work. They know we do a great job for them.

But when she says, "they know our work," she understands all too well that this universe of people who know the value PIE delivers is much smaller than it could or should be. "We've added a few projects and expanded our scope here and there over the past 10 years, but we certainly haven't maximized the ways we could be helping them."

Susie's problem is one we hear from practice leads throughout the expert services industry. You might be doing excellent work, but the opportunities don't just start flooding in on their own.

There Is No *One* Thomson Reuters – and No *One* Opportunity

Susie's challenge is not proving PIE can do the job. She has the best-case study possible: an internal history of doing the work. As she thinks about all the ways PIE could help different buyers within Thomson Reuters, she understands one of the key complexities of her challenge: Thomson Reuters is not one person and it does not represent a single cross-selling opportunity. Thomson Reuters is a collection of professionals who, together, provide critical just-in-time information to legal, corporate, and business customers, helping them keep track of regulatory, tax, transaction, compliance, and news-driven changes. To anthropomorphize this large and complex group by assuming it acts like a single person who "knows" Susie's work – and presents a single opportunity for cross-selling – would be a mistake.

At best, a dozen or so people there know what Susie is doing and that she and her team are delivering excellent work. With a headcount of 25,000 people, most employees have never met each other, much less heard of Susie Krueger. Thomson Reuters, of course, is not an anomaly. Most corporations resemble a brand umbrella spread over a spider web of practices, industrial foci, and geographies, cobbled together over many years of organic growth and acquisition.

So, what are the distinct opportunities for growth within Thomson Reuters that Susie can and should consider? After interviewing rainmakers at accounting, law, engineering, IT, marketing, and consulting firms, both large and small, we've learned that experts who focus on growth of existing clients think about opportunities in six distinct ways. Each of these opportunities carries with it great promise, as well as unique challenges requiring different tactics and skillsets to successfully execute.

MORE: Doing more of the same work you are already doing with the same buyer in a client company

EXPAND: Doing different work (within your existing service lines) with the same buyer

EXTEND: Doing more of the same work you are already doing with a *different* buyer in the organization

REACH: Doing different work (within our existing services lines) with a different buyer in the organization

EVOLVE: Doing new work (that our firm hasn't done before) with the same buyer

INNOVATE: Doing new work (that our firm hasn't done before) with a different buyer in the organization

We're consultants, so naturally we wanted to give pithy names to each of these opportunities, and we wanted a diagram to show how they all relate. To us, the Diamond of Opportunity looks like this:

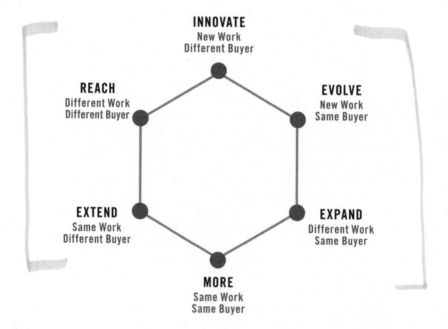

The easiest way to help a client is continuing to do more of what you've proven you can already do, with the buyer who already knows you can do it. This kind of work (MORE) is the base of the diamond. At the peak (INNOVATE) you find the most challenging kinds of opportunities – finding a way to help someone *different* in the organization (with whom you've never worked) doing a type of work that is *new* to you and your firm. In these instances, the bar for earning both trust and credibility is extremely high, making these projects tough to win. Between these poles are four other distinct opportunities to help clients; each requires a mix of skills needed to introduce your additional capabilities to clients and establish relationships with new buyers.

Opportunity 1: MORE

The most straightforward way to grow within a client is to capitalize on previous good work with a buyer to do more of that same work for the same buyer. We call this MORE work. It falls at the bottom of our diamond and is the easiest avenue to being more helpful. Same work for the same buyer. Just more of it.

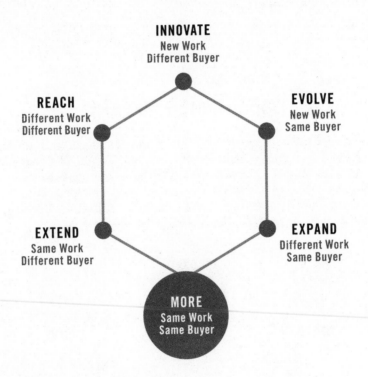

What Might This Look Like for You?

Maybe you recruited diversity and inclusion (D&I) machinist candidates for a client's Seattle manufacturing facility. Your client won a big defense department contract, and you suggested you do *more* D&I machinist recruiting for them.

Maybe you were asked to do quality of earnings (Q-of-E) calls on behalf of a private equity firm partner in the course of their due diligence around an acquisition. Soon, you were doing Q-of-E calls on all this partner's deals, excited to be doing *more* of this work for which you are qualified.

What Might This Look Like for Susie?

With Thomson Reuters, PIE began the engagement by convening a group of Am Law 100 CIOs quarterly for our buyer. Due to the success of the engagement, Susie was able to help her buyer with MORE of this work, by expanding the contract to also convene CFOs from the same companies at the same cadence.

The Diamond of Opportunity in Action

- MORE. Susie has grown the contract to include more of the same work for the same buyer (virtual peer exchange facilitation).

Opportunity 2: EXPAND

The second opportunity to grow our footprint in a client is to focus on doing different sorts of jobs – ones we have experience doing for other clients – with the same buyer. We call this EXPAND work. Our buyer already knows us, trusts us, and knows the quality of our work. It is natural to do additional work that is not exactly what we have done for them before, but that is adjacent to that work. We're asking our buyer to let us be helpful to them in an additional way.

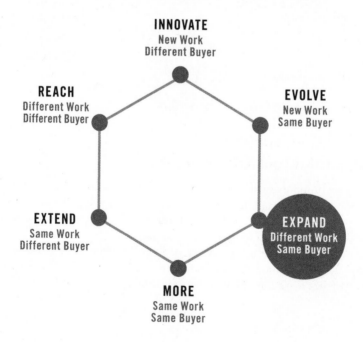

INNOVATE
New Work
Different Buyer

REACH
Different Work
Different Buyer

EVOLVE
New Work
Same Buyer

EXTEND
Same Work
Different Buyer

EXPAND
Different Work
Same Buyer

MORE
Same Work
Same Buyer

What Might This Look Like for You?

Maybe you write whitepapers for a utilities practice in a large consulting firm. You also have speechwriting experience, so you decide to ask the partner you work with if you might write a draft of a speech he is scheduled to make at the SEPA Utilities Conference in Las Vegas next year. He says yes.

Maybe you perform outsourced revenue recognition analysis for second-tier telecommunications services (TELCOs). You decide to pitch your clients, who are heads of revenue recognition, on projects that will ready them for the changes they will need to put in place around the management of their collections lists once the California Commerce Act (and its new privacy requirements) is up and running. Your team has already done this for a few firms in different industries. They said they didn't know you did that work, but quickly agree.

What Might This Look Like for Susie?

With Thomson Reuters, Susie has been able to EXPAND the relationship by introducing live events to the scope of work. Susie explains, "After we'd been convening these networks of CIOs and CFOs on their behalf for a few years, the timing was right to discuss how we could make the peer network even more deeply engaged by bringing the executives together in person – incorporating both facilitated discussion and a social event."

Although our work with Thomson Reuters up to this point had been exclusively virtual events, this was a natural progression, and Susie was able to speak to dozens of case studies that demonstrated how PIE had successfully convened in-person events for other clients.

The Diamond of Opportunity in Action

- MORE. Susie has grown the contract to include more of the same work for the same buyer (virtual peer exchange facilitation).
- EXPAND. Susie expanded this relationship by offering an adjacent service (facilitated live events) to her same buyer.

Opportunity 3: EXTEND

The third opportunity identified by successful experts to grow key accounts is to do more of what we have already proven we can do for that client, but to do it with new buyers within the client. In a way, this often feels like marching across a client's various verticals or business units to see whether they might also benefit from our help. We call this EXTEND work: helping other buyers – often parallel to our current buyer – in the same way we're helping our current buyer.

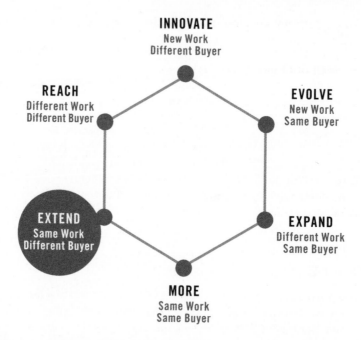

What Might This Look Like for You?

Maybe you run a boutique intellectual property (IP) practice that works for the general counsel of an ad firm, and this firm is part of a large public holding company. You ask the general counsel if she'd make a warm introduction to her sister companies. No reason why you can't help with the same type of IP work for them as well.

Maybe you lead a team that stands up a large consulting firm's customer experience summit every year. Over drinks after the last event, you ask the marketing director you work with if you can write up your experience with the summit and pass it around to her marketing event colleagues in the firm's other practices. You're interested in helping make all of their events equally successful.

What Might This Look Like for Susie?

With Thomson Reuters, Susie knows her current client has a specific target audience: Am Law 100 CIOs and CFOs. However, she also knows that her buyer has peers in his organization whose target audiences are slightly different but are equally focused on deepening relationships with current and potential clients. Susie finds out through conversations with her current buyer that he has a peer in the organization whose mandate is to build the same kind of relationships in the media and telecommunications space. She asks him to put her in touch with the woman who leads this practice and Susie is able to help develop the exact same kind of programs for this new buyer. She's already demonstrated PIE can deliver this work successfully for Thomson Reuters and can now expand to other practice areas.

The Diamond of Opportunity in Action

- MORE. Susie has grown the contract to include more of the same work for the same buyer (virtual peer exchange facilitation).
- EXPAND. Susie expanded this relationship by offering an adjacent service (facilitated live events) to her same buyer.
- EXTEND. Susie extended this relationship by offering the same work to a new buyer (building a new virtual peer exchange group in the media and tele-communications space for a new buyer).

Opportunity 4: REACH

Our fourth opportunity for helping clients is what we call REACH work: offering work to a different buyer in the organization that is one of our existing service lines but is different from work we've done for this client before. We may have strong case studies for this work with other clients, but no one internally can speak to our work in this specific area – *and* we're trying to deliver this service to someone we've never worked with before. In this instance, we're required to work extra hard to earn both trust and credibility, because we're starting with neither right out of the gate.

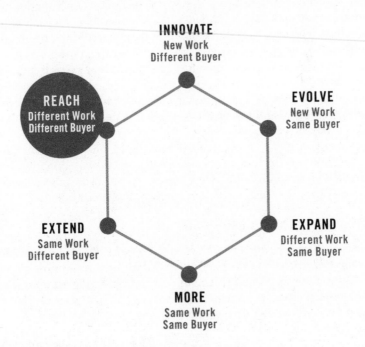

What Might This Look Like for You?

Maybe you do real estate strategy consulting for large retailers, and recently you finished helping a buyer, who is responsible for customer experience, with a location strategy and footprint for their new stores in New York. During a round of on-site visits, you meet the chief human resources officer who mentions that they're thinking of moving to an open-concept office plan for their New York headquarters, and you share some examples of how your firm has helped other major offices in the city make the switch. You'd be happy to help her.

Maybe you did the design work for a print ad campaign for a large athletic-apparel company. The advertising director you worked for passes your name to their head of sponsorships because she likes the work you did and is looking for some similar-themed event graphics at an upcoming race they're sponsoring. She's in luck, as this is right in your wheelhouse.

What Might This Look Like for Susie?

In the course of Susie's discussions with her buyer at Thomson Reuters, she might ask about the initiatives underway in their research department. Susie has ample experience leading research projects at PIE, she just hasn't done this work yet with Thomson Reuters. After checking in about this every so often over the past couple years, her client responds one day by saying he heard earlier that week from a colleague on the research team about a current project that made him think of PIE. They were looking to interview 50 Am Law 100 HR directors to understand buying decision factors for HRIS solutions, and it sounded like the team might need some help. Susie's ears perk up immediately at this – recruiting executives to participate in studies, interviewing them, and synthesizing those interviews into a whitepaper is exactly in line with how PIE has helped other clients before. Susie's client gives her the name of his colleague leading the research effort so she can follow up and offer to help. This is how we REACH with our clients – helping a different buyer with different work they haven't previously hired us for, but which we have strong experience completing.

We can lean on a little bit of extended trust (they know our current buyer, who is also from Thomson Reuters, trusts us) and a little bit of credibility (we've done this kind of work successfully for other clients) – but both of these are far more tenuous than if we have done this *kind* of work for this *same* person.

The Diamond of Opportunity in Action

- MORE. Susie has grown the contract to include more of the same work for the same buyer (virtual peer-exchange facilitation).
- EXPAND. Susie expanded this relationship by offering an adjacent service (facilitated live events) to her same buyer.

- EXTEND. Susie extended this relationship by offering the same work to a new buyer (building a new virtual peer-exchange group in the media and tele-communications space for a new buyer).
- REACH. Susie reached to help a new buyer in Thomson Reuters with a research project, a service with which she has strong experience but has never performed for Thomson Reuters.

Opportunity 5: EVOLVE

The fifth opportunity for growth within a client is to EVOLVE – or, do work for our current buyer that is work we and our firm have never done before. With this opportunity, we are presented the new challenge of trying to win work for which we have no case studies showing our success – neither inside nor outside of that client. Of course, we know we are *capable* of doing this new work based on our team's competencies, but we haven't done this specific kind of work before. This requires maximum trust from our client, and enough earned credibility that they believe we're capable of doing the work, even if we've never done it before.

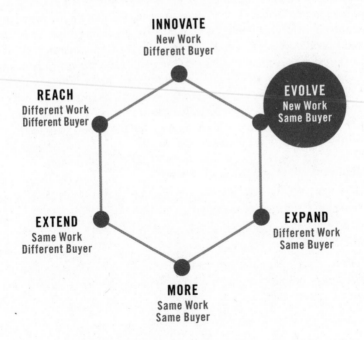

INNOVATE
New Work
Different Buyer

REACH
Different Work
Different Buyer

EVOLVE
New Work
Same Buyer

EXTEND
Same Work
Different Buyer

EXPAND
Different Work
Same Buyer

MORE
Same Work
Same Buyer

What Might This Look Like for You?

Maybe you've been working with the marketing director of a statewide bank for the last five years to produce their local TV advertisements. Now she's thinking about integrating some longer-form video content into their website (such as interviews with employees and customers), and wonders whether you'd be up for the task. You welcome the opportunity. You haven't produced this type of content before, but you know their tone and branding like the back of your hand and you're confident you're the right one for the job.

Maybe you do Salesforce implementation work for small companies in the Midwest. You've been working closely with the IT director at one organization, who is not only a client but also a classmate from college. You've known each other for decades and he trusts you, so you're not surprised when he asks you to come in and do a full Salesforce training for multiple teams within his company. You haven't done this before, but after a successful training session you start to think this is something you should begin offering to other clients.

What Might This Look Like for Susie?

With Thomson Reuters, Susie might come up with a creative new way to evolve the work she is doing for her current buyer. Perhaps her client mentions in passing that some internal visual collateral to help his team get to know these CIOs a bit better would be effective. Susie and her client brainstorm together and decide to produce a series of "getting to know you" video interviews with various member CIOs for Thomson Reuters to share internally and among the group members. Although Susie and her team haven't contracted with clients for this specific type of work before, her demonstrated skills with interviewing executives and the trust she has developed with this client have earned her the ability to help her client in this new way – to EVOLVE the relationship.

The Diamond of Opportunity in Action

- MORE. Susie has grown the contract to include more of the same work for the same buyer (virtual peer-exchange facilitation).
- EXPAND. Susie expanded this relationship by offering an adjacent service (facilitated live events) to her same buyer.
- EXTEND. Susie extended this relationship by offering the same work to a new buyer (building a new virtual peer-exchange group in the media and tele-communications space for a new buyer).

- REACH. Susie reached to help a new buyer in Thomson Reuters with a research project, a service with which she has strong experience but has never performed for Thomson Reuters.
- EVOLVE. Susie evolved her relationship with Thomson Reuters, leveraging the trust she's built with her client and the skillsets she and her team have developed to find a way to help her current client with something *new*, something that PIE has not previously done.

Opportunity 6: INNOVATE

The sixth opportunity for growth within a client is what we call INNOVATE work: work we've never done before with a buyer who has never worked with us. This is the double black diamond run. It's the hardest kind of work to win, as the bars for credibility and trust are highest for us to prove our ability to help. Sometimes it comes from opportunistically listening for where our skillsets can be helpful in different ways across different parts of the organization. Firms looking to reinvent themselves might also be particularly focused on these types of opportunities.

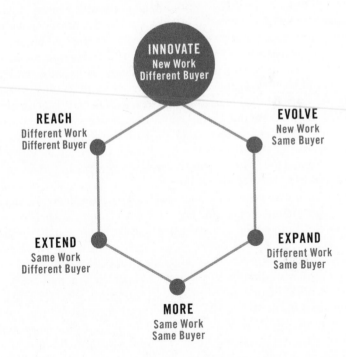

What Might This Look Like for You?

Maybe you started as a firm doing a ton of Sarbanes Oxley compliance work, but when that was done, you had to reinvent yourselves as a risk consultancy, developing new service offerings that were sold to different parts of client organizations.

Maybe you help companies install and integrate SAP Hana, but it is getting to be a crowded space and margins are dropping. You're thinking of broadening your offerings to include outsourced IT and managed services to be more competitive. The thing is your main relationship in your clients is with IT directors. When you pitch managed services, it's above their pay grade and they don't think it's a company priority, so they push you away. So, you have started approaching the CIO directly, someone you do not know with a service offering you have never done before.

What Might This Look Like for Susie?

For example, Susie might recognize a need to create executive engagement throughout the year as a supplement to the Thomson Reuters annual conference. Most specifically, the participants of this event mentioned that with forthcoming changes to California privacy law, a monthly podcast with experts discussing the latest legislative developments could be useful. Susie recognizes that this type of engagement requires interviewing to prepare experts, strong facilitation, and incorporation of key themes expressed by the attendees. While this may not be something Susie and her team have directly performed for clients before, Susie feels confident that PIE's skills in facilitation are transferrable enough to make her an excellent fit for this job. She leans on the credibility she's earned in her work facilitating roundtables to INNOVATE with her client: winning *new* work with a *new* buyer.

For example, Susie might meet a subject natter expert (SME) from Thomson Reuters during one of the live events she's helped put together for her current buyer in New York. This SME is an expert in California privacy law, and she mentions to Susie during the reception after the event that they're working to put together a weekly podcast featuring their various Thomson Reuters experts, as well as some clients, around the ongoing changes in the California legal landscape. She thinks having a facilitator for the podcast would be helpful; she's noticed Susie's facilitation skills in the context of the virtual peer exchange discussions and asks whether Susie has podcast facilitation experience. While this may not be something Susie and her team have directly performed for clients before, Susie feels confident that PIE's skills in facilitation are transferrable enough to make her an excellent fit for this job. She leans on the small amount of trust she's earned through this one interaction with the SME, as well as the small amount of credibility she's earned through demonstrating tangential skills and good work for Thomson Reuters, to INNOVATE with her client: winning *new* work with a *new* buyer.

The Diamond of Opportunity in Action

- MORE. Susie has grown the contract to include more of the same work for the same buyer (virtual peer-exchange facilitation).
- EXPAND. Susie expanded this relationship by offering an adjacent service (facilitated live events) to her same buyer.
- EXTEND. Susie extended this relationship by offering the same work to a new buyer (building a new virtual peer-exchange group in the media and tele-communications space for a new buyer).
- REACH. Susie reached to help a new buyer in Thomson Reuters with a research project, a service with which she has strong experience but has never performed for Thomson Reuters.
- EVOLVE. Susie evolved her relationship with Thomson Reuters, leveraging the trust she's built with her client and the skillsets she and her team have to find a way to help her current client with something *new*, something that PIE has not previously done.
- INNOVATE. Susie innovated with Thomson Reuters finding a way to leverage PIE's skills in a *new* way (a service we haven't performed before), to help a different buyer at Thomson Reuters solve a problem.

Although this might seem overwhelming, it is exciting and allows us to ask more precise questions in account planning sessions.

"What are our top-three ancillary services for which we have strong case studies we might introduce to our current buyer (EXPAND)?"

"We have done good work delivering on CPA-driven accounting projects for the baby-care division. How can we do similar work in other divisions (EXTEND)?"

"What does the client need that we do not currently offer but around which we might hire and stand up a new practice (INNOVATE)?"

This new precision also begs the question, "How should we think about force ranking these opportunities?"

To answer this, first we need to understand why Thomson Reuters isn't just calling Susie up and asking her to do more work. Are there systemic barriers that keep us from engaging more fully with current clients and if there are, what are they?

Section 3: The Challenges

4

The Challenge of Knowing Too Much about the Wrong Thing

Andi Baldwin is on Delta's Minneapolis-to-Seattle flight, thinking the only benefit of traveling as much as she does is that she inevitably gets Platinum status every year (frustratingly, not quite to Diamond). Her seatmate leans over just as the plane starts its descent and says, "What takes you to Seattle?"

That's the courtesy, isn't it? Begin the conversation as the wheels are about to go down. If you start the conversation at lift off, then everyone's faced with that awkward moment-of-disengagement just as the chime sounds at 10,000 feet, letting you know you can use your laptop.

"I'm in consulting," says Andi, stowing her noise-canceling headphones in her bag.

Anyone in consulting knows this fact: Saying you are in consulting is an easy conversation killer. No one knows what consultants do. Andi is a partner at PIE and sometimes she wonders if her closest friends know what she does.

But Andi's seatmate persists. He's downed two Dewar's on ice and his mood is expansive.

"What kind of consulting?"
"My company helps expert services firms drive business development, primarily through sponsored peer-exchange discussions."

"Oh, so you kind of help consultants build relationships in the c-suite to sell more work. Kind of like a BD wingman?"

"Exactly." Andi laughs, having heard this analogy before. "How about you?" she says, trying to pivot away from herself. "What do you do?"

"I'm a sales trainer. I contract with the big ERP software companies."

This piques Andi's interest. Suddenly she starts thinking time will run short before she gets to ask a few questions. Then she remembers that when Delta lands in Seattle, it feels like you are driving to Canada as they make their way across the tarmac to the terminal. There will be plenty of time.

"I've got a question for you, since you're probably an expert on this."

"Shoot."

"In professional services, we always think about the importance of expanding existing client relationships, not just finding new clients. But for some reason, farming existing clients is never as easy as it seems – why do you think that is?"

"Great question. We think what we know about how to win new clients applies to getting more work inside an existing client. But it's not true. It's like that Steve Martin joke, 'It is so hard to understand the French. They have a different word for everything.' It's that way when you are trying to do more work for a client. It's a completely different language of selling than you use to bring on new logos."

We agree with Andi's seatmate. There are, indeed, two different "languages" – or at least two different ways of approaching how we think about our ability to offer our breadths of services to various buyers – and this is the first obstacle. What we know about attracting new clients has little overlap with what helps us expand client relationships.

In our earlier book, *How Clients Buy*, we discussed the seven elements that lead to success in landing *new* clients in expert services. Let's find out where there are cognates – and stumbling blocks – as we learn this new language of farming.

The Seven Elements

How Clients Buy unpacked the set of preconditions that have to be present before a client elects to engage with an expert services provider. Prospective clients must:

1. Be **aware** of our existence.
2. **Understand** what we do and how we are unique.
3. Be **interested** in our service offering. Our services must be relevant to their goals.
4. Believe we have **credibility**; they must respect our work and be confident in our ability to do what we say we can do.*

---

*Close readers will note that in *How Clients Buy*, the word *respect* was used here instead of *credibility*. Upon further study and reflection, the authors think *credibility* – or *respect for one's work* – is the best term to characterize this element.

5. **Trust** us to have their best interests at heart.
6. Have the **ability** to engage with us, meaning they have sufficient authority, budget, and organizational support.
7. Be **ready** to act. The timing must be right. Sometimes all other conditions are met but some other priority supersedes.

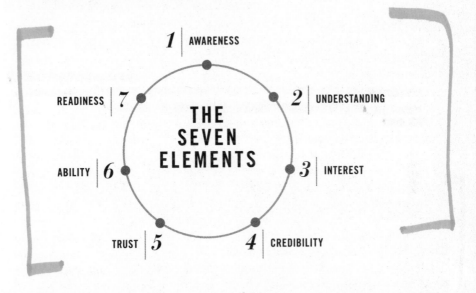

Mutually Exclusive and Collectively Exhaustive

In 335 BC, Athens was conquered by the Macedonians. Aristotle, then a man of 50, returned to Athens after living overseas. There, he set up a school in the Lyceum outside the walls of the city. He'd lecture in the morning, with a particular emphasis on his great love – logic. The following classic example of a categorical syllogism demonstrates how he thought about logic:

All men are mortal.
Socrates is a man.
Therefore: Socrates is mortal.

Aristotle was particularly focused on what he called "categories" since he believed thinking clearly about how elements relate to each other was the ground from which deduction grew. "Men" is a category. It has a characteristic, called "mortality." Socrates is a member of the "men" category; therefore, it follows that Socrates participates in that category's characteristic, "mortality." In the *Organon*, Aristotle wrote that for categories to be useful, they must be distinct from each other: "Of things said without any combination, each signifies either substance or quantity . . ." Aristotle is saying that, assuming there is no overlap in categories (that's the "without combination" part), most categories relate to each other substantively or in number.

In 1963, a full 2,298 years later, McKinsey hired Barbara Minto. She was the first woman with an MBA brought on as a professional at McKinsey. Though she only worked for the firm for 10 years, her impact is still felt. Barbara argued, giving due credit to Aristotle, that when describing what has caused a problem, or how it should be fixed, the description of the parts should be "mutually exclusive and collectively exhaustive," what she called MECE. Though this is most commonly pronounced "mee-cee," Barbara said it should be pronounced "meece," like "Greece." As she put it, "I invented it, so I get to decide how it is pronounced."

For example, if we are asked to list competitors to Ford Motor Company, we would want to include all other car companies (e.g., Chevy, Fiat, Porsche) and not leave any out for the list to be "collectively exhaustive." At the same time, each of the companies on the list of competitors should be completely distinct from each other, or "mutually exclusive." Porsche is owned by the Volkswagen Group and Fiat owns Chrysler, Dodge, and Alfa Romeo; so, for the list to be MECE, we'd want to specify whether it is a list of corporations or brands. Barbara argued that when comparing apples, we need to make sure not to add in any oranges or the result will be muddled thinking.

Barbara was our inspiration when asking the question: How do clients buy expert services? Each of the seven elements is logically distinct and together they represent an accurate picture of the whole. For example, a prospect needs to *understand* what we do in order to engage with us. Separately, they need to be *able* to buy from us or all the understanding in the world won't lead to them scoping a project with our firm. And the list goes on; in order to buy, all seven elements need to be present.

Any Step Can Be the First

The Seven Elements paradigm is not a series of steps to be climbed. We can enter the set of preconditions from anywhere on the circle. *Understanding* what our capabilities are does not necessarily precede the need for a potential client to *trust* us implicitly.

For example, you might have known a woman from church for 10 years, voted for her to join the congregation's leadership council, and thanked her for writing a college recommendation for your son, without ever knowing she was an expert at integrating stand-alone accounting software plug-ins with Salesforce. You trusted her completely as a person before ever understanding what her service offering was (or that she even had one).

The opposite can be true as well. You might have always known there was a franchise attorney the next town over named Frank, but you've never known whether he was any good. Then one day, you're having coffee with the CEO of a housecleaning franchise at the International Franchise Association Annual Convention in Las Vegas, and he raves about Frank. You trust this CEO's opinion. Hearing his description of the excellent work Frank did for them, you can feel your trust in Frank grow, as a potential representative of your own interests. You may have *understood* what Frank's services were for the past decade, but until now, you wouldn't have known he was the right one to *trust* with your business.

The seven elements are a set of preconditions that must be present before clients engage with a new expert services provider.

How Do the Seven Elements Apply?

Using the seven elements as our guide, engaging more deeply with an existing client *should* be easy.

Clients are already *aware* of our firm.

Clients *understand* what our firm does.

Clients have an *interest* in us because we're already helping them on a project.

Clients respect our work, meaning we've earned *credibility* as they know we'll get the job done.

Clients *trust* us because in ways large and small, we have demonstrated we have their back.

You *should* only have to wait until:

- They have budget and are *able* to pull the trigger on new projects.
- They have support organizationally and are *ready* to pull the trigger.

Sadly, it's not that easy. You pole-vaulted over the high bar once to win the work, but now you're running 1,000-meter hurdles.

Awareness

If you work for a client, they know who you are. That's self-evident. Maybe you have been working shoulder-to-shoulder with them for the past 36 months, building a hiring, training, and retention model that will support their growing workforce needs. They know you. You've gone out to Ruth Chris's for fancy steaks that cost more than an upgrade on United. You've eaten mushroom and sausage pizza late at night as you worked to get a project phase done before your client had a status presentation due. You've visited them in their shop, and they have visited you. You've swapped Netflix suggestions. You know each other.

But, do your buyer's *colleagues* know you? The answer, probably, is no. We all run into this. Our buyer's colleagues *might* have heard of our firm, but, just as possible, they have a vague impression that our buyer is simply "doing good work on that initiative" on his own. Although we may feel like 'insiders,' we may still be completely unknown to others in the company.

> *Hurdle 1:* We are not known outside a small cadre of people with whom we are collaborating on a specific project. We lack broad **awareness** within the client organization.

Understanding

When we work with a client, they know what we do.

Maybe you offered to audit their marketing mix and how efficiently their spending was generating traffic. When you show up in their offices, they know you to be the "marketing analytics team." They definitely know what you do and your capabilities, because when they first engaged with you, they called references and asked questions like, "Did you feel like the quality of their marketing analytics work stood up to firm-wide scrutiny?" You know they understand what you do because when they have a problem making sense of marketing data given to them by online sites or media buyers, they turn the data over to you and ask you to make sense of it for them.

But perhaps they've come to think that your firm *only* specializes in marketing analytics. Do they know your firm also does media buying, graphic design, and copywriting? Or do they just think of you as the data folks?

> *Hurdle 2:* The full range of our capabilities is not known – even to clients who know us well – because they have come to define us in terms of the capabilities we offer them now. They lack a complete **understanding** of *all* the services we are equally capable of offering them.

Interest

Our clients would not have engaged with us if we had not been responding to a felt need on their part. All business objectives lace their way through an analysis of causes and a strategy on their way to a statement of a problem to be solved. For example, a client may want to raise revenues and decides that its poorly trained sales force is the reason it is not selling as much as benchmark companies. The chief sales officer of a company asks her head of training to throw out a net to people they know to identify great sales trainers. Your name is given to the head of training by a satisfied client who was asked for suggestions, and you get the gig. Perfect. In short order you're invited to solve precisely the kind of problem you have decades of experience addressing.

But, once you're in and doing your thing, there's no guarantee you'll get a shot at the next problem you are qualified to solve. Maybe you do some sales trainings that go well. But you quickly see that the client also needs to do a better job of recruiting experienced salespeople and updating their compensation system to better align with the goals they are trying to achieve. However, your project lead inside the company, the head of sales training, has a single task he or she has been assigned – to beef up sales training – and has no interest in your other ideas or services. You don't have access to the chief sales officer who decided the secret to more sales is better sales training, leaving you unable to get either the chief sales officer or the head of sales training interested in your additional services.

> *Hurdle 3:* Our client has identified a nail and we were hired as a hammer. Sometimes, however, we see a problem where a Phillips-head screwdriver is a better solution, but the buyer with whom we are working has no **interest.**

Credibility

We've earned credibility when a client knows and respects our work. A client might say, "Joe was on my team when I was at AT&T. He's on his own now, but no one knows revenue recovery better." If you're Joe, this is the kind of experience-based recommendation that leads to new work. Hopefully, once we are engaged with the client, our work is shining on its own, lighting the way to new engagements. When we first pitched the client, we were at a disadvantage, having to talk about our work. Expert services work, however, is better demonstrated than described. When we work next to someone in the trenches, we may come to believe he or she is tenacious, insightful, highly capable, and possessed of sound judgment. Once we are working on a project inside a client, the credibility bar is much lower than when we were on the outside peeking in. They have seen first-hand that we can do the work.

This is harder, though, when we try and do work for new buyers within a client who don't know us, or when we try to tell current buyers that we're capable of different kinds of services.

> *Hurdle 4:* Our client knows the quality of our work, but we struggle to get others in the organization to see that quality. Or, we do good work and offer to perform a new service only to find our clients think of us as a one-trick pony. Our **credibility** is hard to scale – across services and across relationships.

Trust

When we work with clients, we have the opportunity to do the right thing when their backs are turned, and we can demonstrate that we can be trusted with caring for their interests.

We are sometimes given a choice between leaning in the direction of our client – prioritizing transparency and investing in the relationship – or leaning in the direction of ourselves and our interests. Say, for example, you're in a meeting with your buyer and her boss, presenting to the boss on the results of a project you've just completed. Her boss is giving you high praise for the work your firm has done. You notice your buyer looks frustrated for the lack of acknowledgment she's getting (even though you did in fact do 90% of the work). One option is to accept that praise fully and take this as an opportunity to try to win more work from the boss. Instead, you use this as an opportunity to praise your buyer in front of her boss – underscoring the team effort of the project and how great she was to work with. This is how trust is created – one act at a time. You're investing in the long game.

Once we are working with a client, we no longer need to say, "You can trust me!" We have been afforded the opportunity to *show* our clients we have their best interests at heart.

But, like credibility, trust doesn't transfer quite as easily as we might like to other potential buyers in the client company. The more degrees of separation from our buyer, the less you can lean on your hard-earned trust. Client organizations can be big – perhaps hundreds of potential buyers – and the further away from our buyer we get, the harder we have to work to rebuild trust with others. Additionally, we often run into competing circles of trust – where incumbent relationships may box us out from even being able to prove our integrity.

Rob Benson, chief sales officer for Kele Inc., explains,

> If you're in there doing something really well, you may want to offer another service that your company provides. If the customer has an incumbent in there doing those services already and they're doing a really good job, it can be hard to win that business, especially if that incumbent is doing a good job and the customer does not see a need to make a change. It's a risky situation because if you're saying, "Oh, just give us a shot. Give us a try," that's risky as that could cause the customer to consider other options for your existing services. It can be tough to break through that incumbent relationship.

When trying to walk across a client company, we need to remember that our credibility – our reputation for doing work – often travels more easily than our ability to prove our trustworthiness.

> *Hurdle 5:* Our client trusts us implicitly, but our reputation for being trustworthy doesn't always travel as quickly or as broadly as we'd like. Just because our buyer trusts us, does not mean that the buyer's counterpart in Johannesburg will **trust** us automatically. There may also be competing circles of trust that hinder our ability to even prove our integrity to other potential buyers in the organization.

Ability and Readiness

Almost by definition, if we have engaged with a client, the client must have been ready and had the ability to pull the trigger on a contract with us. The company was prosperous enough to enable an engagement and, importantly, the project lead inside the client company was personally ready to tackle a new initiative and had the support of his or her boss.

It's a mistake, however, to think just because the ability and readiness stars aligned in one division of the company, they similarly align in other divisions – even if we are trying to engage with someone who is the functional equivalent of our current buyer. Likewise, we can never assume that just because a client was ready and able to engage with us around one of our service lines that the client is equally ready and able to engage with us around other service lines.

> *Hurdle 6:* Clients need to have the resources and bandwidth to take on new projects. That they are ready and able to engage with us on one project doesn't mean that they are able to engage with us on a second, related project or that their peers in other parts of a client organization are similarly **ready** and **able** to engage.

The First Challenge

The first challenge to expanding our relationship with a client is that the language we learned as hunters doesn't serve us well in the world of farming. Both hunting and farming bring in new revenues, but this fact masks other, more profound differences. The seven elements describe how clients come to know us, understand what we do, and ultimately engage our services. That description, however, is not helpful as we think about how to expand our mandates with current clients. It is not enough that, as professionals, we weren't trained in business development; now we learn that what we know about landing new clients bears little resemblance to the skillset needed to grow that client.

5

The Challenge of Complex Organizations

A combination of organizational and individual barriers within *our own* firms makes farming difficult. The sheer complexity of people, skills, relationships, and networks within an organization often creates roadblocks that limit our ability to seamlessly capture and act on opportunities for growth. In this chapter, we dig into the internal barriers that may stymie efforts to grow within a client before you even get out of the office door.

We Do That?

In large organizations, practice leads may not know each other or their respective expertise. In an age of online organization charts, this seems like it can hardly be true. With a couple of keystrokes, you should be able to identify the exact right expert in your firm to help a client with a problem they face. And yet the rapid pace of change within organizations today makes this task deceptively hard. Mergers and acquisitions upset existing organizational structures and people frequently switch roles, divisions, or even companies. It's hard to keep up with everything your company does and the people who have the expertise you need.

Chris Mirro, senior vice president, responsible for sales and business development for MAXIMUS's health and human services practice in the United States, has seen this challenge firsthand. He says, "I think the biggest challenge in cross-selling is that people inside organizations quite often are experts in their own domain and not necessarily experts in the broader domains of what the company does. Creating enough knowledge across those broader domains to have the first client conversation to generate awareness is often one of the big limiting factors."

Even if you know of the right expert to call into a client project, you might feel unsure in your ability to introduce that new expert to your client. Says Kenneth Guernsey, who for many years ran the law firm Cooley, "It's a challenge for me to know enough about the expertise that my colleagues have, and how to pitch it, to be an effective cross-seller. I can do it, and I do, but it's always a challenge to do it well and to make as effective of a pitch as they could make themselves, given the opportunity."

Who's on First?

Big expert services firms are triple-matrixed by geography, industry, and functional capabilities. In that context, it's hard for practice leads to know where to go in their own firm when they see opportunities. For example, in a technology consultancy, someone might fairly ask whether the Ford Motor account belongs to the automotive vertical, the supply chain practice, or the Detroit office. These matrices can cause firms to lose track of "who's on first" when it comes to client care.

Most larger firms work to tame the matrix by appointing a partner to "hold" the client relationship and through which all outreach to the client must pass. We've heard them called "client account leads," "lead partners," "key account managers," and "key relationship partners," among others. Regardless of their title, these account leads have the unintended consequence of standing in the way of growing a client relationship. Yes, they keep your firm from confusing or annoying your client. The last thing you want is for a client to say, "You're the third person from your firm to talk to me about your cybersecurity services." However, in the context of trying to grow work within a client, account leads are gatekeepers. They add an additional administrative hoop through which others in the firm must jump before reaching out to the client to talk about new work. Although these relationship holders can help pave the way for great growth within a client, they have the potential to make growing work exponentially harder by actively blocking the efforts of others to broaden a firm's suite of engagements to ensure they can keep any wins for themselves.

The Stories We Tell

Unhelpful self-talk is one of the fastest ways experts shoot themselves in the feet and limit opportunities for growth within a client. We often hear experts say they hate sales, that it's not their "thing." Sometimes experts fear that upsetting the status quo and making the easiest ask on the Diamond of Opportunity – to do MORE work with a client – will invite criticism for the work they have already done. Additionally, many experts simply don't like to *ask* . . . for work, help on an article, another beer . . . anything! Experts like to help and asking *others* for something can feel like the opposite of that.

Much of this can be fixed by reframing our stories. If we suggest that we do MORE work for a buyer, it is because we believe we have added value and that it is in their best interest to engage with us further. If, in the process of doing that, they give us feedback that allows us to delight them even further, then that is an added boon – we are communicating well with our buyer. Finally, if you dislike asking for help, adjust the language: Don't view it as asking *them* for more work; view it as asking how *you* can be more helpful.

Winging It

Accountants go to school to learn accounting. Attorneys go to school to learn the law. Strategy consultants go to school to learn about business models, sources of competitive advantage, and market characteristics. No one learns skills for business development at these schools. MBA classes related to sales are inevitably focused on selling products, not on the art of hunting or farming clients in the world of expert services. Practice leaders don't get training in account management. They are trained to be good lawyers or accountants or strategists, but not trained in the art of expanding relationships.

Says Professor Christopher Stevens of Gonzaga Business School, "We don't spend enough time on [business development] in business school. The logic is that we need the time to cover all the technical aspects of the degree, but I think listening, so you really understand what someone is doing, is the single skill that is most important in business."

The result of the lack of formalized training is that too many expert services providers wing it – sending out a case study in a whitespace vertical, talking on a panel at a conference, following up on a couple of leads forwarded by marketing, and taking a handful of clients out to lunch – unsure what works or how the various efforts work together.

Messed Up Incentives

Too often, enthralled with the lure of incentives as a behavioral driver, professional services firms concoct elaborate attribution models for work they have won. Points are awarded for team participation, for previous contact, for introductions, and for presentations. Based on those points and in combination with points awarded for other firm-building activities like leadership, training, recruitment, and product development, money is doled out at the end of the year. If the road to hell is paved with good intentions, these algorithms often lose their power to incent in their complexity. Wander the halls of a consulting firm and you hear, "The incentive system is a black box. I'm not sure how it works."

Traditional incentive systems fail to drive practice leads to refer work to one another and create gamesmanship. Senior consultants report they spend valuable time trying to quantify how much they may have "touched" a prospect to make themselves eligible for commissions. No matter how hard you work to deepen a relationship with a current buyer or another executive inside the client company, it seems like someone else in your firm "touched them at some point" and can lay claim to being part of the firm's relationship with that client. We have a friend at a boutique Fifth Avenue investment banking firm who says, "When there's a win around here, it's like antelope down on the Serengeti. Everyone stops by my office to make the case for their piece of fee." In the same way that hyenas, vultures, and other predators come out of nowhere to feast, consultants fly out of their offices to shout, "I took her to lunch last month!" or "I introduced you to him at a conference!" or "I've been building trust with her since we attended prep school together!" to try to get a piece of the commission and stake their claim.

Refer at Your Own Risk

An expert at a services firm might be charged with a project that is a several-hundred-million-dollar engagement. Her ability to pay for her kid's college depends on that project. She has a vested interest in not damaging the relationship. While the expert knows she is supposed to go to market as one firm, the truth is that unless she personally knows the partner she is referring and knows the quality of his work intimately, she is not likely to endanger the cash cow that is her client.

Walt Shill, head of client services at the engineering and safety firm Environmental Resources Management (ERM), says,

People don't call folks in other parts of their organization because most firms are organized by expertise or service and, so, almost by definition, a person wouldn't know people in another area. They won't call them into a client because they don't trust them. If you've got a good thing going at a client, introducing someone you don't know to do a new service could hurt your own account. So, there's risk in doing it.

If a practice lead refers a big client across the organization, the risk of substandard work reflecting poorly on the practice lead can exceed the perceived win for the firm. Says Shill, "We have a sterling reputation as a firm, but the truth is that quality varies depending on which partner you work with. That said, I try and ask questions about partners in advance of making an introduction, but some of the guys who are two years away from retirement don't even try. They are solely focused on their two or three biggest clients."

Then there is the problem of losing control of an account. Longtime CEO of Accenture, Bill Green, says, "If you're an account executive and you have your best account, it's not a natural act for you to bring in one of your colleagues, who is an expert in an adjacent area, and who, gee whiz, the customer might like better than they like you."

The Second Challenge

The second challenge of winning new work with existing clients is the systemic barriers that stand in the way of referring work inside expert services firms. You would think firms would be strongly aligned on what is good for the firm, preaching the gospel of "When the firm wins, we all win," but instead you find eddies of behavior that cause individuals in the firm not to act in a way that aligns with the wider firm's success.

6

The Challenge of Serving Complex Networks

Sitting outside at a picnic table on PIE's campus, Tom enjoys a salad as he notices one of PIE's college interns reading something intently on his phone.

Tom's interest is sparked, "What has you glued to your phone?"

The intern, not sheepish at all, spins his phone around for Tom to see. There on the screen is a sleek profile of another young adult. There is information about the woman's hobbies – whitewater kayaking, downhill skiing, and backpacking – which Tom knew to be the same as the intern's hobbies.

Always curious, Tom asks, "How exactly does the app make such a perfect match?"

The intern dives in: "The app – Hinge – uses a Nobel-Prize-winning algorithm to help you zero in on the right person for you. You're eight times more likely to have a great date with someone you actually like by using the app. It uses your interests in the algorithm."

Tom lets this sink in. With an algorithm that strong, why is his smart, funny intern still single?

He softens his thoughts verbally, "Okay. This is interesting. Is the algorithm working for you?"

The intern chuckles. He knows Tom well and could read his tone. "Well, Hinge has been working okay for me, but I haven't found the perfect girl yet. It connects you based on mutual interests, but the connection ends there, really. My friend who is in San Francisco just started using this other app, The League, that goes beyond just matching based on mutual stuff. It matches people together based on belonging to the same networks of people or having overlapping networks."

Tom thinks about how he met Mary nearly 30 years ago – introduced through a friend's mother they both knew and trusted. This whole idea of using an app seems too wild. "I don't get it."

The intern pulls up the website on his iPhone and shows Tom: "See – you have to apply to become a member of the dating app, and you are vetted based on having gone to a certain school – see here, you enter your LinkedIn URL – so you are vetted based on your education network. And see here – you enter your social media information, so you can only be connected if you have some overlap in the same social circles."

The intern laughs at the skeptical look on Tom's face.

Standing up to go back inside, the intern says, "I mean, here in Montana where the dating pool is small, there isn't quite as much need for something like Hinge, but all my friends in the city use it religiously. I mean, can you even imagine trying to find your perfect person in the sea of people in Boston or New York? Impossible."

The intern heads inside the office, leaving Tom to his thoughts.

Long gone are the days of serendipitously meeting the love of your life at the dog park. In the new world of dating, one is not left to navigate the complex ecosystem of meeting someone without technological aid. In this twenty-first-century iteration of the ancient art of finding a needle in a haystack, we see evidence of what social scientists call a trusted network, where each of the participating people on the apps are nodes, strongly linked with friends and alumni in social and professional networks, and, through degrees of separation, weakly linked with a much wider set of nodes.

It turns out that dating-app matchmaking has a lot to teach us about how experts in expert services firms connect with others in a client to grow work within and across that client organization.

When Networks Kiss

The intern's dating challenge *is* the challenge of connecting in the expert services industry, or more precisely, the dating app's challenge is the labyrinth of the expert services industry. That is because a dating app sits at the interface of two infinite networks, just like experts do.

The numbers get big because when one network kisses another, the potential number of connections between nodes explodes.

Take for example, the 55 men who drafted the US Constitution. Each of these framers was unique – they were different ages, came from different places, were informed by different experiences, with their own body of influencing friends, and their own differently balanced frontal cortexes. Less a single body – a Constitutional Convention – they were really 55 nodes in a network. That means that there were 1,485 unique combinations of those nodes – subsets of the 55 who might agree to go out for hot brandy punch after debating all day.

You see where we are going with this. With the number of educated, informed, experience-based experts proliferating, the chance of the exact right butterfly surgeon in Nairobi linking just in time with the exact right lepidopterist nursing a Monarch back to health in western China is unlikely at best. It seems to be one of the key questions of our time: How do two people efficiently connect – one with a problem and the other with a body of experience and resources that could be extremely helpful?

On a smaller scale, this is the problem you face with trying to engage more deeply with a client. As the number of possible connections increases – say, your partner in the Shanghai office using you to connect with the chief human resources officer (CHRO) out of Luxembourg charged with Asia Pacific (ASPAC) hiring through a relationship that you used to work with in San Francisco – the likelihood of a connection occurring goes down.

Two Universes

As with The League, there are two networks at play. On one side, there are all the partners in your firm that could be providing their help to a client. That creates the kind of complexity we described in the last chapter. Then there is a second network – all the buyers in a client company with whom you could engage. Dozens of you trying to connect with dozens of them.

Diana Buxton is the chief marketing officer for Cognizant's Banking, Financial Services & Insurance Business Unit. She is a game-changing revenue digital marketer and is responsible for creating new business relationships with clients and prospects, transforming digital connections through conversation, and driving revenue by forging deeper bonds with Cognizant's new buying centers. She rolls up to Cognizant's Global executive vice president and chief marketing officer (EVP&CMO), Gaurav Chand, as do the CMOs for the four other business units.

Diana also knows a huge number of executive leadership team (ELT) leaders in the firm, the functional clients of her services, as well as leaders of other back-office functions, like the person who rents office space for the company and the team with whom she connects on budget and procurement issues.

This universe of contacts in Diana's Cognizant network is characterized by countless nodes and both strong and weak ties to others in the organization. As a firm that provides services to Diana, part of PIE's puzzle is how to leverage our relationship with Diana in order to connect with other possible buyers within Cognizant. As Diana would say, her Cognizant network is her net worth.

The Opportunity Network

PIE's Service Offering	Diana's Network
Business Development as a Service	Diana Buxton, CMO banking, financial services, & insurance (BFS)
	Anna Walsh, CMO retail, consumer goods, hospitality, & travel (RCGHT)
	Antonella Bonanni, CMO healthcare & life sciences (HCLS)
	Tony Viola, CMO manufacturing, logistics, energy, & logistics (MLEU)
	Corey Olfert, communications, media, & tech (CMT); Phil Walsh, global VP, field marketing

When we do account planning, we focus on how we can plug into Diana's network, knowing that the work we have done for her will serve as a proof point to others.

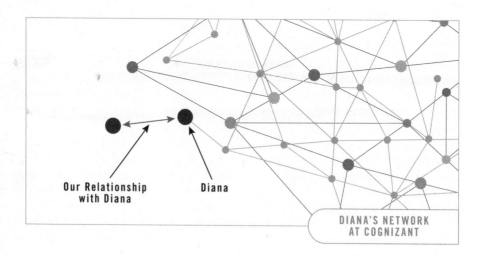

But as we know from dating apps, this is not the whole story. Although this first map describes the many places we could engage within Cognizant around our ability to help, there is also the map of all of our colleagues who would also like to help Diana's friends with their areas of expertise.

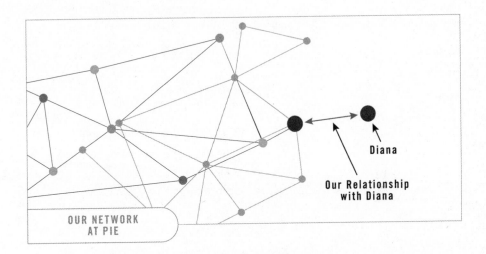

PIE provides business development as a service for Diana. We think our firm might do for Diana other sorts of work we have done for others. We call that the Capability Network.

The Capability Network

PIE's Service Offerings	Diana
Expert at business development as a service	Diana Buxton, CMO banking, financial services, & insurance (BFS)
Expert at writing whitepapers	
Expert at recruiting	
Expert at sales enablement	
Expert at event management	

Kiss the two networks and, again, the numbers get big:

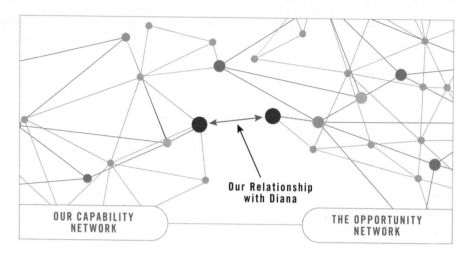

OUR CAPABILITY
NETWORK

Our Relationship
with Diana

THE OPPORTUNITY
NETWORK

If only there were a dating app for expert services.

The Myth of Referral

Let's stipulate that against all odds, you have a match – you've found someone at your firm who could help someone in a client firm your buyer knows. All you need to do is broker the introduction.

Bad news. Buyers rarely refer you or your colleagues around their firm. Here's why.

Secret Sauce

If we as experts have succeeded in our work by adding value to a client, that makes the person who advocated hiring us look good. Never underestimate their desire to keep the "secret sauce" of their success to themselves. Buyers internalize referrals, telling themselves, "I discovered them," not "They showed me the way." After all, if any project manager in their company can simply work with us and effect monstrously impressive outcomes, doesn't that diminish our project manager's part in the equation? Our project manager got accolades across their unit for their good work. Their supervisor gave them a spot bonus, but what if credit for the project was a zero-sum game? What if the more credit we got for the success of our work, the less credit our manager received? That wouldn't be good and goes a long way to describing why some project managers aren't exactly eager to spread the word.

Perception of Risk

People balance risk and reward. Yes, if there is an initiative that will double our firm's revenues, we want to be on the team. At the same time, if the boss puts out an all-points bulletin for new talent, asking everyone to post something on their LinkedIn and Facebook accounts, we might hesitate to push the opportunity to our sit-around-all-day brother-in-law on the theory that if Shawn did get hired, it might come back to nip us in the rear. We can just hear it now: "Why didn't you tell me his fight to understand words was like a blue whale pushing through slushy Arctic waters?" We aren't sure we want to post the job opening because, although there's a gain in doing so – our boss asked for help and she will be grateful if we respond – there is risk in it as well.

Clients think the same way. Passing on our name to others across the organization carries with it some reward. If we perform well, they might get a nod or a pleasant word in the lunchroom: "Shirley, thanks for the name of that vendor. They've been great." With some luck, their boss might even notice as well: "Thanks for helping me push best practices across the division. That was real leadership." It might even get noticed by the organization as a whole: "Shirley saves the company $4MM in payroll expense" blares the company newsletter.

But there's risk as well. For reasons separate from our expertise, we might not perform on a project as well as we would like. Suddenly Shirley is avoiding the lunchroom for fear of running into her colleague: "Thanks, Shirley, I have about even chances of not being terminated next Monday for hiring that vendor you sent in my direction. Remind me to return the favor sometime." Shirley's boss isn't happy either: "In the future, I'd appreciate you running your ideas about how to run the other divisions by me before you run your mouth." And, finally, the organization might notice: "5,000 laid off in a selective reduction in force as a result of Shirley's referral."

The first day selling insurance at State Farm, the sales trainer says, "Never leave the scene of a conversation without two referrals." That may be true for a relatively nonconsequential decision like what kind of highly rated life insurance to buy; there's little actual risk in that decision because there really aren't any bad choices. However, it's not true in career-ending decisions like whom to choose as your firm's accounting advisor and who will customize the instance of SAP your firm recently purchased. This risk is not insurmountable, but it is a headwind.

Vertical Silos

Phil Ensor, an employee of Goodyear Tire and Rubber for 33 years, first used *silos* as a metaphor for how various functional parts of a large organization get walled off from each other. An organizational development and employee relations pro, he wrote an article for the Association for Manufacturing Excellence's *Target* magazine, called "The Functional Silo Syndrome," that still informs how we think of complex organizations. He wrote, "People across the organization do not share common goals. Their goals are primarily functional. Communication is heavily top-down – on the vertical axis. Little is shared on the horizontal axis."

Note Ensor's emphasis on communication. Accounting has a hard time talking to research and development (R&D) because their goals are different. One is measured on accuracy and compliance, the other on new product success. If functions within a company feel siloed from one another, they may feel that they don't understand one another enough to make confident referrals. This is where strong listening comes in on an expert's part, which will be explored more deeply in Part II.

It's Not You, It's Them

Aside from the interpersonal dynamics at play in every firm, there will always be organizational issues that are out of your control. The best thing you can do is acknowledge that these things exist and stay informed about them.

Budget

Your client's budget is a near-perfect expression of its strategy and priorities. Company leaders have a right – it's their job – to shift direction in the face of a changing market landscape and competition. PIE had a very large client (our largest at the time, actually) decide several years ago to focus on digital transformation of its clients. That bet paid off handsomely, even if it meant that in the short run they scraped all the budget away from our buyers to fund this new initiative. Was it the quality of our work that caused the sharp shift down in our billings to them? No. It was a thoughtful reaction to changes in their markets.

Politics

Doing more with a buyer means your buyer has some wood to chop before saying "Yes" to your proposal. Companies are social stews full of competing personalities, loyalties, and differing opinions. Just because you have done good work, doesn't mean your buyer, who may very much want to double your contract, has the political juice inside the client to make it happen.

The Buyer's Ability

Closely related to the question of political juice is your buyer's ability to pitch the expansion of your work for the client internally. In the arena of resource allocation, making a case for a project is everything, but not everyone is equally gifted at making a case. Indeed, almost by definition, you – the expert – are better at making the case for a project than your buyer. You are in the bowels of the ship and see the water pouring in. You are intimately familiar with all you have done to stem the seawater and how the welds are holding up. And yet, almost inevitably, someone else is carrying your message to decision makers or veto-holders.

Concentration Risk

Many clients with whom we've worked at PIE perceive risk in giving one firm all of their work. They carry in their heads the notion that by having multiple consultants in-house, they are creating a sense of competition that holds down price and protects them from "vendor concentration."

The Third Challenge

The third challenge that stands in the way of us winning new work with a client is the complexity inherent in two networks trying to interact. Like a young person trying to leverage his or her network to meet a possible date, the sheer number of possible connections is overwhelming. The likelihood of connection is low and is further frustrated by our buyers' natural instincts to not refer us around their web of connections.

7

The Challenge of Introducing Your Colleagues

A s an elementary school student in Paris, Thierry Chassaing loved three things: chorale, soccer, and mathematics.

I went to Sainte-Croix de Neuilly, a small diocesan school just a little west of the Arc de Triomphe. My father was a commercial executive in an advertising company, and the school was near where we lived.

Housed in a beautiful nineteenth-century four-story building adorned with gables and blue shutters, the school set Thierry on a path along which he has been walking for more than 50 years.

Football continues to be a passion of mine. I can't help but root for Paris Saint-Germain and bleed blue and red. I still love choral singing, especially anything by Bach, and mathematics became my academic concentration. I like finding harmony and order in complexity. Both Bach and mathematics feed that in me.

Today, Thierry runs worldwide marketing for Boston Consulting Group (BCG) out of their Washington, DC offices as a managing director and senior partner.

French people like Washington, DC. George Washington commissioned Pierre Charles L'Enfant to plan the new federal city. I feel very at home in a city designed by a Frenchman.

Sitting down with Thierry, he points to the importance of being able to leverage colleagues in client relationships that you have personally originated.

You hear junior people in our firm talk about looking for new opportunities to help inside a client, and that is important. Equally important, however, is the need to introduce the client to other experts from BCG. It is a mistake to think that you will see or even recognize all the opportunities to bring value to a client. Others in your firm will bring their perspective to a client and plant their own flags, which has a way of driving exponential growth.

Introducing Other Experts

When thinking about how to expand your firm's remit inside a client, it is easy to focus on the opportunities for growth – how you might do MORE of the same work you are doing now for a buyer, how you might INNOVATE by doing new work with new buyers within the client, or how you might EVOLVE by doing fresh work with the same buyer, but it is easy to overlook – or even avoid – the need to bring in others from your firm early on who will be running the new projects.

Says Thierry, "I bring in other experts who have done what I am proposing 5 or 10 times before. They add to our understanding about what is going to be different in this case versus every case we have done before. Bringing in other partners is extremely helpful."

Expanding the number of projects within a client often requires the expert who sold the project to pass along the baton of ownership to others. As Thierry notes, this passing of the baton is beneficial, because bringing in more experts brings in more knowledge. At the same time, the passing of the baton may peel back layers of trust and credibility that had been built up over years of project work between the original expert and the original buyer. In the expert services industry, it is common to say, "We are the product." Our offering is our unique experience, expertise, and insight. That unique perspective is not easily replicated or extended into other people. And the client knows it.

It's one thing for a buyer to invite a trusted expert to a cocktail party and introduce her to their colleague from a different division by saying, "I wanted the two of you to meet. Carol does great work for us." That introduction transfers trust (or perhaps more accurately, suspends distrust), opening the door for the Carol to EXTEND her work across the organization to the new buyer. However, trust diminishes when Carol, the expert, introduces a different person within her service firm to the new buyer. Carol explains to the new buyer, "My colleague, Henrik, does the same work I do, only in your geography." The work may be the same but now both the buyer *and* the provider of the work, or expert, are different. With increasing degrees of separation, the rope of trust weakens.

Likewise, it is one thing for a buyer to engage a trusted expert to do different work – to EXPAND. But the bonds of both credibility and trust weaken when that buyer introduces the trusted expert to a colleague to do different work. This goes back to REACH work, where the work is different and the buyer is different but now, on top of that, the expert is, too. In both cases, you can see how introducing a new expert to any type of work on the Diamond of Opportunity weakens the transfer of trust and credibility built by the original expert.

Walt Shill of Enterprise Risk Management (ERM) is cautious when reflecting on the opportunity to do more work with a client by introducing other partners into the equation:

> No doubt about it. Expanding within a client is a massive opportunity, and I think many professional services firms don't take full advantage of it. But I also know you have to be very careful because, on multiple occasions in my career, I have had clients call me and say, "Can you call the dogs off?" or even more extreme, "We don't want this person back here at our company." I remember one client describing it as inviting dinner guests to stay with you, and they go to the bathroom, only to find out they are going through the closets in your bedroom. You feel violated. So, yes, there's an opportunity, but I also think it has to be done carefully, and thoughtfully, and respectfully.

It is one thing to say that the practice of expert services is a team sport, but there are structural challenges that stand in the way of effortlessly adding colleagues to a client team. Let's look more closely at three of those challenges:

Our Client Doesn't Know if the New Person Is Any Good

If you are hoping to expand how a client thinks about your capabilities and you bring in an expert from your firm, the new expert may stumble in a way that causes the client to hesitate about engaging with him or her.

Bruce Wilson of Wilson Allen shines light on this barrier:

> This was when I started my first business. As our workload grew, I brought in other people. And then, I moved on to looking for the next opportunity and other people did the work. Well, fast forward about 10 years and we're trying to do some conversion work through Thomson Reuters for the same client, and I get a call saying, "They don't want to work with you." And I said, "We've worked with them for years. Why would they not want to work with us?" Then I dig down and find out that one individual who had been there originally felt that we did what they called a "bait and switch" – basically, that I went in and sold myself and then put other people who were less capable on the project to do the work.

You Might Not Know Your Colleague

At smaller firms like PIE, we know our colleagues well. We go skiing together, visit each other in the hospital when we have babies, and we see each other's partners and spouses at the holiday party. In large firms, however, that's not always the case. It is quite possible that the firm's expert on tax policy might live in the Netherlands and not only will we not have met them before, but we might have no idea about their character and ability other than the relatively weak notion that "our firm hires the best."

Rob Benson, chief sales officer for Kele Inc., explains why experts are often hesitant to introduce new colleagues to a client project:

> The problem that I've found is, we've got this great customer, they love us. If I bring another colleague from my company in to offer what they do, they're just going to screw up my account, right? It was this mentality of fear about what a colleague might do to the account really, that tended to create a barrier that prevented cross-selling.

In addition to the fear inherent in introducing others, we may not even know what others have to offer. Gonzaga Associate Professor of Entrepreneurship Christopher Stevens comments,

> Professionals in law, accounting, and consulting organizations have a hard time breaking out of their silos. Everybody's got their head so focused on their specific discipline, their specific specialization, they can't look beyond that and see the bigger picture. And in most organizations, I don't think they really make it a priority.

Reports DXL Group's Harvey Kanter, "One of the greatest challenges when you first engage in building a partnership is understanding if the partner will provide value. And how confident are you in that early on and how much are you going to trust in that?"

You Have to Build Relationships Anew

"What makes cross-selling a bit difficult," says Cambridge Group Managing Partner, Chris Fosdick, "is chemistry":

> Once you find a client you've got that strong chemistry with, it's great. It's great for the client. They feel really good about working with you. It's great for you because you really move away from selling work to just being there to help solve a problem. But it's delicate. And when you introduce a new person, you're hoping that the chemistry will continue without disruption, but sometimes it doesn't quite mesh.

Strong business relationships are formed from built-up trust and credibility. In the expert services industry, relationships between expert and client may, after time, start to feel like relationships between colleagues. As Fosdick notes, this sort of chemistry cannot be transferred in an instant.

Loss of Control

It is hard to introduce colleagues because we want to control the relationships with the client. We want to make sure our values (looking out for the clients' best interests) and our standards (making sure all the work we do for a client is up to snuff) are uniformly expressed across all touchpoints between our firm and a client. We also recognize that these relationships represent the potential for additional work and retaining them for yourself could lead to increased incentive compensation.

For example, in our firm, Stephanie Cole, one of PIE's managing directors and a black diamond traveler, works with Diana and her colleagues at Cognizant. Stephanie brings along Cavin and Erika and five other practice leads from our firm, each with his or her own separate and perhaps completely different network of 10 inside Cognizant. This order-of-magnitude leap in the number of relationships and projects can quickly make Stephanie feel like she is skating on thin ice as she represents PIE to Diana. Is she sure of everything that is going on?

We see it all the time. A project leader does good work for a client and they want us to do more. As we bring on additional people, do different sorts of work for the client, and march away from our first buyer to multiple buyers in different divisions, it produces a kind of anxiety in the first deliverer and, even, resistance.

"Great news!" Erika announces at a company meeting, "I reached out to Cognizant's chief marketing officer, and they are going to hire us to put together a whitepaper series."

"I think you should have talked to me first," says Stephanie, the original deliverer within the client. "My client reports to the CMO. I don't want her to think we went around her."

The Fourth Challenge

The fourth challenge as we strive to win new work with existing clients is the difficulty in including our fellow colleagues, even when we should. Our colleagues will bring equal (maybe even greater) value to those we seek to serve.

CHAPTER

8

The Challenge of Scale

Captain Mark Fithian looked out from the bridge of his pilot boat and estimated the waves at 10 feet. Tonight marked the first time he'd been asked to dock a boat of this size, and the weather wasn't cooperating. Construction to widen the Panama Canal and support larger ships had just been completed, and the Captain had hoped he would get the opportunity to ride along in a larger vessel before taking the lead himself.

The wind gauge read 20 knots. Everywhere there were whitecaps, the spray blowing back his unruly shocks. His guide boat bounced forward, bursting through the swells. Shortly after midnight, Captain Fithian saw the dim outlines of the massive *Rania*, a Panama-flagged container ship looming in the distance.

As he closed in on his charge, he could feel his pulse quicken. Docking the big boats never grew old and the *Rania* was 50% wider and 25% longer than anything he had worked with. At 1,090 feet from stem to stern, the *Rania*, if it was stood up on its propellers, would rise up into the sky nearly as high as the Empire State Building. With a carrying volume equivalent to 15 *Hindenburgs*, it was a beast.

Peering through the murk, he could see the Rania turn to its starboard, blocking the wind and creating a pocket of relative calm on its lee side. Captain Fithian nosed his vessel alongside, tied up, crawled up the short ladder to the hatch in the hull, and made his way to the bridge where he shook hands with Captain Nick Watts. They would be the team that brought the Rania in, with Watts navigating the channels and the bridges before handing over the helm to Fithian, who would bring the vessel into dock.

Watts squinted toward the lights at the shore. Baltimore Harbor is a naturally deep-water port, but for a boat this size, he had to carefully follow a 17-mile zig-zag trail of dredged sections to keep it from running aground. And then there were the bridges.

As he approached the Bay Bridge, Watts slowed, ordering the master to have the crew ready the anchors in case there was an emergency. Then he spotted construction barges and slowed further.

Watts had to pass under the two spans of the Bay Bridge and then the Francis Scott Key Bridge before he handed off the wheel to Fithian. The air draft of the Bay Bridge was 182 feet. The Key Bridge was listed at 185 feet and, fully laden, the *Rania* would clear both easily. Still he was alert because the suspension bridges could sag.

After he passed under both bridges, he wheeled the *Rania* hard to starboard to enter the side channel leading to the SeaGirt Marine Terminal. There he was met by a pair of tugs.

Captain Fithian's job was to bring the boat in the last several hundred meters, and he too was focused. The Rania was carrying 8,402 twenty-foot shipping containers piled high on the deck. He was mindful how the winds might catch the big stack of Conex boxes and whip the ship around, and the wind was picking up, blowing at 25 knots.

He radioed the tugs to begin pulling the Rania vessel toward the wind to keep the boat from banging into the dock. Finally, at 5:25 a.m., the Rania was safely moored.

Economies of Scale on the Panama Canal

Ships carrying freight from Asia, or the West Coast of the United States to East Coast ports, pass through the 51-mile Panama Canal, where the size of the locks that lift boats up from the Pacific to Gatun Lake and then back down the Atlantic, limits the size of the ships. The locks were 33 meters long when originally built by John Stevens and General George Goethals in the decade before World War I. But in 2016 the Panamanian government spent five billion dollars upgrading the canal, including the locks, so that it could handle ships 50% wider and 25% longer. These boats, like the *Rania*, are called post-Panamex ships.

Almost immediately, large shipping companies ordered larger ships, boats that could carry one-third more cargo. Danish shipping giant Maersk placed the first order for 20 of the new, larger ships, each costing $185 million, five years before the canal improvements were scheduled to be complete. They were betting that reduced per-ton shipping costs would boost profits – what economists call "economies of scale."

Economies of scale exist when we are able to produce more units or goods on a large scale with lower fixed costs. Maersk bought bigger boats that can haul more cargo with the same crews and other fixed costs, driving up its revenue/cost, which now gives it a competitive advantage over companies with smaller boats.

Seemingly overnight, Captains Watts and Fithian had to learn how to navigate bigger boats. Their boats got bigger because shipping companies like Maersk leverage the advantage that comes with increasing capacity and driving down their fixed costs.

Scale Advantage in the Expert Services Industry

We see examples of companies across a wide variety of industries leveraging economies of scale. However, economies of scale rest on the relationship between fixed costs and units of production and, as we know, expert services industries are based upon exchanging expertise, help, and service, not goods.

This begs the question:

Do economies of scale exist in our world of expert services?

The answer might appear to be no. The expert services industry is based on humans spending time tackling challenges on behalf of clients. Time is a fixed resource. We are limited by the availability of new work but also, importantly, by the number of hours in the day.

But when we dig deeper, we see evidence of how experts have worked hard to create leverage on their services and, in doing so, create scale advantage.

Scale Through Technology

A Big Four accounting firm creates an enterprise tax compliance solution that harnesses robotic process automation (RPA) to allow it to help big companies satisfy the many compliance requirements they face. The firm uses this software, assuming price is constant, to reduce their cost of having to employ an army of tax preparers and drive up profits. The volume of the firm's work and the size of its contracts produce the capital necessary to create the RPA-driven suite of tax provision tools.

Scale Time on High-Dollar Work

Three friends from law school form a legal firm focused on wrongful termination cases. Their business model is to take cases on contingency. The client pays nothing, but the firm makes 30% of any settlement. To make the model work, they need to be choosy about whom they take on as clients – some cases are more likely to be successful than others and some cases have a higher likelihood of large settlements. The only way to figure out which are the good cases is to interview potential clients and hear the facts of the case. Instead of doing this separating-the-wheat-from-the-chaff work themselves (their highest and best use is prosecuting the winning cases), they hire a sharp paralegal to talk to potential clients and prepare likely-to-pay briefs for the attorneys to review. By hiring help with an average per-hour cost lower than their own, they are able to drive down their average cost of "production" and drive up profits.

Scale Through Buying Power

A small marketing firm that helps design, shoot, and place winning television commercials negotiates a large order discount with each of the top five television stations in their market. By pooling the buying power of all their clients together, they are able to get lower rates, which they can pass on to their clients and gain market share or they keep it for themselves and take the kids to Disneyland for spring break.

Diseconomies of Scale in the Expert Services Industry

However, bigger isn't always better.

Our great uncle dies, and, as part of the estate, we inherit a mining lease in Butte, Montana. We rummage through the files and discover our uncle recently hired a team of geologists to drill and assay a series of core samples from the claim. Looking down at the report, we are hardly able to believe our luck – there is gold in those hills!

We borrow against our 401(k) and set up a small mining operation. After our first year of operation, the news is all positive. There indeed is a productive vein of gold on the claim. We are able to tunnel in, get access to the vein for $100,000, pull out 300 ounces of gold, and sell it for $400,000. We pocket $200,000 and use the remaining $200,000 not only to go back in for a second helping but to open a second tunnel. But then we notice something – the two mines produce 500 ounces of gold. Our average yield is down from 300 ounces/mine to 250 ounces/mine. We sit down with the geologists at the M&M Cigar Store (our favorite bar in Butte that once rebranded as a cigar shop to throw off the feds). Over bourbons, they tell us the bad news: While there is more gold on our claim, it's concentrated in a single small pocket. Our first year, we tunneled into the center of that lode but as we exhausted that vein, the gold, while still there, is more diffusely distributed. The geologists recommend we close the tunnels and instead dig an open pit mine and sift through the large amount of earth to extract the gold. The problem is this will cost us $400,000 a year and will likely only produce a total of 400 ounces/year.

Not only did we strike gold, but we hit on the immutable wall of diseconomies of scale: In some businesses, the costs of production go up, not down, with growth.

As it turns out, expert services firms also face diseconomies of scale, and understanding and overcoming the diseconomy of scale present in our industry is key in growing our work with current clients.

In the early days of PIE, all of our employees "delivered" our services. When we were crammed into 1,500 square feet on Peach Street, all five of us would pitch clients, recruit the executives whom our clients wanted in the peer groups, pre-interview the participating executives, and facilitate peer group conversations that included our clients. There was very little overhead. What accounting there was, we did at night. Whatever technology needs we had got solved over the weekend. We didn't have a website.

Fast forward 20 years, and we have 40 professionals in two buildings. We have a CEO, a COO, a management team, and we talk of getting a controller, an HR manager, and a CIO. Assuming we keep our pricing to our clients the same, we are facing gale-force diseconomies of scale. We will have to figure out a way to get leverage on our service offering, raise prices, or accept lower margins on our work. Although it is true that the specialization of work doesn't necessarily mean lower margins, we have found that big means more bureaucratic friction – a very real form of diseconomy.

We know a mid-sized engineering firm that faces the same headwind. The firm oversees the construction of dams, tunnels, pipelines, and power transmission facilities. It prides itself on being able to mount a small army of engineers to tackle almost any project. "Everything is fine when we have projects," a manager at the firm states. "But sometimes it feels like everyone is back from the field stacked on top of each other in our offices with no income coming in as we burn through cash." Like many expert services businesses, it can feel like feast or famine.

Part of the danger of scale is that, as the gigs get bigger, so do a firm's fixed labor costs even as project flow is unpredictable and discontinuous. "You keep folks on and don't lay anyone off so you can jump on any project you win, but delays, poor business development pipeline, and reduction in project scopes can kill you," reports the engineering firm's COO, highlighting what are the negative impacts of flexibility.

There Is No "I" in "Team"

Matt Ulrich went to Northwestern University, where he was the captain of the football team. After graduating, he signed on with the Indianapolis Colts. He reflects, "I had a chance to play with Peyton Manning and under Coach Dungy. I feel really lucky. They were some of the best. I was in the league for three years before there was someone quicker and stronger ready to take my place. A lot of guys say 'NFL' stands for 'Not for Long'!"

Today Matt is a managing director in charge of our growth at PIE. He says,

It's getting harder as we get bigger. It used to be we'd get a prospective client in our sights, we'd huddle up in the conference room, and I'd say, "What industries do they serve? What are their various lines of expertise? What geographies are they trying to serve?" Once we understood their areas of opportunity, we'd start to dig into their strategic priorities by reading articles on the company and watching YouTube videos of their CEO speaking. You can usually get a sense of their focus and that's where we would put our attention.

Matt sits at his desk. A large man – his teammates called him "Chest" – he leans back in a chair that seems to barely contain him and starts to gesticulate as he warms to the subject.

Then we'd brainstorm theses. If they'd had a lot of success building a data and analytics practice in healthcare, shouldn't they want to extend that franchise to Canada? Let's build them a group of Heads of Data and Analytics in Provincial healthcare providers. Or, maybe they built a practice helping boards of directors pressure-test cybersecurity risks. Seems like the firm would be in a good position to develop privacy policies for the same boards as well as protocols for data governance. Let's propose the idea that we would aggregate a group of Chairs of Risk Committees and another one focused on Chief Privacy Officers.

The wind rustles the aspens outside his office and there is a hint of snow in the air, but we can see the moisture starting to gather on his forehead, betraying the fierce intensity he brings to his work.

I felt like a quarterback in the huddle, giving my teammates direction. Cavin, you come up with a list of F250 companies with Chief Privacy Officers. John, you dig into our databases and identify which consulting firms have cyber and privacy practices as well as the names of the practice leads. Kristin, you figure out emails and contact info for them. Carlie, draft a deck, but let's come up with some new slides that show the work we have done with Chief Information Security Officers. They will respond to that. Jacob, you and Steph work the list. Let's push and report back to each other next Monday.

But we're starting to lose that. The huddle is getting too big, and we are starting to get siloed. We aren't checking in as often to see if someone else at PIE has a relationship with the person we are trying to meet. As we get bigger, communication is getting less perfect. Sometimes I feel like we are the gang that can't shoot straight, with the left hand not knowing what the right hand is doing. To boot, we are losing the advantage of what was our cognitive diversity.

The worst is I feel like we are losing our urgency. Everyone is so busy delivering projects, it's starting to feel like people are not trying as hard as when we were just a small team worried about how we were going to keep the lights on.

Matt is grinding his hands together now, each as large as a head of lettuce, his elbows on his desk, two helmets on the credenza behind him. We can feel his frustration.

The funny thing is I know scale is starting to hurt how we do business development but that's not what bothers me most. It's the feeling I get. I used to get pumped, like we were hunting as a pack. Now I have a feeling of sluggishness. There are always fields I have to fill out in the CRM [customer relations management] and someone I need to call and check with before I can just crank out an email or pick up the phone. Call it business development sclerosis.

Matt is spot on. One of the biggest obstacles to expanding relationships inside key clients has nothing to do with them. It has to do with us, and the internal diseconomies associated with coordinating the efforts of human beings at scale. Small firms are lean, hungry, and nimble. Large companies become rule-driven, hidebound, and satisfied, which makes "getting out of our own way" one of our biggest challenges.

The Tug-of-War Guy

We would not be blamed for thinking farmers and ranchers are agronomists and specialists in animal husbandry. They are, of course, but less obvious is that they are also engineers. There is always a culvert to dig, a tractor to repair, a corral to reinforce, or water to be moved uphill.

Max Ringlemann grew up in Paris in the latter half of the nineteenth century. A strong student, he studied at the National Institute of Agronomy and became interested in this overlap between engineering and farming, taking a number of courses at the National School of Roads and Bridges.

In 1881, he became what might now be called an extension agent, teaching a course on practical agriculture in Grand-Jouan, a quiet farming town halfway between Rennes and Nantes known for its Sancerre. He also wrote a column for the *Journal of Practical Agriculture*. His interest in engineering, however, had him soon testing farm equipment. This work caught the eye of the Minister of Agriculture who, flush with the promise of the

Industrial Revolution, asked Max to set up a center focused on the testing of tractors, threshers, harvesters, and loaders to be able to better recommend farmers on what the Minister could see was a coming industrialization of agriculture.

Max's first task was to develop various dynamometers to measure the torque and rotational speed to understand the capacity and limits of the machines he was testing. Like anyone who has invented a useful tool, he couldn't help but ask what else these dynamometers could measure.

Seeing a group of men in a tug-of-war contest one day, he decided to use a dynamometer to test the force of men pulling on a rope. That's when he noticed something interesting, what we call to this day the "Ringlemann Effect." He noticed that the more men on one side of the rope, the less average pulling force was produced by the team as measured by taking the total force generated and dividing it by the number of men on the team.

As kids, we were told, "Many hands make for light work," but, as it turns out that's partly because we aren't pulling as hard: There is an inverse relationship between the number of hands on a project and their individual contribution.

Ringlemann writes,

> When employing men, or draught animals, better use is achieved when the source of motive power works alone: As soon as one couples two or several such sources to the same load, the work performed by each of them, at the same level of fatigue, decreases . . .

Social psychologists call this the "social loafing principal" and report that humans, when performing a joint task, abrogate responsibility for the task to the whole and stop taking personal responsibility for its success. Even though they *feel* they are giving a task their all, subconsciously they are relying on the others to get the project across the finish line.

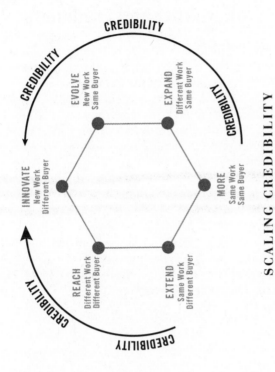

SCALING CREDIBILITY

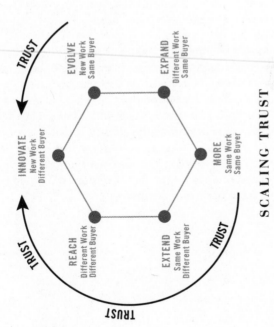

SCALING TRUST

Scaling Trust and Credibility

Assuming we get past the internal challenge of scaling our efforts to tackle larger projects, there exists a second set of challenges – this time external to our firms. It turns out that there are diseconomies of scale at work when we try to extend trust and credibility to those we seek to serve in client organizations.

Trust is the ability to build integrity and strong relationships with our clients that assure them we have their best interests at heart. *Credibility* is the ability to deliver good work and to earn the appreciation, validation, and reputation for excellence in our clients' eyes.

A small expert team working with a small client group soon learns to trust the others and to value the other side's experience and perspective. But as soon as the groups on either side get large, diverse, or geographically dispersed, both credibility and trust diminish.

Interestingly, though – and this is where we are starting to break free and begin to understand where we should put our effort if we hope to build our presence in a client – trust and credibility scale *differently* depending on which type of growth we are chasing on the Diamond of Opportunity.

Scaling Trust

As we work our way up the left side of the diamond toward doing EXTEND work – more of what we already have done but with a new buyer – we have less to prove around the quality of our work.

Say, for example, PIE convenes a community of F500 CFOs for the head of the finance practice in a large consulting firm. If we hope to engage with the marketing practice around convening a CMO group, our credibility is a given. We know how to do our work and hit our marks with the CFO group. The head of the marketing practice will assume that if we promise her a CMO, we will deliver. That's not what keeps us from winning the work. It is that she doesn't know us and doesn't particularly know her colleagues over in the finance practice. She wonders who we are and if we can be trusted to advance her interests. How will we act with her firm's top clients? Will we make the same decisions she would make or is it possible that we might act in our own self-interest?

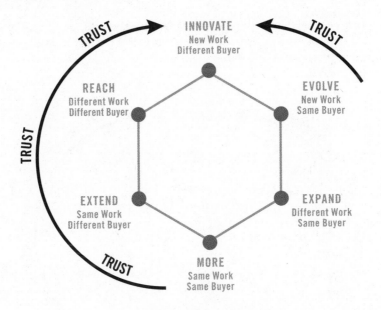

SCALING TRUST

Scaling Credibility

As we march up the right side of the diamond, our challenge is wholly different because the challenge of engaging a given buyer at a client with an expanded set of capabilities is the challenge of scaling credibility, not trust. Our buyer already trusts us. We have had their back in a pinch. But she is not sure we can do this work we promise that is so different from how she has come to know us.

Our job is to show her we have the chops to do what we say we can do.

If we have a neighbor who is a knee surgeon, and she successfully operates on our father, we might come out of the experience feeling that we can trust her to do knee surgery on us if we ever bust ourselves up on the ski slope. But if our aging Nissan Sentra breaks down, and as we are puzzling over why the engine doesn't turn over, the good doctor passes by and says, "Feels like the planetary gear set. Let's get this bucket of bolts over to my house, drop the trannie, and see what I can do," we might pause.

"You ever do this kind of work before?" we might say.

We *trust* her implicitly. We believe she would do the right thing if our backs were turned, but does she have the right experience to work on our transmission? That's a whole different matter. We trust our babysitter with our child's life, but that doesn't mean she has the ability to captain a digital transformation at our thousand-person firm.

As Ford Harding, author of *Cross-Selling Success*, writes, quoting Bob Prieto, former chairman of Parson Brinckerhoff: "(I) called the client to ask for his reaction to the proposal. The client responded, 'There is only one weakness – you have no telecom experience.'"

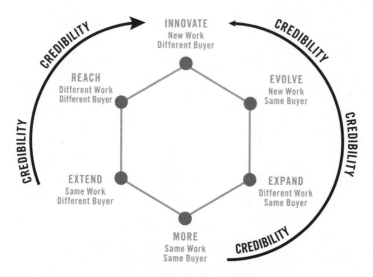

SCALING CREDIBILITY

The Fifth Challenge

The fifth challenge if you want to win more work with a client is the difficulty in getting the trust and credibility you have built with one buyer to transfer over to another buyer. It is one of the reasons our phone doesn't ring with new client work even when we have executed on projects for a buyer with exceptional expertise and insight.

Ouch.

If you are like us, your shoulders are bent from the weight of these challenges.

When the boss came in and said, "Let's come up with a plan for growing the Porsche account," we knew it wouldn't just be a layup.

But we had no idea the extent to which the odds were stacked against us.

But this has been important work. Unless we understand the problem, we are up against; it will be hard to come up with a plan to solve it.

But let's now turn the page on what makes winning new work with current clients hard. Let's see how expert service pros chose where to place their bets on the Diamond of Opportunity.

How We Can Help

In 1995 Dr. Angus Wallace boarded a flight and expected a routine trip, consuming peanuts and perusing the *SkyMall* magazine. Midway through the flight, a call came across the loudspeaker: "Is there a doctor on board?"

Dr. Wallace did what any doctor would do: He offered to help in any way that he could. A 39-year-old woman had fallen off her motorcycle on the way to the airport and developed a potentially lethal condition. Chest percussion and auscultation were rendered ineffective because of the noise from the plane's engines. Dr. Wallace and a junior resident on board, Dr. Tom Wang, sprang into action.

A scalpel and a 14-gauge catheter were available in the aircraft medical kit. (Wallace) created a chest drain with these items along with a coat hanger (made into a trocar for the catheter), a bottle of Evian water (with two holes punched in the cap for an underwater seal drain), oxygen tubing (to attach the catheter to the drain), and Sellotape (to seal the catheter to the drain). Xylocard (100 mg of lignocaine in 10 mL) was the local anesthetic, and the disinfectant for the introducer was a bottle of five-star brandy! As soon as the drain was connected, the patient was operated upon in her seat. Air was released from the pleural cavity, and within 5 minutes she had almost fully recovered. She settled down to enjoy her meal and the in-flight entertainment.

There is no better analogy for the way we should think about business development in the context of expert services.

It would seem arrogant and unnecessary for Dr. Wallace to step on board the plane, grab the PA from the flight attendant, and let everybody know that he is a doctor and available for consultations should any be required. Similarly, it would be downright unethical (and likely illegal) for a doctor to jump on the plane and start passing out prescriptions ("You look a skosh anxious to me, have a little Xanax!" "You look like you need to get some sleep, here's an Ambien . . .").

So too with expert services practitioners looking to develop new work. There is a balance to strike between overt self-promotion on subways or billboards and sitting in your office assuming everyone will just start calling you to put your considerable consulting prowess to work. Diagnosing a problem, and making yourself available to help are key in any professional context. In the same way that a dermatologist has a moral obligation to tell you that you have a cancerous spot on your neck, an expert services provider should feel an obligation to solve challenges on behalf of clients. Strong business developers know how to listen for opportunities to create value.

We can take this one step further as we zero in on developing more work with existing clients. If we are the doctor, then our clients are the passengers sitting nearest us. If one of our clients is choking on a peanut one row up and two seats over – we should know, and we should jump into action. We should be ready and available to help before the flight attendant even picks up the PA to ask.

Section 4: Farming for Knowledge

CHAPTER

9

Know Thyself

In the 2003 Christmas blockbuster *Elf*, Will Ferrell played a character named Buddy the Elf. Buddy has more Christmas spirit than anyone, the greatest enthusiasm for toy making, and lives rule number 1 of the Elf Code to the fullest extent possible: Treat every day like it's Christmas. What's abundantly clear to the viewer – but not to Buddy – is that he is not like the other elves, being two feet taller than the rest of the North Pole population. Also, he doesn't possess the rapid-arm-movement capacity of the other elves that is required for efficient toy creation. His production numbers are pathetic: He creates 85 Etch A Sketches in a day, leaving him 915 off the average. He's useful when a light bulb needs to be changed, but that is not the core skillset they hire for at the North Pole.

Buddy the Elf apparently is not a Marcus Buckingham "Know your Strengths" kind of guy. However, Buddy's not alone. Too many expert services providers make the same error as Buddy: They bring an 85 Etch A Sketch capacity to a marketplace that already produces 1,000 units per day, instead of going to market with their light-bulb-changing service. The light-bulb-changing service may seem like a smaller or less appealing market, but it's one in which they have the right to win.

We see this often in nascent consulting organizations where there is a lack of definition around the product or service being brought to market. This isn't surprising: The majority of new consulting organizations are spinouts of much larger firms; alumni of large firms create their own independent consultancies to solve client challenges with greater autonomy and to enjoy a larger proportion of the profits. Unfortunately, one vestige of the large consulting mindset is often brought with them: They have experience solving a multitude of client problems across various geographies and industries. Now leading a smaller firm, they lack the resources, case studies, and credentials to fully serve their former clients.

Like Buddy, they need to focus their offering.

When looking at the Diamond of Opportunity one of the first questions we should ask ourselves is, "Where do we have a right to succeed?" Because if we don't have a right to succeed – we have never done the work before or are playing in a wholly unfamiliar industry or geography – and a competitor does have the right to succeed in that space, we will lose every time.

Indeed, there is a raft of questions, which, if honestly answered, will steer us away from the longshot points on the diamond and toward our best opportunities to expand with clients.

Size

Are we a big firm with offices across the globe or a small firm with limited reach and resources? Do we strive to be a big firm, or do we like being a well-regarded niche player?

Take, for example, PricewaterhouseCoopers (PwC), which is currently investing in robotic process automation (RPA)- and artificial intelligence (AI)-driven tax preparation tools. They can do that because their revenues are a little north of $42 billion. The kind of investment they can make in future technologies, which may take years before they can monetize them, is beyond the ability of a boutique tax preparation firm. In the language of the Diamond, PwC has the scale to INNOVATE, developing solutions they do not now offer to buyers that they may not have yet met. In this case size is destiny.

Boutique Firm Opportunities

Boutique firms tend to be known for a narrow band of expertise. They should focus on opportunities to do MORE, to EXTEND, and to EXPAND but stay away from EVOLVE and INNOVATE, which are not adjacent to the work they currently perform. They could enter a new line of work, but in many ways, it would be like starting a whole new firm just when they are finally getting traction on their current line. Doing MORE of what they already do for their current buyer, EXTENDing their offerings to others in the client company, and EXPANDing the offerings to adjacent service lines is what they should be doing. They have a right to succeed in winning this work. When we talk to small firm owners, they tell us that a single successful project at a client company tends to beget other similar assignments.

Interestingly boutique firms have a right to win REACH and EVOLVE work – assignments that involve them doing jobs they have never done before if they are hyperaware of opportunities as they arise. Their size and nimbleness earn them the right to take on small assignments often with short timelines, slightly outside of their core competency, but close enough that they can quickly pivot, repurposing their skillsets.

Boutique firms have distinct advantages that uniquely enable them to grow their work:

Culture

There's truth to the old adage, "Culture eats strategy for breakfast." Small firms have strong cultures and can adapt to change. In many small firms, it feels like everybody is engaged in the fight. The trappings of hierarchy, HR processes, and other big-company governance do not eat at their power to innovate and deliver. In a smaller firm, ideas are less likely to be squashed while making their way through the kind of long approval and implementation processes that stymie innovation in larger companies. In a small company, you might scooter down the hall and ask the CEO if you can implement a new program management system. A simple yes green-lights your idea. In a larger company, that same ask might take months, by which time the luster on your idea has begun to rust.

Agility

Small organizations are agile. Large organizations invest considerable resources into agile business strategies to try to achieve a percentage of what small firms come by without effort. Big firms may have to run the traps on exploring an adjacency before they can even bid on it. The questions of "Have we run this through the pricing and proposal committee?" "Have you completed the conflict check?" and "Who else on the account team needs to be notified?" may mitigate risk, but they also stifle. The small firm, by contrast, has limited bureaucracy and can act quickly in responding to client challenges.

Storytelling

Stories sell. When we first started PIE, the stories of the firm seemed to belong to every employee. We all had lived and died every new client gain and loss. As small firms grow, however, the stories become diffused across the organization. Indeed, you see small firms create structures to feed their cultures to ensure their ability to keep telling stories.

Big Firm Opportunities

Nothing should be beyond the reach of a big firm. They have experts in every industry, every service line, and in every geography. But this breadth can hobble them at the same time. When you are known for everything, are you known for anything? Big firms often have a hard time growing clients because the world, including partners in the firm, don't have a good sense of all the firm is able to deliver to clients. Indeed, big firms must be intentional about the structure and technology to create widespread understanding of various offerings and solutions. Big firms have the advantage of housing an expansive set of services and expertise, but if experts in the firm don't know what's in the company toolbox, they will come up short even on simple construction projects. Where they do have an unfair advantage is in the following:

Technology

Large firms do well when clients require, or will require, new enabling technology that only large firms are able to develop. They also do well when they invest in technology that details firm offerings and house libraries of case studies and success stories. Customer relationship management systems (CRMS) allow us to take good notes, keep client conversations seamless, and scale trust and credibility across our organizations. Furthermore, technology that connects experts within a firm allows those individuals to note where their colleague's capabilities may help grow their own work. As technology improves, our expectation is that these systems will become increasingly predictive and enable new work by suggesting complementary services to the ones being currently delivered. That value will be mined as soon as someone figures out how to get professional practitioners to input data into the CRMS.

Global Reach

As the importance of bringing localized expertise to global work becomes more sought after by clients, big firms can capitalize on the opportunity to expand work with clients as they grow. If you're a US-based manufacturer opening your first facility in Latin America, you'll likely hire a Big Four accounting firm with a presence in the region to give you tax advice – not your personal accountant from a 50-person firm in Omaha. As business becomes increasingly global, big corporations want to partner with firms that can be helpful across the world, not across the street. This globalization also changes the way that relationships are developed for consulting engagements. Long gone are the days of rubbing shoulders with your potential clients at the local country club. Increasingly, services are not specific to a location, but specific to an audience. Big firms can resource experts on the ground – and around the world – to tailor solutions and services to fit a particular need.

It is these advantages that have expanding with clients on all points of the Diamond of Opportunity as long as the job is big enough. Interestingly, they regularly leave the crumbs of additional work on the table in order to put their scale advantage to better use.

Structure

How does your matrixed organization affect how you go to market?

Most large expert services firms are organized by geography, industry, and service line. The only more complicated matrix is the relationship between Neo and Morpheus. Acquisitions aimed at a particular geography or service and infrequent large-scale mergers only add to the complexity. Add in nine enterprise resource planning (ERP) systems and it's enough to give anyone a headache. Given the complexity, structure can be a challenge or it can be a key tool to improve collaboration and jumpstart growth.

First, your operating model should reflect the way your buyers want to engage. Are you serving international clients with the need for specific resources across multiple geographies? Are you working in an industry like oil/gas that has a very narrow geographic footprint and a high number of regulations? Do your services apply to multiple buyers or one specific executive function?

Second, your structure should be used to shape your internal culture and operations. Are you trying to foster a culture that is less dependent on travel? If so, structure by regional office in a way that allows people to serve clients locally. Are you trying to expose people to multiple industries, sectors, and cultures as part of the development process? Structure around travel and cross-functional collaboration. Are you trying to scale the time and talents of a few key experts or leaders? Structure in a way that ensures experts are spending time talking to key customers or prospects and are not bogged down in administrative minutiae.

There is no one right answer. We've seen dozens of "reorgs" in all types and sizes of our client firms. The frequency of these changes would seem to suggest that these firms got it wrong the first time and are course correcting, but that is not the case. Reorganization drives many desired outcomes:

- It brings fresh people and fresh ideas into a particular service offering.
- It creates collaboration and fosters relationship development with the business units, which in turn increases the awareness of service offerings and increases the likelihood of cooperative pitches.
- It creates career path options for an employee base made up of high performers who are frequently on the lookout for the next big opportunity.
- It creates innovation: rotating one highly capable consultant out in favor of another highly capable consultant reduces the risk that the services will become stagnant over time, and increases the likelihood that each new leader will look to improve upon what has been done before.

Take stock of how your firm is structured. This can be a good indication of your firm's goals and values, and what leadership is looking to optimize. Know, however, that how you go to market will affect where you should play on the Diamond of Opportunity. If you emphasize the regional nature of your firm, it might be harder to work with other buyers who might be in different geographies (EXTEND, REACH, or INNOVATE). You will want to focus on the Diamond points that have you working more fully to serve the one buyer who is in your region. Likewise, if you go to market primarily by way of your service lines, it is going to be easier for you to do MORE and EXTEND your work than it will be to introduce other professionals from other functional areas in your firm to your client. It is not that it can't be done, it just requires that many more gymnastics.

Growth Strategy

How does your firm plan to grow – organically or through acquisitions? Each path – both worthy for different reasons – will color your relative success in chasing various points on the diamond.

Organic Growth

At Arthur Andersen, the concept of "one firm" was a critical cultural component and, as a result, the firm was not acquisitive. Instead, Arthur Andersen made an intentional and strategic decision to grow the firm from the inside out. Aside from an occasional lateral partner hire, the growth was all organic.

Arthur Andersen demonstrated that adopting a one-firm approach solidifies culture across the organization. It allowed the firm's culture to spread naturally throughout and reduced the need for forced culture-building events. Andersen folks were lifers. If you speak to people from Andersen about their time at the firm, they still wax poetic about the collegial culture of the firm, a culture cemented in the early days of employment as employees went through training at the legendary St. Charles center.

This may not be the easiest way to grow – developing new service lines from the ground up is hard. Organic growth contains a startup cost that can be avoided when you acquire niche firms and these challenges are multiplied when a firm is trying to work across cultural, geographic, and industry boundaries.

When we say Andersen had a strong culture, we are saying that the company seemed small. People knew each other across service lines, geographies, and industrial sectors. They had come in young, gone through the same St. Charles bootcamp, survived, and thrived. There was not a lot of coming and going. They were lifers and they were there for each other. When you needed help halfway across the world in Beirut, the person who picked up the phone didn't need incentive pay to collaborate. They gave you a hand because it was the Andersen way. They knew one day they'd be giving you a call.

For this reason, firms that have decided to grow organically are better at introducing their colleagues into the mix than firms that have grown through acquisition where you may not know anyone in the newly acquired firm. Organically, grown firms do well with EXPAND, EVOLVE, and REACH, each points that often include bringing your colleagues into your client.

Mergers and Acquisitions Growth

When you are focused on rapid growth, growth through acquisition can be a strong strategy. This type of growth can be used to achieve certain metrics on behalf of a demanding marketplace or private equity partner. It is a good strategy in a "land rush" market, where there is a race among competitors to get to scale first. Even better is when this growth is accretive, meaning the acquiring firm can buy a smaller firm for one multiple of earnings and "sell" those earnings to a public market that values that same earnings stream at a higher multiple. Acquisitions can also be helpful when trying to develop new service lines or enter new industries or geographies. Wipfli acquired Bauerle and Company in Denver, Colorado, to build a construction and real estate practice. Bauerle was a dominant firm in the Rocky Mountain region construction and real estate (CRE) market and was a seamless bolt-on to the existing Wipfli CRE practice in other markets. This mitigated the risk of what would have been a years-long process of developing relationships, winning work, and becoming an established player in the market.

If your firm is focused on growth through acquisition, you will struggle with creating a culture that emphasizes refer-and-assist behavior (the very points on the diamond that organically grown firms will excel at). However, you will have a sweet spot in anything that requires you to do new or different work (EXPAND, EVOLVE, REACH, or INNOVATE) because you can always buy your way into these new offerings. Whereas it might have taken Andersen years to build up software writing capabilities, you can acquire those skills for a seven-times multiple in less than nine months.

Experienced Hires

The middle ground between these two growth strategies – and something that many expert services firms choose to pursue – is the hiring of single smart professional to beef up the capabilities. Rainmakers say this can be a good strategy if you mind these points:

- **Vetting** – Get clarity between the two parties on the expectations. Are you expecting content knowledge? Are you expecting them to bring a slew of new relationships and business development? What are your goals and metrics for success and are they achievable?
- **Compensation** – Get clarity on the compensation package. It's incumbent upon the firm to give a clear picture of the compensation system and appropriate expectations for the incoming partner. Potential commission is not a replacement for base salary.
- **Cultural assessment** – Take the time to understand the cultural fit. Create a social activity and allow staff to interact with potential hires. Have the lateral partner spend a full day in the office as part of the interview process so both parties can determine if it is a good fit. The same axiom is true in lateral hires as it is in others: Hire slow and fire fast. Years ago, PIE tried our first lateral hire and got nearly everything wrong. We saw it as a chance to "up our game" and hire someone who could have real impact by leveraging her network. We ignored the advice of our current employees and assumed they were intimidated by a competitor. But our people were right. The fit was terrible. Our people found her antagonistic, arrogant, and uncollaborative. She left our firm less than a year into her tenure; we were left with a temporarily bruised culture and plenty of lessons learned.
- **A lot about a little** – Workplace happiness can be a lot about a little and things vary dramatically from firm to firm. It's important to give a fulsome picture of "a day in the life in our firm." Will this person have administrative support? Will they write their own proposals? Will they be able to utilize budget if a new idea arises? These are some of the pitfalls that can make a lateral hire go the wrong direction.

Your Team

Next question: Who's on deck?

Developing a deeper understanding of our capabilities and the potential of our colleagues and our team is critical to knowing where our firm has the right to succeed and is best positioned for growth. It might seem obvious but the difference between REACH (doing different work with a new buyer) and Innovate (doing new work – work no one in the firm has ever done before) is the difference between Jasmine's ability code or not.

Thierry Chassaing of BCG notes the importance of knowing his firm's capabilities and his colleagues' capabilities as he prepares for a project:

> Carefully selecting what we sell is very important to me. I've always trained my teams to make sure we don't do the wrong project. When we do the wrong project, we damage our relationship and create an unhappy client. The BCG brand should be one of guaranteed success. Working on the right project with a client is number one for me, and then making sure every step of the way that we bring the right experts and seniority to the table so that we can exceed expectation in terms of quality. Part of picking the right project is being sure, if we are being hired to create a change, that the change is doable and that we know how to make it stick. If it doesn't stick, again it's a total waste of time and money.

Taking the time to get to know, understand, and build trust and strong relationships with our colleagues can accelerate our ability to work our way around the diamond.

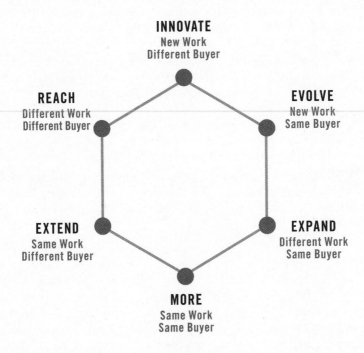

Let's go back to Susie's work with Thomson Reuters to explore the benefits of leveraging others in your firm. We saw how Susie might expand her work with Thomson Reuters through the six opportunities:

1. MORE. Susie has grown the contract to include more of the same work with the same buyer (virtual peer exchange facilitation).
2. EXPAND. Susie expanded this relationship by offering an adjacent service (facilitated live events) to her same buyer.
3. EXTEND. Susie extended this relationship by offering the same work to a new buyer (building a new virtual peer exchange group of Media and Telecommunications CMOs for a new buyer).
4. REACH. Susie reached to help a new buyer in Thomson Reuters with a research project, a service she has strong experience with, but has never performed for Thomson Reuters previously.
5. EVOLVE. Susie evolved her relationship with Thomson Reuters, leveraging the trust she's built with her client and the skillsets she and her team have to find a way to help her current client with something *new*, something that PIE has not previously done.
6. INNOVATE. Susie innovated with Thomson Reuters, finding a way to leverage PIE's skills in a *new* way (a service we haven't performed before), to help a different buyer at Thomson Reuters solve a problem.

However, it took Susie a full 10 years to access some of the new opportunities for work. What would happen if Susie brought in additional members of her team to accelerate the growth of her partnership with Thomson Reuters?

1. MORE. Susie brings in a junior colleague to facilitate four additional virtual peer exchanges per year with her Am Law 100 group. Because her colleague is now on board, Susie's time is freed up to pursue additional growth opportunities.
2. EXPAND. Susie introduces the Thomson Reuters team to a new hire at PIE who specializes in event planning and live-event facilitation. Credibility is immediately scaled because Susie's colleague has 20 years of experience in events.
3. EXTEND. Susie brings in two talented colleagues who facilitate a number of virtual peer communities – one specializes in CIOs and one in CFOs. Thomson Reuters expands its contract with PIE to include two new groups with each of these new facilitators.
4. REACH. The new hire at PIE who specializes in live-event planning and facilitation has a contact from college at Thomson Reuters. Susie and her colleague reach out to the new buyer and sign a contract to help plan and facilitate breakout sessions at Thomson Reuter's annual conference.

5. EVOLVE. Susie introduces her client to one of her colleagues at PIE, who comes from a technology background and sees an opportunity to help integrate PIE into Thomson Reuters' CRM system. Susie's colleague hasn't done this but has the core skillset and wins the work based on the trust that Susie has built up with the client.

6. INNOVATE. Susie's colleague with the Thomson Reuters connection sees an opportunity to lead all of Thomson Reuters' account managers in an offsite around landing and expanding new work. Susie and her colleague are able to leverage PIE's skills in a *new* way to help a different buyer at Thomson Reuters solve a problem.

Your Personal Brand

How well have we established our own brand in our firm?

We are charged with getting to know experts across our firm so we can introduce them to our best clients and continue to win and deliver excellent work. By the same token, we should be building our brand inside our own firm so that others will pull us into *their* best clients. It is incumbent on us to let others in our firm know of our expertise and experience helping clients. Greg Engel at KPMG shares, "You have to find a niche you are passionate about. It is a very fast way for you to be an in-demand expert, and being an in-demand expert is a good way to get yourself in front of people and win work."

Cindy Hannafey remembers her early days at the accounting and financial services advisory firm UHY:

> When I first came to UHY, Steve McCarty, who is now our CEO, was the first partner who called me in and gave me a chance with one of his customers. We absolutely killed it. We did a plant move – generating significant revenues for the firm – and it was a big success. The customer said it was their best executed plant move. That experience opened many doors for me and my team at UHY and with our customers.

We can't expect our colleagues to remember everything we are able to do. Leave them with one or two specific client examples. Walt Shill of ERM explains:

> You have to sell internally to the client account manager. You have to convince the account manager that you can do a good job. And while you can make a long list of reasons you shouldn't have to do it in big organizations and small, you have to. Some of our partners at Accenture would get very angry and say, "Why do I have to sell internally?" And I said, "Look, that's just a fact. Why should this guy introduce you to the client that's going pretty well?" We would teach the service area leads how to get credibility with the area managers or with the account managers. Often, they would want to go into the technical details of shared services, or cybersecurity, or

remediation when, in fact, that doesn't help the area manager or the account manager. That actually makes them *more* nervous because now the service lead is bringing up all this technical shit that the client lead knows the client isn't going to be interested in.

So, we had to teach those service managers the way you sell to the account manager is by bringing in specific client examples. Here's what we did for Amazon. Here's what we did for Citibank. Here's what we did for the State of North Dakota. Here was the issue. Here was what we did. And here was the result.

Experts tell us that once we become our firm's go-to person on a subject – communicating clearly to our partners how we can help their clients – that is when it begins to rain. Sharing our expertise with our colleagues is the easiest business development action we can take.

By extension, if we are in a firm that is populated by professionals who have bright, highly differentiated brands, it is easier to know whom to call when you see your client in need. Have a client who is facing a wrongful termination lawsuit? You know to call George because he is was recently named one of the top employment litigators in the nation. A firm that is full of strong personal brands will find it easier to EXTEND and EXPAND.

Your Niche

What is your firm's niche?

Experts report that they spend as much time brainstorming opportunities to grow inside a client as they spend force ranking those opportunities around where they have a right to succeed and their capabilities. Expert services firms should work to own a niche – to be the largest board advisory firm, or the oldest, or the most-admired – and lay stake to a claim they can rightly make.

Amidst the plethora of firms advertising this or that service, buyers have a hard time remembering who does what. Tight niching builds brand recognition and highlights a signature service or specialty that separates you from the noise. A firm that claims expertise in being able to help with any problem under the sun diffuses its brand in the marketplace. However, a firm that is known as the best board advisory firm working with middle-market software companies is much more likely to be top of mind when a middle market software company encounters a challenge with its board. Even Buddy the Elf recognizes the power of a good niche. When Buddy wants to treat his crush to a warm winter drink, he heads straight for the New York City shop advertising the world's best cup of coffee. If that same shop suddenly claimed to be home to the world's best apple pie, best pizza, best vegetable dumplings, *and* best martini, we might start to question their claim to coffee. Can anyone really be the "best" at everything all at the same time?

Kris Timmermans of Accenture explains:

I've personally created a brand for zero-based budgeting. We became a market leader doing $1 billion and more in strategy and consulting work in zero-based. In this particular area, our brand is present. We published a book, we're known everywhere, and we've got ten times the number of engagements that the second strategy firm would have in this space. So, in very meaty areas, you can build this, but it's been a five- to ten-year investment to get there.

A niche is powerful, both because it communicates a sharply defined value proposition, and also because it paves the way for efficient marketing. It allows a practice to begin to narrow the number of seeds they plant in their business-development garden. This narrowcasting keeps everyone focused on making friends with the exact 200–500 executives who are most likely to use the firm, as well as publishing consistent and useful thought leadership targeted toward that cohort.

Many firms worry that they can't make a claim to being first or biggest in their industry.

The trick is to narrow the claim. You can be the *world's largest* doughnut company in the world – Dunkin' Donuts at 11,000 units and $1.3 billion in revenues. But if that's not available to you, then you are Tim Horton's and *Canada's largest* purveyor of doughnuts. Short of that, you are Lucky's Doughnuts on Main Street and are voted *Vancouver's best* doughnuts. Find and own whatever superlative helps you stand out.

As you look at the Diamond of Opportunity, you might be tempted to stretch in the face of client need and offer to do work that is out of your niche. "Yes, we can develop software," you say (INNOVATE) as you think about whom you might hire to onboard that capability. But do you want to? Or in your stretching for new revenues are you actually watering down your brand?

Beware the Brand Prison

As we build a brand and cement our niched reputation, that very brand can become a moated, bars-on-the-windows prison, out of which it is difficult to talk about new capabilities. This, of course, is the opposite of what we just described. Sharply niched brands are the most effective way to bring in new business, but they stand in the way of expanding our portfolio of services that we offer, making it challenging to EXPAND, EVOLVE, or INNOVATE. To expand our set of service offerings, we have to build a new brand, and that takes time, work, and money. It also takes the ability to *demonstrate* our new abilities.

Nichole Jordan of Grant Thornton explains,

Sometimes we get an opportunity in an area where we do not have brand permission to play. We have to be able to show, rather than tell, what we have done in other areas. We have to be able to say, "With these three peer companies, we have done this type of enterprise risk management project and it has brought them these outcomes. Please feel free to speak with them." It is about showing what we have delivered.

Alternatively, you can refer business you stumble on if you want to stay true to your niche. Says CPA Carrie VanDyken,

We try to stay within our wheelhouse because we are a professional firm and we have to be careful of how much we advise on and consult on anything outside of our expertise. Often, though, clients call us with questions about a government program, employee discrimination law, insurance, etc. They come to us first and we refer to others we know.

This is all to say that having a strongly niched brand doesn't block you from doing new work; just go into new work with your eyes open.

Fortunately, the very work of *knowing thyself* better holds the keys to breaking out of brand prison. As you gain a deeper understanding of your firm, your team, and your own capabilities, you are able to identify your core skillsets, which, if redeployed, could yield an adjacent opportunity.

At PIE, for example, our core skillset lies in recruiting and interviewing executives, synthesizing content, facilitating conversations, and guiding clients on strategic business development follow-up. Several years ago, we asked ourselves, where else might some of our core skills apply? For example, where else are our clients recruiting and interviewing executives? That process yielded new service lines in research and loss review work, both of which involve getting time on busy executives' calendars and thoughtfully interviewing them. In our effort to expand our service lines and encourage our clients to leverage us to solve additional challenges, we look first to where we have a right to succeed. From there, we can identify the kind of services we might offer that our client already believes we can do even if we have not done it with them before. We lean on hard-won trust with existing clients to make our way out of the brand prison.

Our ability to serve our clients and grow our work begins with intimately knowing our firm, our team, and our own capabilities. However, that foundation is not enough to win us new work. Just as we spend time getting to know ourselves, we must get to know and understand our clients, their needs, their challenges, and their opportunities.

CHAPTER

10

Know Thy Client

Every rainmaker we interviewed shared a common, strongly held belief: that it is important to study your client to understand their strategic intent. Only by knowing our clients as we know ourselves can we best identify where our breadth of expertise matches their breadth of challenges and needs. Here is how Will Williams of KPMG puts it:

> You've got to be a deep, deep student of the client and understand the business challenges that they face and the strategic imperative that they are trying to execute against. You want to have a culture where you are always saying, "Hey, if we want be an all-star player, a world-class professional, we need to never stop being a student of our clients." You never want to put yourself in a box where you're just delivering your one piece of expertise. You want to try to bring the whole power of your firm and help in as many ways as you can.

So, let's sharpen our pencils and head back to school. How do we become A+ students of our clients?

Leverage Your "Insider" Status

First, let's acknowledge that we're being graded on a curve. When we interviewed a number of experts, they reported three advantages to already being on the "inside" when we're working to better know your client, compared to those trying to win the same client as a new logo:

1. **Implied Trust:** If we are in the building, we have gotten past security; we are not an outsider. Large companies, in particular, have hordes of would-be experts trying to scale the walls of their corporations, so they dig psychological moats to keep the multitudes at bay. When we are inside a company, we are among the chosen.

2. **Hard Information:** Half the battle of trying to navigate a company for expanded opportunity is knowing just who is doing what. When we are on the inside, hard information like organizational charts comes much more easily and that helps. Depending on the project we are working on, we might also have access to confidential information like divisional P&Ls, budgets, advanced knowledge of new software implementation, cuts, strategies, and initiatives. We can't snoop around a client like 007 – that's a sure trust destroyer – but we can honestly process what we see in a way that is useful to our efforts to grow an account.

3. **Soft Information:** One expert we interviewed from a large engineering firm said simply, "Live where you work." When we are on site, we form relationships, not only with our buyer team, but with others as well. It is in the context of trusted relationships that people start to let their guard down and begin to talk about what might be true (educated guess), what should be true (point of view), and who it might be true for (gossip). This fuzzy world of not-yet-fact is how experts begin to engage with client executives before the request for proposal (RFP) is issued. Rumors are a sign of coming changes, and changes are the fertile fields for experts to farm their client relationships.

Banish the Brochure

"But, we're unique." If experts had a nickel for every time they heard this – from every type of executive in every type of industry – they'd all retire at 30. As we all know, this is the result of consultants constantly showing up at a buyer's door with a slick five-step brochure that purports to have the silver bullet to everything. These pitches are often met with pushback, such as "We have 14 ERP instances, a decentralized back office, and an incentive structure that misaligns with that approach."

The expert has no chance at this point; they have exposed that they don't understand the specific – or "unique" – issues that this organization is facing.

While successful case studies are definitely important, pitching something that worked someplace else as a boilerplate for success can seem insulting to executives leading complex organizations with tens of thousands of people, especially ones that you purport to know based on an existing client relationship. Abandon the brochure. Ask questions. These questions should be aimed at understanding the client's overall strategy, the role of the group you are serving, and how your capabilities might be leveraged to achieve those goals.

Surprisingly (or not so surprisingly), demonstrating curiosity can be a key contributor to growing a client relationship – and a lack of curiosity can have the opposite effect. Dave Lubowe of Ernst & Young (EY) agrees: "The CEO of one of my long-term clients told me that he had turned down another consulting firm because they didn't have a 'Dave' showing up to ask questions, whether he was selling or not."

Listen Effectively

As we're demonstrating curiosity by asking smart questions, it's equally important that we listen to the answers. If we only start listening when an opportunity arises, it's too late. Listening is a critical portion of developing new business, but it has to be a constant habit as we work to deeply know our clients. And we shouldn't only ask questions of – and listen to – our individual buyer. The best experts are constantly gathering information from multiple stakeholders to get clarity on the direction of the organization. If we've taken a break from listening, it's likely that a defter expert has won our assignment.

There are a handful of questions that experts should constantly have in the back of their minds as they think about their client relationships. If we've been listening well, we should be able to answer all these at any point in time, while understanding the answers may always be evolving.

Questions you should always be able to answer about your client:

- What is their budget cycle and fiscal year?
- How does each individual involved with this project define its success? How does the firm measure success?
- Is this initiative tied to a larger strategic project? How do we ensure we are aligning to those outcomes? Who else should I be connecting with to ensure that's happening throughout the project?
- How does this project interface with other business units in the organization?

- Whose support do we need to earn to make this implementation go smoothly (and to renew this contract)?
- What external factors (e.g., regulatory environment, talent shortages, etc.) are acting on this business or industry that may impact this project or our future partnership?
- What is the change management process for this project? Can we include some lessons that we've learned in driving effective change as part of the scope?

If we realize we've lost sight of an answer, it's time to start asking questions again – and listening more closely.

Growing Relationships Through Change Management

Walt Shill of Environmental Resource Management (ERM) highlights the value of incorporating change management into any scope of work. "Any time you're doing a project of any potential impact on the organization – and you shouldn't be doing it if it's *not* going to have an impact – there is almost always a major change management element to that. It's crazy not to include it in your scope of work, because you won't be successful if you don't."

Expert services providers are incentivized to find creative solutions to big challenges in corporations. Pithy models and enhanced techniques are often the result of years of experience and painstaking research. Having gone through the work, experts are frequently guilty of viewing a newly developed solution as a panacea. This ignores the reality that large corporations are collections of people trying to achieve specified outcomes. The collection of people brings political considerations, hierarchy constraints, and other factors that make change an incredibly important part of any engagement. You can't "bolt on" a new finance operating model with a one-size-fits-all approach.

This approach of incorporating change management has many benefits:

- It increases likelihood of project success.
- It broadens relationships and support for the project within the organization to minimize key client departure risk. These relationships are the seeds for additional work as people move to other firms.
- It deepens understanding of client priorities and uncovers nebulous political considerations.
- It lays the groundwork for other growth opportunities.

This final benefit of including change management highlights the tremendous opportunity this presents to do more of the same kind of work (MORE and EXTEND work) within a client organization. As Shill describes, "It requires that you meet a lot of people when you include change management. And if you've met them, now you've opened up the door. Then you need to go back and share with them the results because, if they're in the change management piece, they would see it. And then they'd go, 'Oh, wow. Here's someone who's gotten results.' To me, it's so obvious but so few people do it."

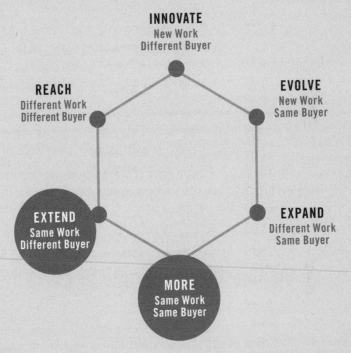

The key is building the relationships upfront. Buyers are naturally distrustful of consultants who roam the halls with 20-page decks touting how successful their recent projects were. Including a broad swath of decisionmakers in the change management context provides a natural communication channel to describe value creation that doesn't feel like a pitch. The easiest growth opportunities come from good work being seen by key decision makers. If experts believe in their services, they should do everything they can to expose them, in action, to more people. Change management is a fruitful way to do this authentically.

Understand the Political Dynamics at Play

Clearly, consulting engagements should represent a creation of value beyond the cost of the project. This could come in the form of cost reduction, revenue growth, or risk reduction, but it's rarely black-and-white. Astute consultants understand the impact that a project will have on the overall organization, the way work is completed at that organization, and perhaps most importantly, the impact on individual employees with whom the work is done.

Years ago, we invited a chief operating officer (COO) and a chief financial officer (CFO) from the same Fortune 500 company to an event we were hosting, and both agreed to attend. Through the registration and pre-event planning process, we learned that there was a lot of animosity between the two executives. Once they learned of each other's commitment, they both canceled their attendance. Clearly, we did not have a good understanding of the political dynamics on this leadership team. We lost a shot at engaging either of them by inviting both.

Understanding the importance of individual outcomes allows experts to develop deep trust and position themselves for future opportunities. When possible, we should look for opportunities to elevate key people on the project in front of decision makers. Engagements are most effective when we understand the hierarchy at play and build a strategy that accounts for unique reporting relationships and seniority differences. Experts can separate themselves from competitors by understanding individual goals and going the extra mile to help their clients achieve those.

Be Mindful of Budget Cycles

Ask a junior person at a large consulting firm if they know their client's fiscal year, and you will usually be disappointed. Ask a senior partner the same question, and they will likely say, "October 1" without hesitation. Rainmakers work to understand a client's budget cycle. It is invaluable to know, for example, that first-round budget requests are sent by March 1, your client gets a rough cut back on the total budget by June 1 with a second chance for input, and then they get the final budget on October 15. Without this knowledge, you're hindering your ability to help.

If you don't know when to play the game, you can't win the match.

Cozy Up to Their Technology

Bits, bytes, cables, and modems promise to connect us and, yet, sadly, sometimes they keep us apart. It is our job to bridge that divide. If I am a Mac person and the client is all PC, it is on me to play nice with them. Not *vice versa*. We should try to integrate into their technological ecosystem. Rather than sending over data in a spreadsheet for one of their clerks to input into their enterprise software, we should aim to get a seat in that software and own the actions.

At PIE, we're focused on assisting services companies with business development in targeted markets. Recently, we've added CRM integration as part of the engagement. This allows us to track wins, hold business developers accountable, and find opportunities for improvement. As an added benefit, having someone who actually inputs information into CRM is a value-add on its own. Marketing consultants create deeper relationships, better engagement, and more success when they integrate with a client's CRM system. This form of technological engagement improves the stature of the expert because they are now "part of the team," and less of an outsider.

Stay Alert on the Outside

We may not learn *everything* on the inside. Gather information regularly from publicly available news sources. Google Alerts are an effective and efficient tool for staying up to date on newsworthy items. A chief information officer (CIO) leaving our client organization may indicate a move toward information technology (IT) centralization. The acquisition of a small technology company may indicate a strategy shift. Earnings calls may describe previously unforeseen risks on the horizon. We should use these pieces of information as the basis for future exploration and questioning, not for giving a diagnosis or prescription.

Conduct Loss Analysis

Rainmakers at leading expert services firms report they regularly use loss analysis firms to understand when they have failed to win a competitively bid project. If a practice lead for Deloitte has burned through three weekends preparing an RFP only to lose the bid, they want to know why. How often have we heard, "I just don't get it. We were the best ones for the job." Maybe you were within 5% of the low bid, you got the top scores on all the rubrics, but this particular project went to your competitor. If you've developed a good enough relationship with your client, and you're doing good work for them in other ways already, you should be in a very strong position to gather information about why you weren't the one best suited to help them in this other way. Maybe the other firm had stronger case studies in that specific line of work. Maybe it was cost because budgets are tight. Maybe that particular buyer has a longstanding relationship with the firm that won the bid. If you're already on the inside, you should work hard to gather the intel so you're better equipped to win the work next time.

Playing Defense

The email from our marquee, but relatively new, client comes scooting in after quitting time. Jacob's watching Arizona tape on ESPN wondering how the Gonzaga basketball game will turn out on Saturday. Tom's getting ready to throw some elk burgers on the grill.

"I wanted you to know first," the email from our client says. "I'm off to my next adventure. Friday's my last day. I'll introduce you to my colleague, Jennifer."

We pay close attention to these sorts of transitions because it can be a dangerous time in a relationship. If the first buyer earned institutional credit for building the program we run, where does that leave their successor? Often, they will get credit for extending the program or enhancing it in an important way, which can be good for us, but inevitably, along comes a buyer who sees the opportunity to make their mark by rationalizing our efforts. That can mean cuts or even a new provider.

It doesn't matter if the key stakeholder moves to another position within the client, gets recruited to go to another firm, or gets fired. The effect is often the same: We have a new buyer who doesn't know us and with whom we need to create a trusted relationship, *pronto*. Absent our ability to create that trust, we could lose work as the new buyer moves to *her* trusted relationships. We have to re-prove ourselves with a new buyer. In this circumstance, just continuing business as usual feels like we're doing EXTEND work – it parallels the challenge of doing the same work with a new buyer in a client organization.

What do we do when our buyer bails?

- **We go meet the new stakeholder in person.** When we hop on a plane, we communicate that we do not take the relationship for granted. We are telling our new stakeholder, "You are powerful, and you are important to me." Many of the service providers our new buyer oversees will not do that. Travel makes us stand out. And, yes, there is no better way to accelerate the creation of trust than to meet face-to-face.
- **We learn more.** Before we land, we pay attention to newsworthy items about the client, gathering information on "deep background" from other people we know in the organization. We once met with a mid-sized consulting firm in New England. The COO there told us, "I tell my consultants, the goal is to become so familiar with a stakeholder that you're starting to share gossip." Relationships like that, no matter the level, can help fill out the picture.
- **We ask them about their priorities, and we listen; we don't pitch.** As we're walking inside, a voice in our head will say, "This person doesn't know what we do or how good we are. I need to tell them."

We work to ignore this voice. Although we haven't yet built all the trust and credibility we would like, we have some. If nothing else, we have inertia. It is a mistake to ignore what has transferred. Understanding the context in which our old buyer left is important. If they were fired, it could be that all of their initiatives are toxic, and a new person has a vested stake in remaking the world in their own image. If our old buyer was promoted and is currently a darling in the company for having engaged with us, we might have an opportunity to make our new buyer an even bigger hero.

- **We make adjustments.** No one takes over a program and says, "I want to keep it *exactly* the same." They've been elevated to run the department because their views are valued by their firm. They need, want, and deserve a chance to give voice to those views. They want to put their mark on anything under their control. The last thing we should catch ourselves saying is, "Well, that's not how Joe wanted it." It does us no good. Like it or not, we have a new boss, and we should be working hard to align with their goals.
- **We add value.** Jeff LeSage, Former Vice Chair of Tax for KPMG, describes being very aware of these kinds of transitions:

We relationship map professionals who are critical to an organization's success. These key professionals include decision-makers and those we believe will have an impact on the long-term success of these companies. We need to feel confident with regard to who is in line for successorship. What we have found works really well is presenting these key individuals with a first-100-day playbook. This guide provides useful information that will help ensure they remain focused on what they should be thinking about in their first 100 days and offers suggestions to help promote success.

While we have a standard first-100-day playbook, our teams make an effort to personalize the playbook for each organization. We want to make sure the new leader knows we are thinking about them and trying to help them to be successful. It goes a long way in building trust and establishing a strong relationship within a company.

Like Jeff, we think it is important to add value to a new buyer on an account, whether it is by presenting a PowerPoint summarizing a project to date or providing a platform to discuss the following year's budget.

Finally, there is one bit of housekeeping to do before we plow forward with our new relationship, and that is staying connected to our old stakeholder. Inevitably, she has moved across the company or to a new company where we might be able to do new work. If we haven't already, we connect with her on LinkedIn, having invested valuable time demonstrating we can do good work for her and have her back. We don't want to let that go. Life is long.

Open the Aperture

So, we've asked all the right questions, listened intently in all the right places, and gathered all the knowledge we possibly can about our client. What do we do with this gold star we've earned? We help.

As Dave Lubowe of EY puts it,

> We look for trends within and between industries. We try to understand how new technological advances can be used to get more value or to drive improvements in businesses. Then we will go to clients and say, "Hey, based on our understanding of your company, we think you might be interested in this point of view." It's a way to have a conversation with the client. It's not, strictly speaking, selling, but it's intended to open the aperture a little bit. It says a few things. First of all, "I care enough about you to make this phone call." The second thing is, "I've actually thought enough about your business to suggest what might be relevant to you." And then the third thing is, "You can tell me if you want to pursue this or not. I'm not selling it to you. We're just talking about it."

It's time to look at our Diamond of Opportunity and start putting the puzzle together. Let's use all this knowledge to see where and how we can help.

11

The Secrets of Diamond Account Planning

We have a friend who is a senior partner at one of the strategy firms that spun out of a Big Four accounting firm. She lives in White Rock, just outside of Santa Fe. She and her husband are big fans of Georgia O'Keeffe and she loves to paint the rich hues of Diablo Canyon and the Rio Grande at dusk in watercolors. Between hobbies, volunteering at church, and video chatting with her three grandchildren, she keeps busy. Her consultant days are over, but not so distant that she doesn't remember the annual budget thrash well.

> Every summer, we were asked for our numbers as the organization built its budget and worked to reverse engineer earnings projections. Of course, we were asked to project our headcount and expense lines, but we were also asked to project revenues, which is hard.

> It was hard because the "answer" came from on high.

We would get a mandate to increase key client accounts by a certain percentage, say 10%. Our job was to build a plan that would achieve that number.

We are talking to our friend by phone on a bluebird February day. She reports the skiing that morning at Taos was excellent and that she made short work of the four inches of new powder the hill had received the night before. She continues her story,

We would fly everyone who touched an account into a meeting space and the client account lead would lead us through an exercise where we would review the work we were doing, look at an organization chart of the client, and look at our services lines as we tried to answer the question, "Where will the new work come from?" When a client gets big, this work is daunting because the numbers are so large. If we did $100 million of work, a ten percent increase is $10 million more, which is not like picking daisies in a meadow.

It was an exercise in coordination because, like all consulting firms, we were organized by geography, industry, and functional expertise so there were lots of fingers that touched the client. I was on the industry side of things, focused on healthcare management, but others might be located where a client had their headquarters or had specific expertise around, say, pricing, out of which they served lots of clients, including ones outside of healthcare.

Aligning the Stars

We've spent so much time getting to deeply know ourselves and our clients for one key reason: We want to align the stars in the strongest, brightest way as we evaluate our opportunities to help. For every expert services firm and every client, there will be a unique set of opportunities on the diamond that will equate to maximum helpfulness. At its best, account planning can help us fill the entire diamond, pushing us to be creative with our own work in the right ways, and guiding us toward our highest and best use for our clients.

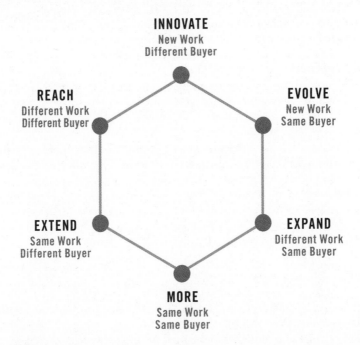

INNOVATE
New Work
Different Buyer

REACH
Different Work
Different Buyer

EVOLVE
New Work
Same Buyer

EXTEND
Same Work
Different Buyer

EXPAND
Different Work
Same Buyer

MORE
Same Work
Same Buyer

Active, ongoing account planning is an essential part of expanding relationships with existing clients. Experts we spoke to shared that they use a variety of structures and strategies to achieve a couple key goals as they think about their account planning process:

- Where do our services align with the specific desired outcomes of the client?
- Where do we have the trust and credibility to win that work?
- How can we develop relationships with key buyers who are not currently working with us?
- How can we introduce our additional capabilities to this client to help them in other ways?

Laura Smith, vice president for North America Technical Sales & Summit Program at IBM, describes how her firm approaches account planning, underscoring the importance of viewing the entire exercise from the perspective of the client's needs:

Our account planning starts with what the client's challenges are. Then it's the application of, "Okay, what do we have in the portfolio that can help them in those challenges?" But there's also another piece of account planning, which is the art of the possible. What are the areas, because we have knowledge around the industry and around the client, where we can say, "Here are places you're not even thinking about that maybe you need to think about. And here's how we can help you think about an area that you hadn't even considered yet."

In a small organization, account planning may be as simple as two key employees brainstorming relationship depth and opportunity for value creation, then making a plan to achieve those goals. This makes sense, as most small firms have fewer than five service lines and that lends itself to a simpler planning process. As organizations grow larger, the complexity of leveraging different services, different experts, and different geographies is magnified. This size requires formalized planning and relationship mapping in order to expand the work being done.

Dave Lubowe of Ernst & Young (EY) shares with us the eight key steps of his account planning process, some of which vary based on the size of a particular client. His strategy is clearly rooted in deep knowledge of the client, and of EY. Woven throughout the process is a theme of building on existing trust and credibility:

1. First, we gather relevant partners and business developers on an annual basis. This may include consulting, tax, assurance, or mergers and acquisitions (M&A), depending on the work being done currently with the client.

2. Then we look for interlocking opportunities across the matrix of services, geographies, and industries, and align those to the structure of the client.

3. Once an account plan has been established, teams will make investments to increase the likelihood of winning that work. Investments might include training, marketing, or asset development (this could include research, modeling, or thought leadership that solidifies credibility to operate in a particular industry or service line). These investments often require collaboration across internal groups and engagement of third parties.

4. We host regular meetings and conference calls to stay abreast of the changing landscape within a client and adjust the strategy regularly.

5. We make sure we describe the opportunities to serve that client across our business units. We utilize relationship mapping to identify the functional areas within the client where we have established trust. This also develops a view of the competitive landscape. Sometimes, an executive has a strong affinity for a particular firm because he or she is an alumnus of that firm. In those cases, developing relationships with the leadership group one level below the executive will foster opportunities when that leader moves on to a new role.

6. We force rank the opportunities based on the intersection of client trust, strength of offering, and internal capacity.

7. We pursue the opportunities.

8. Repeat.

Expanding Your Capability Reach

Rainmakers at expert services firms have a handful of best practices they use to systematically expand how clients think of their firms' expertise. Much of this is focused on REACH and EXTEND work – simply introducing clients to your additional offerings that you've successfully performed for others in the past. But it also includes doing EVOLVE and INNOVATE work – becoming a strong enough partner to your clients that they trust you to dive into new kinds of projects with them as you look to put your skills to work solving their challenges.

Speaking about developing these new kinds of services, Accenture's Kris Timmermans reports,

> In my part of the business, we have huge budgets to innovate. When we invent the newest stuff and we think it has market traction, we reach out to our client account leads (CALs) and the accounts where the possibility for initial success is the highest. That's how we learn, and we get better. Once the innovation has credibility and it has a few cases, we invest in what we call the last mile. You've got to get the innovation in the hands of the CALs and the accounts.

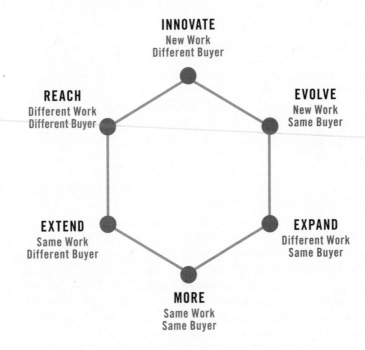

Successful firms are able to expand their capability reach by doing a few things:

- **They limit ancillary services to where they have a right to expand.** Expansion to world domination is a journey of a thousand steps, and the next step is the one closest to the last step. The Cambridge Group's Chris Fosdick puts it this way: "After we do one really strong piece of work, we go on to do more work for them and solve more problems. We systematically say, 'Okay, we did good work, what are the logical one or two things that we can do next to help them further?'"

  If you do cyber work for middle-market law firms in California, being a Clio partner (a well-regarded purveyor of practice management software for law firms) for those same firms makes sense. You have a right to expand in that direction.

  - You already know the buyers – they are the same chief information officers (CIOs) you are already working with.
  - You are known for your technical prowess.
  - You already have geographic coverage and a brand that is known in that geography.
  - You understand how "law firms are different" and have already demonstrated your sensitivity to law firms' unique sensitivity to conflicts and privacy.

    If, however, someone on your team suggests that it would be fun to do strategy consulting for large New York investment banks – you know this isn't a winning strategy. Know thyself; adjacencies are not all created equal. Some naturally spring out of work for which we are already known, and this is where we should seek business development satisfaction first.

- **They allow for limited – or appropriate – scope creep.** As a project unfolds, clients will ask for you to do work that was not in the original statement of work. Best practice is to gently remind them that their request is "out of scope," and that while you're happy to do the work, you will need to adjust the scope engagement to meet their needs – as well as your own. This has to be the rule if you ever hope to hold onto your margin.

  An exception is when a client asks you to do a project out of scope that is exactly where you hope to expand your practice but where you do not yet have great case studies or reputation. When Mark Finlan of Huron talks about testing out these new kinds of work with clients, he says, "These opportunities work best when built on a strong partnership foundation. With the client, I would highlight that this is something that can help them achieve their desired outcomes, and explain why we are the firm best positioned to help them, highlighting where we are willing to invest together."

- **They boost their credibility.** A time-honored way to expand a firm's right to work in adjacent service lines is to import a star. Similarly, firms acquire each other. Maybe a large public accounting firm hires a former Internal Revenue Service (IRS) leader for their Washington office. Maybe they acquire a technology company to help them better deliver tax technology automation solutions to their clients. In many cases making such investments can be a sort of 'fast-track' to credibility as can strategic investments in training or requests to have certain skillsets from elsewhere in your firm seconded to your team.

- **They move from provider to partner.** Over time, the goal is not just to be a vendor, but to be a client's collaborator. One opportunity to do this is during a client's budget process. It is basic account management to know thy client's fiscal year and when the budgeting cycle begins. PIE has a Big Four client whose fiscal year ends in the fall. For them, the spring kicks off a six-month budget process. That always starts with each of our buyers pulling together presentations describing what they have done with the previous year's money, some way to think about measuring that effort's success, a smorgasbord of possible new initiatives, and a recommendation.

  None of our buyers like this process and they welcome our help when we offer it for free. Each year we offer to pull together some slides on the work we did, including some qualitative and quantitative results, and then suggest brainstorming some ideas for the next year. We have never had a client say, "No, thanks" to this offer. And we put work into those slides. It's thrilling when our slides get passed around as internal work product. Volunteering to help clients at the front end of the budget process is one of the surest ways to expand those mandates.

- **They level up.** Your buyer's boss may often be the decision maker on the second set of services you hope to do for a client. You should prioritize developing the trust and credibility there to put yourself in the best position to earn that REACH and INNOVATE work when the time comes.

- **They are "other-centered."** Successful account planning depends on a business development culture focused on helping others, not helping ourselves. Rob Benson of Kele Inc. explains,

> I think you use account management to educate people around the fact that to sell in a new world, you have to do it in an *other-centered* way. That's number one. You have to do it in a way that takes pressure off of people and makes the client the priority, which is what so few good professional salespeople do. It almost always comes across as what are you going to do for me?

All of us are doctors on a plane. We are here to help. Experts should be focused on developing relationships, asking great questions, and exceeding expectations when taking on an assignment. The emphasis should always be on driving outcomes for the client (or patient). Throughout the process of account planning, make it a point to stop and ask, "Is this how we can be most helpful, or position ourselves to be best prepared to help?" Over time, this philosophy will lead to full pipelines, trusted advisor status, and strategic impact.

But how to execute your plan? For that we turn to the Seven Disciplines of Successful Farming.

Section 5: The Seven Disciplines of Successful Farming

12

Discipline 1: Do Good Work

On the edge of Boston's financial district, Bill Green's offices overlook the neo–Art Deco State Street Bank and Trust building. The legendary former CEO of Accenture is known as the leader who laid the foundation upon which Accenture's current market-dominating position is built.

On a foggy fall day, we ask him how to expand his footprint in clients. Leaning back in his chair, he's frank.

"It's fucking hard. You have to start with that, right?" You have to have your best day . . . every day.

Smiling broadly, he goes on to explain that at the heart of expanding in a client is doing good work:

> At Accenture, the money gets made if we have the two thousand largest companies in the world as our clients, period. You don't need to capture all these little guys. You've got to capture the franchise clients – what we call our diamond clients. Clients that are leaders in their industries and appreciate the value we deliver. They're clients you have for life. We have worked with Caterpillar for thirty years. We've had some of our clients for forty years, uninterrupted. A diamond client is one that is over $100 million in revenue per year . . . year after year. We built 150 of those.

He has a point. In the expert services industry, more clients isn't necessarily better (in large part due to the diseconomies of scale we outlined in Chapter 8).

Better is better. Focusing on a few key clients, and growing work within those clients across the Diamond of Opportunity, generates the highest returns.

Green elaborates,

> I think when you say, "land and expand," it's boring. You want to *weave yourself into the fabric* of the world's great companies. To do that you must bring them your best. We always brought the best of Accenture to the table. That's how we operated, regardless of operating group, regardless of geographic boundary, regardless of language skills. The absolute best. Our job was to bring the best ideas to the clients, sometimes way ahead of their time. Sometimes, two or three years before the clients were ready for them, because that was our proposition. That's what I mean by weaving ourselves into the fabric of our customers.

Bill knows what we all know. Mediocre work closes the door on further opportunities with a client, whereas superlative work leads to additional chances to serve. No book on how to expand client relationships can say otherwise. The work comes first. Only after bringing the very best of your firm to a client have you earned the right to make new friends and listen for new opportunities.

Three thousand miles away, Scott Wallace sits in the Seattle office of international law firm Perkins Coie. A partner at the firm, Wallace focuses his practice on Trust & Estate Planning. He puts it this way:

> Business development starts with your work product. I think you have to produce an exceptional work product. And I think secondarily, it's your interactions with others, for lack of a better term, your people skills. If you work hard and have a good work product, and if you can get along with your colleagues and your clients, the business development will naturally happen. That's not to say that you shouldn't go to lunches and coffees and take speaking engagements. But I think if you work hard, produce quality work, and if you are good with people and good to people, around year seven or eight or nine, it will start paying dividends because you'll get client referrals, inter-office referrals, and referrals from colleagues in your field.

Paul Allen, serial entrepreneur and founder of Embark, a financial advisory firm, agrees. He says, "Once a client finds out 'This is a firm we love to work with. They're easy to work with. They're a great value from the perspective of the talent they provide and their capabilities,' they say, 'What else can you do?'"

Brands are built one 2-by-4 at a time, but when they are freestanding, they provide cover and warmth to every future fledging relationship someone in our firm is creating with a new buyer in an existing client.

What You *Can* Control

Doing good work is what causes clients to re-up and expand the scope of a contract. It begins and ends with the work.

Writes Art Gensler, author of *Art's Principles*, "Bringing in business is one thing; winning repeat business is another. The key to loyal clients is to make sure you have excellent delivery of your services. This is a core part of the design process. From your opening conversations until the final handover to the client, you want to refine your delivery process."

At PIE, we say, "Delivery sells."

That's equally true and not always true. A better way to think about this is that "good work" is a necessary but insufficient precondition for growing any type of work within a client, whether that is by doing MORE work, EXPAND work, or INNOVATE work. It's the foundation for growth across the Diamond of Opportunity, but it's not the only thing at play. At PIE, we might nail a project for our client, a consultancy that advises oil and gas companies on land-lease development. The consultancy loves our work, but a major drop in oil prices means our client is facing tighter margins because their buyers are forced to cut budget. Market factors outside our control may force our client to cut additional projects, *even ones that are effective and that they love.*

There is nothing we can do about global demand for oil and change in the commodity markets. What we can control is the work we deliver. We want to put ourselves in the best position to earn that work back when the price of oil starts to tick back up.

In short, our job is to "wow" our clients every day, in whatever ways we can.

Deconstructing "Wow"

When we "wow" our client, we open the door through which more work can walk. We know this, but what does "wowing" a client really mean? For us, it means consistently doing Level IV work:

Level I: Good Work. When experts produce quality results, deliver what they promise, and deliver it on time and under budget, they are thought to have done good work. A client on the receiving end of Level I work might say, "I was pleased with PIE. We had no idea how to best capture the interest areas of the thousands of technology experts attending our upcoming conference. PIE surveyed the community and got the job done within two weeks with very few issues coming up."

Level II: Excellent Work. Good is good, but excellent is better. When clients work with expert services providers who do excellent work, they start recommending them to others. Let's say PIE did excellent work instead of good work. A client might say, "We asked PIE to survey all of the participants planning to attend our upcoming conference. We gave them two weeks, but it was done in five days. They blew me away with their professionalism, understanding of the complexity involved, and the attention to detail they put into the project."

Walt Shill of Environmental Resource Management (ERM) describes a fool-proof way of knowing whether your team is delivering excellent work:

> **Try asking one of your team members for a client reference from a past project to use for a new proposal. [. . .] If they say, "Sure thing," sending you names of multiple references within a few minutes, you know they delivered excellent work.**

Level III: The Lagniappe. At PIE, we take time each month to recognize those in the company doing extraordinary work. We say these people "deliver the lagniappe." Mark Twain can explain what we mean:

> We picked up one excellent word – a word worth travelling to New Orleans to get; a nice limber, expressive, handy word – "lagniappe." They pronounce it *lanny-yap*. It is Spanish – so they said. We discovered it at the head of a column of odds and ends in the *Picayune*, the first day; heard twenty people use it the second; inquired what it meant the third; adopted it and got facility in swinging it the fourth. It has a restricted meaning, but I think the people spread it out a little when they choose. It is the equivalent of the thirteenth roll in a "baker's dozen." It is something thrown in, *gratis*, for good measure. The custom originated in the Spanish quarter of the city. When a child or a servant buys something in a shop – or even the mayor or the governor, for aught I know – he finishes the operation by saying – "Give me something for lagniappe." The shopman always responds; gives the child a bit of licorice-root, gives the servant a cheap cigar or a spool of thread, gives the governor – I don't know what he gives the governor; support, likely. When you are invited to drink, and this does occur now and then in New Orleans – and you say, "What, again? – no, I've had enough"; the other party says, "But just this one time more – this is for lagniappe."

> —Mark Twain, *Life on the Mississippi*

"Lagniappe" means "something extra." When we find a way not just to do excellent work for a client but to give them extra value on the house, we start to step into the world of "wow." We want our buyers to tell their colleagues, "PIE blew us away with their delivery. On top of gathering survey responses from the conference attendees, they sorted through the content to provide briefs for our experts who would be meeting with attendees. They were happy to help connect the dots for us and make us feel well prepared. They saved our event team a ton of time and made our team look good in front of our biggest clients."

Matthew Sunderman, president of the advisory business at HBR Consulting, knows the long-term value of the lagniappe far outweighs any short-term inconvenience or cost:

I mean, for me personally, I think it's been critical to the relationships or the good relationships that I have and the folks that come back for repeat work. The cost of sales of spending four extra hours to make someone happy for "free" versus trying to find a new logo is 1/100th of that time, and the probability of them coming back is a lot more. I think going over and above and beyond for existing clients just for their benefit, even if it doesn't have a direct benefit to the company or your personal bottom line, is worth its weight in gold.

The lagniappe drives client storytelling, the kind of stories that lead to MORE work. Perhaps your buyer's boss put a brutal deadline on a project and your team works the weekend to ensure it is met. This has very little to do with competency and everything to do with demonstrating that you "have their back" – you're building up a mountain of trust when you deliver this kind of lagniappe.

A lagniappe does not need to be large. It can be help with a budget deck that saves your client from having to put one together. For example, you might offer to help and say, "We'd be happy to pull together a couple of slides that talk about the project and the options going forward." It can also be an accumulation of things small and personal, like recipe or movie recommendations. A little "extra" can go a long way.

Caution Scope Creep

The dangerous cousin of the lagniappe is "scope creep," of which there are two kinds.

Army Ranger sharpshooters know that when they fire, the rifle kicks back forcefully. When they mount a telescopic scope on a heavy-recoil rifle, that kickback can cause the scope to slip a thousandth of an inch, resulting in "scope creep" and declining accuracy over time.

That's not what we are talking about here. Scope creep is when a client asks for extra work that was not contemplated in the original statement of work or modifies the scope of work in a way that requires more of our resources. Indeed, it can feel like a bait-and-switch when it happens. We win the work on the basis of a statement of work (SOW) that we have bid in a way that gives us a fair margin. Later, they change the project requirement in a way that bleeds out all our margin. Good for them. Terrible for us.

The difference between the scope creep and the lagniappe is that the former is the client's idea, whereas the latter is ours. This is not about control; it is about scale. Lagniappes are small gestures of extra value, given in service of building good will that we believe will be building blocks for growing the client relationship. Scope creep is about major new requirements that cause a project's profit to hemorrhage.

Level IV: The Pivot. True "wow" lives in the world north of excellent work and freebies. It lives in the world of strategic advice. Experts who ask the purpose of an assignment set themselves up to be able to pivot during an assignment and suggest modifications to the scope of work that *better* deliver against the *why* of the effort.

When helping our conference host we might pivot and say, "We're excited to work with you to conduct a survey of the conference attendees. We thought it might be helpful to create a heat map showing interest areas that come up through the survey so we can look at how those best align with your service offerings. We'd be happy to meet with the various teams to brief them on the results so they can be best prepared."

Even higher-level strategic input happens when you first bid on the work.

In a similar vein, if PIE were to learn that the goal of this survey project is to unearth growth opportunities with individual attendees, we might suggest at the outset that we conduct 1:1 interviews instead of doing an email survey. We might explain how we've used this as a business development tool for other clients and walk through how the in-depth interview approach will allow us to hear specific pain points more fully and map those against their service offerings and specific account teams.

Similar to understanding your buyer's strategic intent is to plug into the white-hot current of your client's strategy as a firm. Perhaps we saw a YouTube clip of our conference host's chief executive officer (CEO) talking about the importance of digital tools in enabling life sciences companies as the industry faces rapid disruption. We could offer to expand the scope of our preconference survey or interview work to create a roundtable of chief digital officers from life sciences companies as an ancillary event at the conference for their largest clients. Or, at the very least, we might suggest incorporating some more targeted questions in the survey or interview process, reflecting our understanding of their firm-wide priorities.

This is the stuff of true partnership. If we've done our job, our buyer starts telling their colleagues things like, "PIE is great. All their work has been excellent, on time, and under budget. But more importantly, I feel like they are partners. They really get our business and always have useful suggestions. If you want a team that knows their stuff and has your back, you should work with them. They're head and shoulders above all the other partners I've worked with on our conferences in the last five years."

How to "Wow" Clients

At PIE, we have a process of delighting customers that we call SHELIE. Our director of quality delivery even has a small stuffed bear on a bookshelf in his office with "SHELIE" embroidered on its t-shirt.

SHELIE-the-bear exists to remind us of the key steps we must take to ensure we're "wowing" our clients.

S	*Set goals with our client:* At PIE, we think about goal setting as a series of meetings.

The **first meeting** is actually the last pitch meeting. The client agrees to engage with us. We've brought a draft SOW, and we go over it with them. The statement of work includes what we will do, how much it will cost, when we will get it done, the resources we will bring to bear on the project, and the metrics that will be used to measure success.

We say, "Let's walk through the SOW. We want to make sure we're getting you where you need to be. As we read through this, keep in mind our objective is to leave you delighted. If there are ways we could improve this draft that would leave you 'wowed,' let's get that in there. Same with the metrics. Let's set up a series of measures that, if we can achieve them, will leave you feeling great about the success of this engagement."

Note that in this first meeting, we're setting the bar at "delighted." We're asserting that if our client tells us what would delight them and we do it, then we have a right to expect them to be, well, delighted.

The **second meeting** is what we call the kickoff meeting. Here we go over the edited version of the scope. Again, we say, "Our goal is to leave you delighted after this engagement is done. We want to make sure we've captured exactly what you are looking for us to do and what, if we do it, will constitute a roaring success in your mind."

You might think this is repetitive, but part of client management success is keeping the client focused on what they hired you to do.

H	*Hit our marks:* We are always on time, we never charge more than we say we will, and we work to move mountains for our clients. To us, these are table stakes if we are committed to doing excellent work.
E	*Be enthusiastic about wins:* Enthusiasm matters not just for the work you do and for the intellectual mountains you are scaling, but for the progress you are making – one piton at a time – along the way.

Our **third meeting** with a client is also the first milestone meeting. It's critical to set periodic checkpoints to ensure that the project is on target and that the goal posts aren't shifting. Say we've gotten the gig to host a roundtable of manufacturing chief information officers (CIOs) for a client. We promise that by the end of 90 days, we will have built a community of 25 CIOs and interviewed at least half of them for the kickoff roundtable session. After three months we gather in the client's conference room, look out their floor-to-ceiling glass windows at the ant people below trundling home, and dive in:

When we gathered together three months ago, we said we would reach out to CIOs for large manufacturing companies and recruit 25 of them to join an ongoing round-table discussion. We've done that and would like to talk about who is in the group, what opportunities for you we've been hearing in the interviews, and the topics the group is interested in discussing during this kickoff session.

Then just before the meeting closes, we say, "Thank you. We're really excited about the progress we're making. Just quickly to review, we said we would recruit 25 CIOs in the first 90 days and interview at least half of those CIOs to uncover their agenda interests. We've done that and, now, according to our schedule, we're going to take a week to incorporate the feedback you gave us and iterate a draft agenda for the first roundtable discussion."

In **meeting four**, we do it again, only this time with more enthusiasm. "This is great. We are on a roll. We love working with your team."

L	*The Lagniappe:* Now we start looking for opportunities to give our client a baker's dozen in **meetings five and beyond**. We might offer to fly out to visit our client and give their boss a briefing on the project to date, or maybe we send a book on business development we were discussing at our last meeting.

If we find ourselves nickeling and diming a client (like the ubiquitous copying charge found at the bottom of a $700/hour attorney's bill), we try to remember to ask, "Why are we doing this? Have we lost the forest for the trees?"

I	*Initiate feedback:* Now, the project is winding down. This is when we ask for feedback in what could be our last meeting or a renewal meeting if the project has potential to be ongoing. We say, "When we started this project, we said our goal was to delight you. We all hammered out a plan we thought would achieve that end. Over the last six months, we have hit our marks and tried to over-deliver on all the metrics you said were important. We know sometimes our plans aren't perfectly conceived. Were you delighted with the project? What have we learned if we continue this program or do another project together?"
E	*Elevate the conversation:* Later in this final or renewal meeting, we pivot to a brainstorm around strategy. We say, "I've kept track of the nice-to-haves you've mentioned over the last few months. For example, you said having a way to track all the opportunities that come up during our 1:1 CIO interviews and roundtable discussions would help your sales team capitalize on those interactions. We do that work all the time and I thought I would share with you a couple of the dashboards we've developed for other clients as well as a recommendation on how we might help with this." This is the moment to venture across the Diamond of Opportunity, but to do so in the context of offering strategic advice. Writes Stephan Schiffman, sales coach and sales trainer, "We cannot assume that our client's plan or reason revolves around our own preconceptions; we must do the work necessary to identify what was originally most important to this decision maker. And, as long as that decision maker remains in the same place, is facing the same situation, and is focusing on the same goals, that plan or reason is what should drive our efforts to retain and upsell to the customer."

Metrics

Some consulting engagements have hard and specific targets that clearly outline the goals of the assignment. For example, cost cutting tends to be a practice with specific and measurable goals both parties understand and work to achieve. (If you can reduce our client's marketing spend by $100 million over two years, that is a real win.) On these assignments, the critical first step of goal setting is relatively easy.

Other projects are more nebulous and require experts to clearly outline the objectives of the project in language that is clear. In practices like innovation or marketing consulting, the objectives are rarely independently measurable. This doesn't mean consultants shouldn't try. Questions like, "What will it feel like when we finish this project and it has been successful?" and "What will others say about this department if we do our job well?" help the expert and the buyer frame language that clearly describes desired objectives.

The Easy Way to *Not* Win More Work

"The quality of their work was terrible, and they were at least six months behind schedule and 50% over budget," says Andy Weas, a director at PIE who helps lead our technology efforts.

Andy is frustrated. He came to us from Perficient and had long experience overseeing IT projects on behalf of demanding clients. Now at PIE, he is having his first experience being on the client side of one of these projects. We've asked him to help lead the purchase and installation of Salesforce into our shop alongside John, one of our managing directors (MDs). They interviewed a dozen integration shops, and spent hours describing the needs and idiosyncrasies of our company in the sort of precise language that could be easily consumed and digested by potential vendors. They scoped the work, gathered bids, and called references. All in all, they executed a flawless purchasing initiative.

For months, Andy piped over our existing data and provided feedback to the contractor at check-in points. He was also eagerly training stakeholders and writing update reports for our management team.

In August, Andy gave the management team an update on progress and said, "I feel confident we will be going live by the first week in September." John nodded his agreement.

Then there was a delay.

At the next update in early September, Andy told the management team, "The contractor came across an unexpected challenge in trying to accommodate a couple of our edge cases."

Andy and John still sounded confident and, importantly, we could still hear them investing their credibility into the project. Drawing on his experience at Perficient, Andy reiterated to management, "This is normal. Just a little snafu."

Then early September slid into mid-September. By October 15, leadership was starting to ask questions. Jacob checked in with Andy and asked, "Everything okay? When do you think we will be up and going?"

Andy started to pale a bit in these conversations. He knew his word was turning to mud. He was worried his personal credibility with his bosses was eroding with every assurance that "We're close." But what could he and John do? Recalls Andy, "I called them every other day and they continued to say, they have just one more thing to tackle and they will be finished."

Around Halloween, the contractor sends Andy and John an email saying that their original bid was not nearly enough to cover the work given what has been unexpected complexity in the project. At this point, Andy feels compelled to put his "developer hat" on to move the project forward and achieve desired outcomes that the vendor couldn't deliver.

"I can't believe it," John says. "We spent hours and hours with them telling them about this complexity." With the anticipated cost overrun becoming meaningful, John suggests a call with the COO of the contracting company. John cuts a deal with the vendor and reports back to the management team. He tells us it is going to cost more, but we have it under control. He says, "I split the difference between what they were asking and the original bid. I felt strongly they needed to take responsibility for their mis-bid in some way. They have told me we will be live by Thanksgiving at the latest. I told them that was a good week because a lot of people will be on vacation and demand on the system will be low."

Now John is in the mud, too, putting his credibility as a manager and negotiator on the line. John was telling his fellow MDs, "I've got this."

Anyone who has ever done a software integration knows where this story is headed. We are writing this December 12, and the instance of Salesforce is still not up or going. We are starting to say to ourselves, "If it is live by the New Year, we can live with that."

Want a sure-fire recipe for *not* getting new work from a client? Over-promise and under-deliver.

We will all be logging our meetings in Salesforce in short order (think, Q1). The work will be done. Indeed, the work might be some of the best work an integrator has ever performed on a project like this. The contractor might even get some award for how clever they were in solving our problems.

But PIE will never, *ever* hire this contractor again. They didn't do what they said they would do. When we realized that, their credibility dropped to zero. Then they didn't communicate with their buyers, Andy and John, in a way that allowed them to build confidence in the project with their stakeholders. They made a fool of our whole team. When we realized that, our trust evaporated like rain dropping on a hot highway.

Contrast that experience with a recent project PIE conducted with AD Creative, a design agency we work with at PIE to bring our visual ideas to life. We needed graphics drawn up to illustrate a few of the concepts in this book and gave them a tight deadline (one week) and (very) rough sketches for what we had in mind. We asked if our request was doable and they responded within minutes, connecting us with a designer and setting up time to talk specifics – shocked they couldn't fully understand our stick figures – to ensure they could deliver the product we wanted. Within four days of our initial ask, AD Creative sent us dozens of shiny new graphics that matched our existing PIE branding and helped clearly communicate the concepts we were looking for. AD Creative even added a few additional examples they thought might be useful to include on top of our initial ask. They know how to "wow" their client.

Companies that prioritize great work and deliver on it know this is the simplest formula for success. Says Sarah Clifford of Seven2, a boutique creative agency,

> I've realized that all clients want is for me to be fully transparent about timelines, budgets, creative, and what's reasonable, and that builds a trust between a client and me. A lot of agencies will say, "Yes, we can get it done," and turn out a really shitty product. Then we get called to fix it. It's happened to us multiple times. The client comes to us and says, "Sorry we didn't go to you guys to begin with." When we take on work, we look at it, we look at our resources, we look at our talent, and say yes or no, or yes, but here are the caveats. And I think that goes a long way with the relationship building.

Imagine if the Salesforce implementation firm we used at PIE had approached the project with that same level of professionalism and had delivered work that not only met our expectations, but surpassed them. For one, we would have been in Salesforce months ago, or at the very least we would have had a more realistic timeline so we could better plan training and data transfer internally. Andy and John would have waltzed into the leadership team's monthly meetings singing praises of the vendor and championing them as a partner. We would have invested in MORE Salesforce work with the firm to meet our need for additional functionality within the system. A year from now, when we realized we need to EXPAND our technology enablement, we may have turned first to that vendor as a partner to see if they could help us with a different type of work. Instead our sights are set elsewhere. Landing anywhere on the Diamond of Opportunity starts with doing good work.

Key Ingredients for Doing Good Work

It sounds easy, right? Just do a good job. But there are a number of things we can do to ensure that, from the outset, we're setting ourselves up for an outcome that we can be proud of and one that leaves our client thrilled with our performance.

Strong Delivery

Experts have to bring the goods when looking to engage on a new project. For a sole proprietor, that expectation is pretty straightforward. It gets more complicated when you win work and then hand it off to a more junior associate. That's how we make money and margin in expert services, but we can't push down too low in the organization or else our team will disappoint. There is a fine line between giving our client "the best, most expensive team" and giving them "the B team."

Mark Finlan, former principal at Bain, sighs as he recalls a past project put at risk and future work likely lost:

> We were working on a large organizational transformation project, and we had a multimillion-dollar extension on the table with our client. There were many other projects we were talking to them about, including that they might want to move their ERP system to the cloud, which could be a massive undertaking. I had recently helped cross-sell a very small project with one of our other practice areas. The client expressed they were having challenges with their analyst on the project, who was not performing well. Because that work was perceived as IT-related, my client voiced concerns about working with our organization on other projects going forward.

Regardless of the size of the project, the quality of the work matters. Every time.

Proper Expectation Setting

Doing good work begins with the initial scope of work. This is when experts need to set expectations. Says Stephen Spears, chief revenue officer for SAP SucessFactors,

> Deliver on what you promise and don't oversell. I think that that's probably the key element of the whole story, knowing what you can't sell and then selling underneath of that to ensure two things: number one, that you are successful and number two, that you'll leave something on the table. You know my wife is famous for a quote, when we go on vacation, we take trips somewhere, you always have to leave one destination that you just don't quite get to because that's the impetus to go back. That's the impetus to require another trip, another at-bat, so to speak. And there are some amazing software professionals that I've worked with over my career that do precisely that.

At PIE, we aggregate likely buyers into peer group discussions. Typically, our clients ask us to do this for three reasons: They want to build their brand; they want to gain market insight so as to better craft service offerings; and, most importantly, they want to build executive relationships in target companies off of which they can scope work. We call it brand awareness, market insight, and relationship development – the three ingredients that we believe can help them systematically win new business.

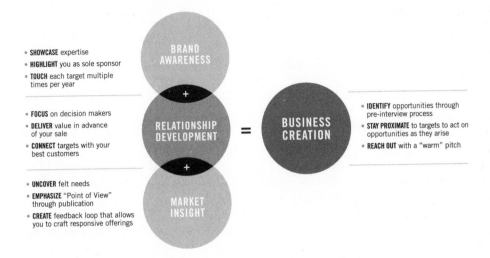

- **SHOWCASE** expertise
- **HIGHLIGHT** you as sole sponsor
- **TOUCH** each target multiple times per year

- **FOCUS** on decision makers
- **DELIVER** value in advance of your sale
- **CONNECT** targets with your best customers

- **UNCOVER** felt needs
- **EMPHASIZE** "Point of View" through publication
- **CREATE** feedback loop that allows you to craft responsive offerings

- **IDENTIFY** opportunities through pre-interview process
- **STAY PROXIMATE** to targets to act on opportunities as they arise
- **REACH OUT** with a "warm" pitch

During the scoping part of a project, we ask our clients to identify which of these three objectives is driving them. If their objectives are a combination of all three, we ask how they will define "success" 12 months down the road. Twenty years of experience has taught us that our clients might say, "We are all about brand and market insight – we don't want to be selling," but then a year later, they will have moved past this, and say, "I am having a hard time with my boss. She's asking where the ROI is on this project."

Instead we push for the hard objective – the one everyone seems to be tip-toeing around initially. We have found that while our clients see these peer exchanges as a chance to build their brand and to learn more about their clients' pressing issues, inevitably, at the end of the year, someone is going to ask about ROI. From the start, we carefully measure business development opportunities that arise, so we are prepared for the ROI question, whether it comes three months or three years after our initial scope.

We know that writing great case studies is hard in expert services – and it's especially hard if we haven't set strong metrics that we can report clearly to potential new buyers. It's hard because we often don't have access to the client data that allows us to make our case.

Say, for example, a diversity and inclusion (D&I) human resources firm successfully pitches a chemical conglomerate on a series of career-day booths at seven different universities with above-average minority chemistry majors. The project scope said the firm would work to generate interest among minority students and gather contact information, which then would be forwarded to the recruiting firm engaged by the chemical company. Check. After one year, the D&I consulting firm finishes its roadshow, having produced 523 referrals. When it comes time to renew the contract, their project manager tells them, "The [chief human resources officer] CHRO was questioning if the career-day strategy was a better use of resources than an investment in social media. She wanted to know how many new hires resulted from the effort." Fair question. But you don't have that data, nor was it part of the metrics that were included in the original scope.

The bottom line: *Scope metrics into your SOW so you can overcome even the hardest objection a new buyer in another division might throw your direction.*

A Killer Case Study

Case studies are how experts scale credibility. We know our buyer well and our buyer trusts us. They are rock solid in their faith that we will, in the immortal words of Spike Lee, "Do the right thing," even when no one is watching.

What they do not know, however, is whether we can take on a new assignment that is somewhat distant from the context in which they know us. We have their trust but have not scaled that trust to do EXTEND work and help others across the organization the same way we've helped our buyer. Similarly, we have not yet earned credibility with our current buyer to help them in different ways, doing EXPAND work.

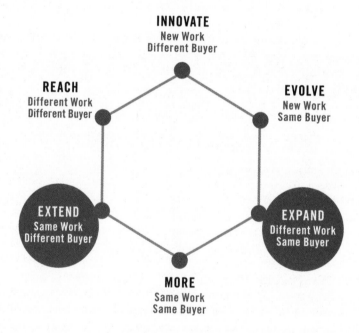

This is where the case study comes in. A great case study illustrates we can do the job by illustrating how we successfully took on and conquered a challenging assignment – either with a different buyer (EXTEND work) or a wholly different client (EXPAND work).

Great case studies have five key elements:

1. **They look like the assignment you hope to do.** At PIE, we work to pick assignments from our past that are most like the client we are now trying to serve. The closer to the size of the client, the scope of the project, the geography of the client, and the task being solved, the better. How many times have you offered up case studies that included your biggest and most renowned clients, only to have the buyer say, "Do you have a case that describes how you worked with a client more our size?" This is even more important when we're speaking to current clients about potential projects. We know them, and we should show that through the case studies we share.

2. **They state the problem solved.** There is an art to framing the challenge you solve for another client in a way that ties to the challenge you hope to take on with your current buyers. Sometimes it is easy and there are a handful of direct analogs available. For example, when looking to expand our work with a client we might say, "You're interested in building a group of financial services CIOs from large retail banks in Canada. We've done that for two other financial services–focused tech firms in the United States."

   But more often, we have to re-frame.

   For example, that same client was investing a bunch of their marketing budget into big conferences and dinners to attract CIOs of large retail banks in Canada. We'd helped this client with a few similar events in the United States but showed them how we built out virtual gatherings for another US-based tech consultancy to connect with CIOs, a cohort that tends to be overbooked and stretched thin on time for travel to in-person conferences. The virtual exchanges helped that client connect with over 100 CIOs on a regular basis throughout the year, and also helped lead to $60 million in new work with three of the CIOs in the forum.

3. **They include challenges overcome.** If we write a case in which we simply say, "*Vini, vidi, vici,*" as if we were with Julius Caesar striding across Gaul, we risk seeming glib at best and naïve at worst. Better is to list how the project was difficult. Not only does it seem more realistic and believable, it gives you the opportunity to put the pain points your would-be buyer feels into the words of others, enabling them to conclude that you have not only done this work before, but have faced the same pressures they feel.

   For example, we might point to a case study where our client was under pressure from leadership to "right the ship" quickly and where we delivered an executive peer group in 80 days, 10 days shorter than our typical timeline for kicking off a new group.

   The client may be focused on the uniqueness of their industry or buyer – maybe they do healthcare consulting and sell to chief medical officers. In this case, we'd want to share case studies demonstrating our experience convening this particular type of executive and working successfully in this industry.

If a client is concerned about budget, we may refer to a case study in which we spread payments over two fiscal years to help with the client's budget constraints or one in which we helped the client win $2 million in new work with the participating executives by the third roundtable, thereby covering the initial investment in the exchange more than 20 times over.

The client may be hesitant to invest in a new strategy, in which case we might share a case study highlighting our net promoter score after one year with a similar-size firm. We might also share a project in which we took the time to meet individually with a dozen different stakeholders in the project to gather their strategic input and deliver a project that exceeded their expectations.

Use your case study to address the elephant in the room and show how you successfully navigated similar concerns with other clients or projects in the past.

4. **They include endorsing quotes.** Use quotes that are both specific in their praise of you and specific around the niche you have chosen to serve.

Weak: "PIE is a competent and trustworthy business development partner."

Strong: "As a managing director and practice lead in one of the biggest professional services firms, my priority is to deliver high strategic value to as many clients as possible. PIE makes my job easy. They keep me close to my clients, help me identify opportunities, and always create interesting, sticky peer conversations that keep my clients coming back."

5. **They include an ROI claim.** Buyers love ROI claims, particularly if our service is focused on increased revenues or decreased costs. Their bosses are asking the ROI question, and, as experts, we need to give our buyers a credible answer. Using quotes for these ROI claims can be particularly effective as well. For example:

> We have used PIE to build communities of senior executives, helping us increase market awareness and build our brand with CEOs and others. In one particular market, we calculated PIE to have a 250% ROI based on the increase in work with CEO member firms during the course of our engagement.

The foundation of doing more with a client is "wowing" them with your service, and then drawing on your experience to showcase how that service is a particularly effective strategy. Boston Consulting Group's Thierry Chassaing defines experience as "having solved this problem before five or six times" in analogous situations, and not using that experience set to create a one-size-fits-all solution, but rather using it to understand how a current client is a lot like the others, but different in important respects. This, he argues, is the road to "customization of solutions," which is where true value is found.

Doing good work, work that WOWs, is the diving board off of which any effort to do more work springs. Nearly every rainmaker with whom we spoke agreed on this fundamental point. It is the absolute and required condition of expanded engagement. But there is more that rainmakers do. Next up is how rain-makers think about the tricky art of putting appropriate incentives in place.

13

Discipline 2: Be a Good Friend

One of Jacob's favorite measures of a client relationship is a term he's dubbed "fridge rights." Jacob has a close childhood friend named Riggs, who now lives in New York City, where he runs a real estate business. Jacob and Riggs know each other's families, colleagues, and even though they live on opposite sides of the country, their friendship never skips a beat. When Jacob is in New York to visit a client and stops by Riggs's West Village townhouse for dinner, a knock is superfluous. After a quick rehash of the latest in both business and family life, Jacob will walk straight to Riggs's fridge and grab his favorite New England IPA or tangerine La Croix. These are fridge rights. And they're earned, over time.

We like to think about setting a goal of "earning fridge rights" with our clients. Not because we want to walk into their kitchen and help ourselves to a Coke. This, obviously, would be a high bar – and perhaps inappropriate. What we want is to approach client relationships with this mentality. It requires us to invest in the relationships and care about them as people – remembering that they just bought a new home, that their daughter is about to have her bat mitzvah, that we should send them a bottle of their favorite Chilean rosé when they get the news that their boss is really happy with the project.

Ford Harding, author of *Cross-Selling Success*, quotes Mike Palmer, a founder and partner at the consulting firm DiamondCluster: "It's sort of like raising children. You need quality time with a client, but you need quantity time, too."

It's not hard, really, it's just a choice: Either we're going to treat our client as a nuisance who is forever making our job harder, or we're going to see them as a human being – beautiful, strange, and interesting – just like us.

Be a Good Friend to Your Colleagues

The effort to be a good friend shouldn't be reserved for your clients, though. This should be a practice you start every day with your internal team and others across your firm. As we know, doing good work is rarely the result of one person's efforts, and more often relies on a team of skilled people. You can't expect to bring your best to a project without first being a good friend to your colleagues.

This sounds simple, but it can take as much discipline as reaching out to potential new buyers. For most experts, investing in colleague relationships falls under the category of important but not urgent. On any given day, you may be struggling with a misunderstanding, for example, that has cropped up between your highway project management team and your client at the Texas Department of Transportation. The last thing on your mind might be checking in with your colleague across the hall to see what new projects she's focused on. Nonetheless, meeting and getting to know others in your firm is vital. Without question, you will eventually want or need to introduce others in your firm to one of your clients. Rainmaking experts tell us they never visit a branch office of their firm without spending half a day meeting the principal players there. It's tempting to blow by the office on the way to a client or pitch – you are fully mobile, after all – but it is a mistake.

It's hard, explains Professor Rita McGrath at Columbia Business School. She says,

> Consultants and services people have always been busy people. But today the expectation is that we need to be on for clients 24 hours a day, returning texts right away. I think it's fraying the patience required to create internal relationships among the people in the firm. People have less time or they're relying on ways of communicating that are less rich than working together. When your only interactions with people are mediated by technology, it's so easy to get stuff wrong, for misunderstandings to pile up, to get attributions wrong. There's been research that shows that if you are interacting with somebody through a technological medium rather than in person, you tend to be a lot meaner. Your remarks tend to be worse, and you tend to be more critical. There's something about not being with another breathing human being that just brings up the worst in us. So, I think that's a clutch of things that really gets in the way of building relationships inside the firm.

In order to truly *know thyself*, you need to invest the time. The goal is two-pronged: to know the full range of your firm's capabilities, and to know your partners well enough that you trust them with *your* best interest, which means introducing them to your best clients.

Implicit to getting to know your colleagues is vetting them. Says Dave Lubowe of Ernst & Young (EY),

> If a colleague asks for an introduction into my client, I'm talking to them first. I am going to vet them myself before I let them talk to the client. I feel I have responsibility to the client to say, "I talked to these people. They are competent. I'm looking forward to hearing what you think about your conversation." When I do that, I am taking personal responsibility for the firm's work as a whole.

You know you've succeeded in scaling trust and credibility *within* your firm when you reach the point of referral without hesitation, as Scott Wallace of Perkins Coie suggests. "I get calls from clients all the time saying things like, 'I need you to help me on a real estate contract.' My expertise is estate planning, so I say, 'Great,' and I send them to one of our real estate attorneys. That's the beauty of Perkins. I have such faith in my colleagues that I will send them work and not touch it again."

You Never Leave McKinsey

Many expert services firms think of their alumni associations as peer groups and a source of new or add-on business. McKinsey is famous for saying that once someone has worked at McKinsey – even if it was just a summer internship – "They'll always be a McKinseyite."

Says, Scott Wallace at Perkins Coie, "We invite (alumni) back for every Christmas party. We take them out to lunch and dinner. They're invited to any functions they want to attend. We've even invited Perkins alumni to company retreats."

Both firms spare no expense on these networks, cultivating the feeling that alumni are inside the "circle of trust" by extending trust to them first. As author Art Gensler writes, "Invest in trust. It is always worth it."

Both McKinsey and Perkins Coie understand alumni networks are a powerful way of adding value to those you most want to serve in advance of them needing your services, strongly positioning you to be of assistance when need presents itself.

Be a Good Friend to Your Clients

Alice Buckley, an associate director at PIE, leads one of our client projects with Boston Consulting Group (BCG). Every chance she gets, Alice flies out to meet her buyer at BCG in person. Yes, they use this time to talk shop, but it's also a chance to get to know her buyer – how he orders his martini, his love of the Rocky Mountains, and the latest on his 16-year-old daughter's birthday plans. Being a good friend means following up on the work as well as the person. It means taking the time to Google an appropriate gift for your client's son's bar mitzvah (a dollar multiple of 18, learned one of our colleagues), and when your client loses someone close, not only sending a thoughtful card of condolences, but showing him or her some grace with your project and doing what you can to ease the burden. Treat the client, in short, like a friend.

Grow Your Circle of Friends

We never pass up the opportunity to hang out with our buyers and their colleagues. Much of our work at PIE is virtual, but often we are asked to facilitate in-person best practice roundtables on behalf of clients at their summits. Our margin on this work is intentionally skinnier. We love the idea of flying across the country, demonstrating our work in front of parts of the organization that might not have been exposed to it, and then meeting with them and getting to know them better in person. That kind of opportunity is like trout fishing in a stocked pond. Says Alice, "The fact we're in the room says that client has endorsed our work, and that eliminates much of the fear people feel around engaging with a vendor. We're safe because we've been vetted." It's indeed one of the best ways for us to scale our trust across an organization.

"And, I always buy the drinks when we hit a milestone," reports Alice. "During our live events, everyone is keyed up, wearing their best clothes and focused on producing a quality experience. And everyone is *always* ready for a drink when it is over." Not only does Alice buy her client a celebratory drink, but she makes sure to ask them to invite their friends and colleagues. "That's my objective. To help make the afterparty a success, too. After toasting to a job well done and getting quality time with my client, I try to sit next to someone I don't know and see what I can learn."

We're social animals. Social interaction is one of the central ways trust is cultivated. Having people we know at our side is reassuring. It allows us, and, importantly, our clients, to extend themselves a little more fully than they might on their own, stuck in cubicles and away from the agar of friends and fellows. Lest we forget, colleagues are the wingmen that make social interactions more fun – and successful.

As you think about making a commitment to grow your circle of friends, a few habits can prove helpful.

Keep Your Head Up

Grinders have their heads down; finders have their heads up. If you are an expert working inside a company and have a chance to attend company events, your job is to make friends. It can be simple:

Say you run into a guy in his early 40s at the hotel bar, halfway through his Stella Artois and checking a few emails on his phone. His name badge shows he's at the same conference as you. You might say, "I am not sure we've met. I'm working with Tim O'Brien on a safety project. What's your role here at Ultra?"

Then follow up with thoughtful questions:

"You're in tax? That's got to be a big job. How many jurisdictions do you file in? Are you seeing widespread automation of compliance or is that still in its infancy? How big a deal was the recent corporate tax cut for Ultra?"

Soon it will be your chance:

"I'm an OSHA guy, but I spent five years as a former general counsel of the agency. I know all the departmental and agency GCs. If you ever want me to introduce you to the GC at the IRS, let me know."

You end the conversation not by asking for an introduction or pitching new work. Instead, you conclude with an offer to help, a pattern that your new friend will remember.

Ford Harding, author of *Cross-Selling Success*, writes that we should be looking for connectors – those people who are naturals at introductions:

"Bridges" is a term devised by Dennis Sullivan, of the Robert E. Nolan & Company, to describe people who work in many parts of an account and so are in a position to introduce you to people in different vertical business units. . . . Although your regular staff contacts are most likely to serve as bridges, anyone who is politically savvy, has influence, and is in a consulting firm is predisposed to help you develop new business and can be considered a "bridge."

Be Friendly and Curious

It sounds trite or, perhaps, unserious, but being friendly is one of the most important skills we can have while working with a client. When we engage with a client, we try to set aside our mind chatter and be present. We work to make new friends, regardless of whether they are on our project. Rainmakers know that everyone they meet in a client organization is a potential buyer – or at minimum an influencer – no matter where they fall in the corporate hierarchy. As Alice says, "We're playing the long game. Chances are some of the people assisting on our projects from the client side are our future program managers. They will get promoted or sent on to different divisions. We want them to say, 'I used to work with PIE. They were great. We should bring them over here.'"

Whenever we step into the elevator on the way up to meet a client, we literally say aloud, "We're happy people and glad to be here." It resets us and puts us in a positive mindset. When we bring that kind of brimming possibility to our clients, they appreciate it. Second, we are question-asking animals. We agree with Michael McLaughlin, who writes, "The quality of your questions is one way you demonstrate your competence."

Bill Burch of ECFX takes it another step and conducts surveys. He says,

> I'd hear from my team, "Hey, we've got to look at these numbers because no one's spending any money right now." And I say, "Okay, so you're telling me you have a company that spends $500 million every year, and suddenly they're spending zero? I don't think that's the case. I think the case is our company and products are not important enough that they want to spend the money they've got on us. What you have to do is go in and find out what's important to them." So, I created customer profile surveys to help us get aligned with their objectives – 10 questions we would ask during account planning.
>
> With a client CIO, for example, I'd tell my team to ask, "What are your five objectives for this year? What are your key goals? What is the company's strategy and what does it mean to you?" They had to go in and get deep to get the answers to those questions. They couldn't just, over lunch say, "Hey, what's your strategy?" If they asked that, the CIO is probably not going to spill the beans.

You get the idea. When we ask questions of people, it communicates that we are interested in them – their goals, their challenges, and what they need. When we express interest in others, there is a natural instinct to reciprocate, and if we ask good questions, that reciprocation will be, "I liked Jacob and Tom. They seemed smart."

Remember Who Your Hero Is

The rookie consultant is tempted to take credit for everything they do. Experienced expert services providers laugh at this naivete. "It's always the client's idea," says Jacob. "If I'm good, I discover great ideas in what my client tells me. They might not remember it was me, but they will say things like, 'I found my work with Jacob to be a good collaboration.' That's what you're looking for. Not credit." Remember, your client has two interests: the collective interests of their firm and their own personal and professional interests.

Sadly, we recently witnessed an intellectual contest between an outside intellectual property (IP) attorney and his client, the assistant general counsel of a logistics company. The attorney seemed to be trying to establish dominance over the client with his deeper knowledge. It is one thing to bring your deep domain expertise to the table, but it is crazy to play subjugation games like this. Our job is to make our clients look good in the eyes of the world. That's it.

Counterintuitively, we get further faster when we brag about our client than we do when we talk up our own prowess. Crowing about all we did is unbecoming. No one wants to hang with boastful people. We would never say something like, "The PIE team drastically improved attendee experience at our client's event by adding facilitated breakout sessions for the various c-suite attendees." That sounds like we are the hero and, perhaps, that our client team is not very smart and wasn't really thinking about attendee experience until we came along.

Better would be to say, "Working with Jamie's team, we were able to build on their long record of great attendee experience among the c-suite and go the extra step of providing focused break out sessions. This proved valuable to both attendees and hosts and participants from your client team who were able to demonstrate expertise in this format. But all the credit goes to Jamie for having the vision and drive to bring about this change."

We can choose to be the hero, but it's better for us to be the Gandalf or Merlin in the story whose sage advice helps the hero succeed. Why? Because, our new buyers inside the client can more easily identify with their colleagues than they can with us. They don't really care if we win; what they care about is whether we can help *them* win.

Brainstorm with Clients

Perhaps the most important skill that rainmaking experts point to when talking about how to successfully introduce new service lines into existing clients, or EXPAND work, is the ability to think on their feet in the presence of a client. Not everyone can do that. It takes a special talent to brainstorm with a client on the fly.

"What do you think about AI? Is it the future?" your client might ask.

You may not be your firm's foremost artificial intelligence (AI) expert, but that doesn't mean you can't share what you *do* know. You might say, "My experience is that AI's going to change how we drive revenues in the company and how we reduce costs over time. You are on the cost side of things. There, I see clients spending 80% of their time using RPA [robotics process automation] to drive out costs, not so much AI – for example, to automate filings and drive down headcount. RPA is the low-hanging fruit right now."

It is these sorts of conversations that lead to new work.

Your client might go on to say, "Aren't RPA improvements just macros?"

Here's where you draw on your experience – and the experience of your colleagues – and respond: "We did a project for a firm in Austin where we tracked their compliance pipeline and then automated the filing process. They cut their labor cost by 13% in one year. This stuff is amazing. I should see if we can get you over there to see what we did. And I can connect you with Helen – she's our expert on this stuff in your industry. I think you'd love chatting with her – I'll set something up."

Being a good friend doesn't mean having all the answers all the time. It means being honest, understanding where your opinion is valued and useful, and knowing when to loop in other resources for the best, most thorough answer.

Grab at the Hard Stuff

Leading experts have a Spidey-sense for what their clients hate or find hard to do. As Jacob says, "We are paid to do the hard shit that no one else wants to do. They outsource the hassle, so they can focus on their more important work." Anytime he hears a moan, groan, grievance, or gripe, it's like a dinner bell, calling him to be helpful. Just as we'd reach out to help a friend who's carrying an overly heavy burden, so should we support our clients.

Take Good Notes

Customer relationship management (CRM) is all about the power of notes. What the database providers do not tell you, however, is why it is important to take notes. Taking good notes gives you the tools to pick up where you left off with a client or potential buyer. On any given day, you might be knee-deep in your retail project. Maybe you have one 20-minute conversation in Atlanta in which you talk about wholesale, but then it is gone from your mind. Your would-be second buyer, however, has been living that wholesale conversation every day since you two last spoke. It is important to take good enough notes that you can continue the conversation where you last left it. Nothing is more frustrating to a potential buyer with whom you have already spent time than going over the basics again – or feeling like they're just another person being pitched. If they told you last time that they were headed to their daughter's graduation, and on the next call you ask them if they have kids – that's exactly how they'll feel. Client whisperers tell us they work hard to keep the conversation seamless.

Making the Move from Provider to Partner

Rainmaking experts know that over time their goal is to move from being seen as a vendor to a client's strategic partner and collaborator. The question becomes less "Would you be open to speaking to me about our integration services" and more "What are we going to do next?"

If we have created real value in an organization, we can feel as though we have a right to march across the client to do more of that work, but this is hubris and a failure to understand the systemic obstacles to that happening easily. It betrays a certain naiveté about how groups of professionals interact with each other. Our job is to *know thy client*, to become a student of how information and recommendations flow inside of our client, and then surf those rivers of reputation and referral to ink new work where we know our experience will help the client better achieve their objectives.

But what about expanding the kinds of work we do with our most trusted clients? Rainmakers tell us that requires us to flex a different muscle.

Level Up

A rookie mistake is to create a close relationship with only your project manager. As we've underscored, top experts invest time into developing relationships across the organization – most importantly, this includes their buyer's boss. The boss is often the decision maker on the second set of services that an expert hopes to provide for a client.

For example, say you work for a technology consultancy that does good work providing cyber-services to a raft of California law firms. The buyer for those services, generally, is the CIO of the law firm. The CIO's boss in these firms is the COO, who as it turns out, is the main decision maker on software that supports case management across the firm. You have built trust with the CIO, and that will be important since someone might ask their opinion about how it has been to work with your cyber-service firm.

But when you say to the CIO, "We see you're thinking about switching to the Clio platform and we'd love to be considered on that project," the CIO may be as likely as not to say, "That's actually a project being driven by the COO and a team of practice leads." Your job is then to ping the COO and say, "As you know, we've been doing a good job helping your CIO and his team with your firm's cyber work. I heard you and the operations team were considering moving to the Clio platform. We've done a number of Clio migrations for California law firms and, if you would find it useful, we'd love to stop by and pass on some key learnings. I want to make sure you avoid some of the mistakes others have made."

Follow Up

When we meet someone at a client firm who is not our buyer but who *could* be, we follow up.

For example, Sarah Matthews works for a data privacy consultancy. She is presenting at a client conference on the general data protection regulation (GDPR)-driven privacy work her firm did. That evening, she meets another partner at the client firm. She wants to learn more about what they do, and she ask lots of questions. Perhaps she can even tie what she hears from them to another client with whom she's worked. She says something like, "That's interesting, we found the same thing when we were trying to rationalize another client's approach to GDPR and the California Consumer Protection Act."

This is not the time to pitch. If they ask what she does, it is fine for Sarah to tell them, "We do cyber security work for your firm around privacy governance." However, this is not the time for Sarah to say, "Do you think we might work with your division in the same way?" If she truly wants to help, Sarah must be patient, reel the fish in slowly without breaking the line, and follow up.

Here's our process at PIE:

- We note that we met a new "contact" in our CRM.
- We wait a week and send them an email:

Sam,

It was great to meet you at the Atlanta event last week. I found what you said about the growing environmental risk to the built environment interesting, especially for Silicon Valley sweethearts who've typically been immune to such disruption. I just read this article with one economist's take on how this risk may disrupt the way we physically organize companies and businesses that I thought you might find interesting. Here is a link.

Next time I'm in New York, it would be fun to grab a cup of coffee. I will reach out the next time I have a trip in your direction.

Tom

We'll likely receive a return email from Sam,

Tom – Great to meet you as well. Thanks for the link. Coffee would be fun. Thanx, Sam

- We reach out the next time we're heading to New York and schedule coffee, following the same email chain so Sam can easily place us. We are also subtly reminding Sam that he said he would be open to coffee.

At coffee, Tom asks, "How's your business? What are you focused on right now?" Tom brags about his program manager, Sam's colleague with whom he works. "Jessica is doing great things in the retail unit. She's been fantastic to work with for our team." This is a sideways pitch. You're floating a fly on the surface of the stream, waiting for the two-pound brown trout to jump out of its hold and strike.

Then we ask: "Would it ever make sense for us to do something like that for you? Maybe I could pull together a short deck that describes how that might look and what we did for Jessica in retail." Note you are not asking to be engaged. You are giving the new buyer something that is easy to say "yes" to. Who says "no" to a deck reviewing someone else's project? No one.

- We send the deck within a business day, and in the cover email we write, "Here's the deck I mentioned that describes our capabilities and the work we did for Jessica's team in retail. I'm happy to schedule some time to walk you through it. Would next week work? Here are a few times." We have found that most busy professionals are bouncing from call to call and back again over the course of a day. When we offer to "walk them through the deck," they are relieved. There is a next step to be taken but it is one that does not involve them trying to read your deck on the train home to Rye.

- After walking Sam through the deck, we ask again, "Could you ever see something like this helping the transportation division?"

He will likely say, "You have to understand that in transportation, things are a little different than they are in retail . . ."

We expect this and we don't panic. It is just Sam asking for more time to digest what we are saying and, importantly, to think about how he is going to navigate the traps he needs to run on his side before he could ever engage with us. We give him time.

We ask a few more questions and then suggest, "You mentioned that Judith and Ravi would need to sign off on this. Would it make sense for us to set up a call where we can give them the brief on what we did over in retail?" We don't make them tell our stories for us – we're the best at telling them anyway.

Ask the Hard Questions

Being a good friend to your client means taking the time to re-hash your March Madness brackets, and it also means taking the time to ask for honest and thoughtful feedback on the work you do for them. During the account planning process, EY invites a key client in to talk about the account and get direct feedback on key questions. While these meetings are useful to understand the health of the account, they are also fertile ground for identifying opportunities for growth across the Diamond of Opportunity. Following is a sample list of questions that EY uses in these meetings:

- What do you like about our performance this year?
- What do you dislike?
- What issues should we be dealing with?
- Are there other areas where we can add value?
- What future events or trends are you watching that might impact your business?

This process is decidedly more impactful than trying to guess at client priorities. It creates clarity on behalf of EY and allows the client to feel valued and heard. Win-Win. But lest we forget, the key to effective questions isn't just remembering to ask them; its also listening to the answers.

Stick with Your Friends

Just as we follow our friends and family members as they navigate through the changes of life, so too must we follow our clients. People change jobs. Indeed, at some of our largest expert services clients, it feels like senior executives stay in their role for about two years. For that reason, it is important for us to keep track of everyone we know and where they land when they leave our orbit. Following people into their new roles is an important tool for growing your business. First, the trust and credibility you earned with them in one role moves with the relationship as it migrates to a new organization. Second, many key relationships, when they move, are getting a promotion that carries with it new responsibilities. Today's analyst is tomorrow's practice lead, captaining their own profit and loss (P&L) and invested with the authority to engage us in heretofore difficult-to-penetrate parts of the organization.

LinkedIn can be a powerful resource for this, especially when someone leaves a company but also when they take on a new role within your client. Setting Google Alerts for everyone we know at a client as well as the client itself is a strong tool for keeping track of the comings and goings as well as announced changes in client strategies and acquisitions.

Saying, "Congratulations on the new gig!" can be a monstrously effective way of starting a conversation along the lines of, "You know us as process engineers, but I wanted you to know that we have a Gartner-recommended practice around oil and gas lease management as well." You've invested in these friendships – maybe you've even earned fridge rights. Don't let that investment get lost in a move.

14

Discipline 3:
Leverage Your Team

A s our colleagues begin to leverage us for their client projects, and we them in ours, our path toward growth and new work smooths and accelerates. Sharing our expertise with our colleagues is the easiest business development action we can take, and mastering the art of leveraging our team is a critical strategy for growing our business. It's impossible to scale our services if we alone are the product. Our time and capabilities are finite. Bringing others into the fold to help scale both trust and credibility allows for new types of work within a client. That said, experts worry about introducing their colleagues and scaling the trust they've built with a client across their team.

Basking in the Warm Glow of Outgroup Homogeneity Bias

In 1980, two Princeton professors, George Quattrone and Ned Jones, published an article in the *Journal of Personality and Social Psychology* about an experiment they ran with Princeton and Rutgers students. In the experiment, they asked student *observers* to watch a videotape in which student *actors* made some simple decisions. The actors were identified by their supposed college affiliation – either Princeton or Rutgers. Then the student observers were asked to predict how the two university populations would make decisions by extrapolating what they had seen with the student actors. Quattrone and Jones found that student observers from Princeton predicted that the Rutgers population was more likely to make decisions similar to "Rutgers" students, whereas Rutgers students predicted that the Princeton population was more likely to make decisions similar to "Princeton" students.

Psychologists call this phenomenon "outgroup homogeneity bias," or the tendency to think that groups of which we are not a part (outgroups) are more alike than groups of which we are a part. Humans tend to think that the group they are part of is diverse but mistakenly assume that other groups are homogeneous and likely to act in the same way.

While not true, this bias tilts a little in our favor when we are introducing colleagues into a client. We worry that our partners' credentials or ability to engender trust in the client won't be as strong as our own and perceive risk in making those introductions, especially if we are at a large firm and do not have experience working with this particular colleague before. We think the trust we've built with our client is so unique to ourselves that it will be difficult to transfer to our colleague.

But we shouldn't be worried. The outgroup homogeneity bias almost guarantees that if our clients have had a good experience with us and find us to be trustworthy and capable, then they will be likely to assume that, as part of our group, our colleague is equally trustworthy and capable.

As we know, leveraging our colleagues is an effective way to scale both trust and credibility and, in doing so, grow our work with a client. Trey Cox notes, "The benefit of double dating is I can talk up the reputation and experience of my colleague in a way they cannot and use that credibility to build trust."

Across the board, experts emphasized the importance of systematically introducing others to our clients, both virtually and in person. Many of those we interviewed suggested it's the most effective way of leveraging our teams and maximizing our ability to do good work.

The Art of the Introduction

There is an art to introducing our colleagues to our clients. Mastering the art requires understanding the variety of ways an introduction can be made and the types of colleagues it behooves us to intentionally introduce. There are three types of introductions:

By Email

Sheila,

I hope this note finds you well. I have a quick favor to ask. Would you be willing to introduce my colleague, the head of our supply chain practice, to your Chief Supply Chain Officer? He is hoping to share some insights on automation our firm has learned in the process of helping a third of the largest OEM manufacturers over the last 20 years.

Let me know if you would be open to something like this. I'd be grateful.

Erica

This is the easiest but weakest form of an introduction. The note is straight-forward and takes two minutes to write but rather than scaling trust, it's a leap of faith. First, Erica doesn't know if Sheila even knows the chief supply chain officer. Second, Erica is implicitly asking Sheila to vouch for someone she does not know in a field in which she is not qualified to vet.

Email introductions work best when they are a follow-up to a conversation:

Sheila,

Thanks for your willingness to talk with my colleague, Stan Murphy [best practice is to hyperlink Stan's LinkedIn page to his name]. I've worked with Stan for a number of years on a variety of assignments, and he's the best. When you said you were having issues secur-ing your mobile network, I knew you two would have a lot to talk about. Stan runs an ace team that works on just these issues for manufacturing companies. I have cc'd him on this note. I will let Stan follow up and find a time to connect.

Best,

Erica

By Phone or Videoconference

Introducing a colleague on a conference call is painless and effective. Before the call, you might email your client and say, "I'm going to invite my partner, Stan, to join us on the call. He's head of our cybersecurity practice. I thought he might be able to help us sort through some of the security aspects of our project and share a few ways we've approached this with other clients."

On the call itself, you introduce Stan. This is no time to hold back. This is the time to brag about your partner; you might say, "I'd like to introduce you to Stan, the head of our cybersecurity practice. We stole him from the NSA where he led the team that successfully hacked Al Qaeda's phone network just after 9/11. He's a Stanford PhD and currently is the chair of the Manufacturing Association's Cyber Council." You can do this because it sets Stan up to be human: "Wow, that was quite the introduction, Erica – not sure I'm worthy of it! Sheila, it is nice to meet you. Let's dig into your issue, and I will try to be helpful."

In Person

The most time-intensive – and effective – way to connect one of our colleagues with a client is to introduce them in person. This can take the form of a client visit, a casual conversation at a conference, or a meeting over drinks or dinner. In any case, the rules are the same:

- **Keep it light.** We try to remember this is not the time for pitching. It is a time to laugh, find points of connection, and build rapport.
- **Be generous.** We know our colleague is the third wheel, so we work hard to pull them into the conversation and ask them for their perspective.
- **Respect the client.** The conversation should be 60% about our client, 30% about big issues our colleague can join in on to demonstrate their chops, and 10% about our colleague and their work and background. We're fine if our airtime is 0%.
- **Segue from our expertise to that of our colleague.** It's not hard to organically move from our client's interests, hobbies, or family to our colleague's interests and experience. It establishes trust, commonality, and rapport. As the conversation drifts to Sheila's new cell phone, you might say something like, "Stan, you're the NSA guy. What phone do you recommend?"

Experts know that when trying to establish a partner's credentials and trustworthiness with one of their clients, their job is to act as a facilitator of the conversation, drawing out commonality and mutual expertise to alchemize a generative and memorable conversation.

Just Dropping By . . .

Experts report that they have two jobs: to harvest best practices in their area of expertise and to offer those best practices to clients. We invite our colleagues into our client to learn from and appreciate what our client is doing well, as well as to bring a fresh perspective about how our firm can best serve them. Spending our time onsite working with a client is the perfect opportunity to have a colleague drop by.

Following are four kinds of colleagues we can have visit.

The Rock Star

The rock star is our lateral hire, the one we've brought on board to scale our credibility in a certain space and win new work. We take advantage of every opportunity we can to introduce our team's star to our clients, perhaps by having them do a roadshow and stop by various offices around a region.

Say you work for a consulting firm that helps municipalities plan parks, open space, and recreational opportunities. You've just hired the former head of HUD's Disaster Recovery Buyout Program, which gives grants to cities to buy damaged buildings if they tear them down and create parks. This is exactly the person you want to introduce to your clients in parks and rec departments across the region, whether it's for lunch, for a quick meet-and-greet, or for client-focused presentations.

Best practice with rock stars is to have them visit bearing gifts – lagniappe value they contribute to the client.

The Boss

When we bring the top brass in our firm out to a client, it elevates everyone's game. Experts share the importance of the "leadership client tour," where firms send a senior partner to visit key clients and ask, "How are we doing?" The value of bringing in a senior partner is that they can have a conversation at a strategic level that the delivery team may be less prepared to hold. This meeting is fertile ground to improve the work being done on a current offering, solidify the relationship at a senior level, and earn the right to win more and different kinds of work in the future.

For this to be successful, smooth, and complete, information transfer between the visiting senior partner and the delivery team is critical. Otherwise, we risk frustration on the part of the client if information is shared with leadership and then not reflected in future work. Furthermore, the boss must come to the table to help, not to sell. Otherwise we run the risk of it feeling like we're bringing in senior leadership to get a better deal or facilitate a transaction and we diminish our trust rather than scale it.

Jim Solan, a Spokane, Washington, attorney, calls this "sending in the gray hair." As he puts it, "In the legal profession, nobody respects you until you have a few gray hairs. It seems like you need those gray hairs to earn their trust for major opportunities." This comment captures the theme that it can often take significant time and hard work – perhaps producing a few gray hairs – before you've earned the credibility and trust to be giving strategic guidance that requires jumps across the Diamond of Opportunity.

Ann Kieffaber of IBM tells us how she's seen this done effectively,

> IBM did this very well. It is called it the PEP program, or the Partnership Executive Program. The IBM partnership executive is typically somebody in the c-suite or someone with specific skills and experience that is of high strategic value to the client. We would pull them into an account on a recurring basis to help strengthen existing and grow new client relationships. Of course, the preparation for these sessions is critical. The PEP executive needs to be familiar with the strategic priorities of the client executives they will meet with and how the IBM account plan aligns with those priorities. Similarly, the client executive needs to be briefed and have input on an initial set of topics to be discussed to ensure the time will be of high value to them. Timing and thinking about the right personality matches are important so that you are able to establish ongoing relationships between the right players at the right time. Optimally the right PEP executive can help the account team on the ground move laterally and vertically within an account. As an example, it is a high-value interaction for Fortune 100 company executives like UnitedHealth Group to meet one-on-one with their peers, say the CEO of IBM.

As Solan and Kieffaber highlight, the boss – or the "gray hair" – can be a helpful player in accelerating the rate at which we can earn trust with new buyers or earn credibility with different work.

The Peer

"When I was a CIO at Jacobs Engineering, I was brought in to assist in the sales process and share the perspective of the buyer we were courting," shares Cora Carmody.

The peer is the colleague we bring in who shares the perspective of our client and can speak to what it's like to be in their shoes. When done properly, it can mitigate the negative characteristics traditionally associated with "selling" services.

The presence of your own CIO in a meeting, for example, describing how a particular challenge was managed and what the resultant deliverables were, can add authenticity and credibility when trying to grow work with a CIO buyer. Of course, they must truly be a peer, or have the ability to speak to a similar challenge, for this to be effective – if your firm has 100 employees and your client's firm has 10,000, then a conversation around technology change management between these two CIOs won't be very useful.

This strategy can also mitigate the phenomenon of "oh, we have a service for that," which some consultants are accused of promulgating. The presence of a peer executive allows the firm to display knowledge around cultural characteristics, systems limitations, and change management concerns. Companies don't want to buy an off-the-shelf solution to their challenge; they want to engage with someone whom they trust to navigate the forthcoming implementation challenges with grace. Inviting the CIO of your company into a CIO pitch can deliver that message in a genuine way. It's critical in these circumstances to properly prepare our peer and ensure they have a fulsome understanding of that client's challenges and opportunities.

The New Talent

Bringing in the new talent is a strategy that experts use to effectively scale both trust and credibility. Asking a client to bring in a training class of our newer hires to learn about an aspect of their company signals that we respect and appreciate their company, and we want to use it as an example for our employees. In doing so, we also scale credibility by telegraphing that we are growing and have plenty of arms and legs to bring to bear on any problem they might be experiencing. Similarly, when we bring in a handful of late-20-somethings to add some brawn as we push toward the deadline, it shows our client that we have resources we can bring to bear to accomplish the impossible on their behalf. Showing off our house full of bright, young, intellectual horsepower can help increase our clients' excitement about the future of our partnership.

The Pack

At PIE, we don't think of ourselves as some corporate behemoth, but neither do we say we are family. Family is something special and wholly apart from the community of people with whom we work. Instead, we call ourselves the "PIE Pack." We live close to Yellowstone Park and have respect for how wolves travel, care for each other, and hunt together. That's the way we think of ourselves. We approach our work as a collective endeavor, not as a solo sport. Interestingly, Chassaing describes BCG in the same language. "We're like wolves or lions. They can't catch anything alone. They hunt in packs and so do we."

Thinking about ourselves as a pack makes it easy for us to think of ourselves as having unique talents and perspectives, which we can and should bring to both our clients and our colleagues' clients. It gives us a sense of collective power, that while any one of us might be small in the face of a challenge, together we are powerful and there is nothing we can't do. This, in the end, is the promise of pulling in others to work with a client: When we combine our best and brightest with our client's best and brightest, together we can pull off magic.

15

Discipline 4: Incent Good Work

❝I don't know why I expect it to change," Jacob tells Tom. "Every time I see the cartoon where Charlie Brown is running to kick the football and Lucy pulls it away at the last moment, I hope she won't do it. Call me an eternal optimist."

Just as it is important to cultivate trust and credibility with a client, we must do the same thing with our internal teams around incentive pay as well. Reneging on a commission agreement is the easiest way to destroy trust with your employees.

Jacob is in charge of the incentive compensation distribution at PIE, and the conversations can be awkward or difficult for people because money is involved. Jacob says the same thing every time he awards a commission to set the proper tone for how PIE views incentives. He says, "Paying you a commission is the best part of my job, because it means we are growing the business. We set the system to drive certain behaviors and you have excelled in those – thank you."

The opposite is also true. If we start moving the goalposts or go back on our word on even one commission, the entire organization will know about it, and trust is the first casualty. The specific circumstance is unimportant. If we feel like we are paying a commission that shouldn't be paid, we should fix the incentive system. If not, our employees will be sending around GIFs of Lucy pulling the football away as a metaphor for our leadership style.

Don't be a Lucy.

Expert Services Needs a Different Yardstick

When Jacob started graduate school at Gonzaga University, he anticipated a collegial environment that would be focused on learning outcomes, not grades as had been his experience in undergrad. "I thought, never again will I have to endure a student in the back of the classroom interrupting a lecture and saying, 'Is this going to be on the exam?' Turns out I was wrong."

Jacob recalls one class in his MBA program called Corporate Financial Reporting. "If I were naming the class," he says, "I would have called it simply 'The Language of Business.'" More than any other, this class prepares future leaders to, at the very least, sound like they know what they are talking about. It's during this class that students gain fluency with terms like *EBITDA*, accrual accounting, and key financial measurement devices like ROA, ROE, and P/E ratio. After the first exam, Jacob was standing with a few classmates who were also finished. One gentleman pulled out his calculator and said: "With the curve, I can get a 44 on the next test and still get a B in the class. Who wants to grab a beer?"

Jacob skipped the 3 p.m. Tuesday drinks and contemplated the oddness of using grades to measure learning. Why, he wondered, didn't universities adjust metrics to measure the outcomes that students desire: job placement, network development, or command of content? Many mid-tier universities that are focused on research tout the work they do publishing in academic journals to display credentials. For Jacob this seems archaic. "No disrespect, but I've published in those journals, and as a metric for measuring a university's success in training future business leaders, it seems irrelevant." I have never had a businessperson come up to me and say, 'I saw that piece you did for Indiana University and it changed my thinking on innovation.'"

Øystein Daljord, an incentives expert and professor at the University of Chicago Booth School of Business, points out a key metrics challenge: "We can measure important things, but not everything that is important can be measured." For instance, knowledge improvement and job placement can be very difficult to track and manage over time but are still key performance qualities in many service sectors. Furthermore, additional metrics are critical in those cases. What do people want in a job placement? Money? Benefits? Work/life balance? While salary has a clear unit of measurement, the other aspects are more ambiguous and harder to put on a pithy slide aimed at attracting the next generation of students. Universities settle for arbitrary metrics like the *US News & World Report* rankings, which impose a success model on universities that may not align with desired student outcomes.

As Jacob compared his MBA experience to what he sees working in expert services every day, he realized they have much in common. The world of expert services is tangled in a very similar web of metric confusion: Measuring – and incentivizing – the right things is often costly, complex, or in rare cases, impossible.

For tasks that have a single unit of performance, measurement can be simple. For instance, Professor Daljord says, "If I'm a fruit picker, it's really easy to assess output and quality of work. I either pick 5 apples in an hour or 500 apples in an hour." A few areas in the expert service industry are easier to measure because of the simplicity of the arrangement. Take cost reduction projects, for example. When a consulting firm comes in and says, "We can save you $100 million over four years by implementing a category management approach to your decentralized procurement, and we will take 20% of the savings," that is easy to measure. Assuming the two parties have a solid definition of how to define savings, and they won't have to debate the delineation between cost savings and cost avoidance during the project, this measurement should be ideal.

Unfortunately, incentive pay is not that easy. Success, especially business development success, has many mothers. Also, developing a new piece of work in expert services – whether with a net new logo or a new buyer in an existing client – is rarely a quick endeavor. Trust and credibility take a long time to develop. In addition, the buyer's circumstances must align with the provider's skillset to create the opportunity. The service must fit into the buyer's overall strategic priorities, budgeting constraints, and align with major corporate initiatives. Because it takes so long, there are invariably a large number of people involved in the project. The longer it is drawn out, the harder it is to accurately track who has responsibility for the work.

Defined Commissionable Activities

Many organizations use clearly defined commissionable activities as a means to distribute incentive compensation. This system allocates specific commissions to activities like origination of relationship, developing new content, or winning an assignment. There are good reasons to take this approach. This creates clarity for members of the firm on exactly how the incentive compensation will be distributed. Additionally, firms can adjust the level of compensation associated with certain commissionable activities. As an example, if you're in a smaller business and have customer concentration concerns, increasing the bonus allocation for net new logos should generate new sales and mitigate that risk. If your EBITDA is slipping, a firm could increase the allocation for new work within an existing client or a particular service line that is exceptionally profitable. This type of measurement system can give leadership a dashboard and clear direction on how to change behavior to drive certain outcomes.

This system sounds ideal internally, but there can be some snags when it comes to aligning with your client's priorities. This type of system can be too inward facing, and without a resilient client-service culture it can produce bad behavior.

A consultant looking to achieve a prescribed goal may engage in a project that has limited upside for the customer in order to meet the quarterly goal and earn their bonus. Furthermore, these specific activities are hard to apply to a collaborative environment, and you may return to the "antelope down on the Serengeti" problem discussed in Chapter 5, with everyone fighting for a piece of the pie.

Worse than fighting for dollars at the review table is the possibility of excluding key players and insights from a potential sale – and failing to win the work because of this. Specific incentives often create a decision point: "Do I bring in the robotic process automation (RPA) expert to close this sale and split the commission, or do I go for it myself and get the entire commission?" If consultants have one thing, it's confidence. The opportunity to sell the entire program alone calls out to us like an injured antelope calling to a hyena. Some consultants joke about this bravado and the mentality of being "often wrong, but never in doubt." When firms want to present the full force and capability of the firm to a would-be client and increase their odds of winning the work, they must develop a system that incentivizes collaboration. This redounds to the benefit of the client in the form of better understanding of capabilities during the sales process (and better services in the long run), and it redounds to the benefit of the expert services firm in the form of more business.

Double Counting

In response to the silo risk that is created by pure commission systems, some firms have moved toward "double counting." In 2010, Jeff LeSage, KPMG's Americas former vice chairman–tax, recognized that the full force and power of KPMG services were not being brought to market. Although it is a collegial environment, a firm that size requires systems to drive collaboration. KPMG, therefore, moved all business development credits to a system of double counting. In the past, if a tax partner and a technology expert collaborated in winning new work, they would evenly split 100 "new business credits" between them. This created a natural incentive to "go at it alone" on pitches, which ultimately reduced the likelihood of winning the work. So, KPMG introduced the concept of double-counting business development credit. In the previous scenario, the tax partner and the technology expert would receive 100 full credits. The same would be true if seven partners collaborated on an opportunity; each partner would receive 100 new business credits.

This is an example of an organization effectively using incentives to drive the right behavior. KPMG is more likely to win additional work and grow as a firm when an engagement team put their best foot – or feet – forward in a pitch, which often requires subject-experts from various parts of the firm to come together and emphasize its one-firm mentality. Breadth and depth of expertise is a competitive advantage for KPMG, and they must have a system that leverages that advantage.

Collaboration Credit

"In circumstances without double credits, there is a penalty for collaborating," says Walt Shill of ERM.

Knowing that collaboration drives results – especially when trying to expand a client relationship – he awards collaboration credits on top of double counting, measuring the frequency with which partners are collaborating in a collaboration index. "What I am trying to avoid is people acting on their own. We had one guy leading an account and only 20% of his sales included other partners."

Top of the Funnel

Typically, top-of-the-funnel metrics like lead generation rarely dictate the majority of incentive compensations, but some firms are adding these metrics to a broad scorecard of activities. These metrics can be useful and allow the incentive structure to flex to the culture and strategy of a specific firm. Bottom-of-the-funnel measurements, like new revenue, can be less strong measurements of actual effort on business development. In most cases, factors like budget, timing, and economic environment introduce luck into the equation.

Firms trying to grow their practice have found success incentivizing the types of behavior that have a long-term impact on growth. This is different than the defined commissionable activities in that those align to a specific deal; these are general behaviors that a firm believes will, if practiced well and consistently over time, pave the way for more business. What are the behaviors that lead to improved business development for a firm? In most cases, they are activities that drive relationship development, even if indirectly.

Toward Better Alignment

How do we balance the need to create value for clients with the need to build value for our own operation? The goals can be at odds with each other.

Take this example: A CPA firm is helping a client shorten the quarterly close. In order to complete this assignment, the CPA firm places four analysts inside the organization and the client is delighted with the effort. The company is now able to close the books in three days, and the time freed up by having four additional CPAs in the office is allowing them to focus on higher-value work. Along the way, one of the analysts notices that a technology solution could reduce manual workflow and improve the process, without employing the four analysts from the CPA firm. The consultant leading the project now has a choice to make:

- Does the CPA firm continue the current process, have a delighted client, and enjoy the gravy train of making a margin on these four analysts?
- Does the CPA firm implement the technology solution in order to maximize value creation for the client in the hope that this trust will open the door for future opportunities?

This example seems simple. The consultant does what is best for the client, right? It's never that simple. What if, in this case, the consultant is 100K short of a massive bonus accelerator? What if this consultant recognizes that this decision will have a considerable impact on his or her own incentive compensation? Designers of incentive plans should never put leaders into this situation. If at all possible, the metrics of success for the consultant should align directly to the metrics of success for the client.

Kris Timmermans, a leader in Accenture's procurement practice, highlights their movement on this: "The incentive scheme pertains to the success of that client, not Accenture's success. The number-one metric is client value generated." We define this progress as the inverted incentive curve. Timmerman's incentive structure abandons internal metrics like new sales and profitability in favor of a simple metric, "Are we creating value for you?" That value can be defined in myriad ways but the only thing that matters is that success is viewed through the client's eyes, not Accenture's. Over time, reviews of projects will have to be done, profitability will have to be assessed, and changes to pricing or delivery models may occur. These are larger strategic questions for the firm to manage and should not infringe upon client success creation and incentives.

Chris Fosdick of The Cambridge Group suggests that viewing success through a client's eyes can also be additive in other ways. He says, "Recently, we went through a process of systematically looking at clients over five years and analyzed their economic and stock performance while we were working with them against their peers' performance." Fosdick was pleased to find out that their clients generally outperformed the market. Sharing this performance view does two things:

1. It solidifies client service as a cultural tenet in the organization. When the view is shifted to client success, the culture naturally evolves in that direction.
2. It opens up business development opportunities via storytelling that is backed by data.

Born versus Bred

It's a fun question, and one we hear often: *Can* great business development skills be developed? Or are some people just "born to sell"? Business development skills, in some capacity, seem to be an important element of most careers and everyday life. In his exceptional book, *To Sell Is Human*, Daniel Pink conducted a study examining what people do at work. He found two key outcomes:

1. People are now spending 40% of their time at work engaged in nonsales selling – persuading, influencing, and convincing others in ways that don't involve anyone making a purchase. Across a range of professions, people devote roughly 24 minutes of every hour to moving others.

2. People consider this aspect of their work crucial to their professional success – even in excess of the considerable amount of time they devote to it.

This data suggests that everybody should develop persuasion techniques as a part of everyday life. It does not suggest that everybody is drawn toward these activities. Many firms recognize that certain personalities are more likely to enjoy – and thus succeed at – business development. If the goal is firm growth, it can be wise to divide and conquer business development and delivery.

Aligning Client and Employee Priorities: Finding the Optimal Structure

Professor Daljord from Chicago Booth's school of business points out that, "In a group of consultants, it's likely that you will have material variation in the way that they respond to the same incentives." It makes sense. A 40-year-old with two kids and a mortgage is likely to value stable compensation and prefer an incentive package that emphasizes salary and health benefits. A 23-year-old who is sharing a two-bedroom Peter Cooper Village apartment in NYC with five roommates might prefer to take on the riskier incentive compensation and pursue a big payday (if only to escape that apartment). Different responses to incentives points to tailored incentive packages.

Scott Wallace, an attorney at Perkins Coie, outlines how his firm organizes business development and delivery to make the best use of each expert's unique skills:

> Some attorneys are natural BD attorneys, some might call those rainmakers, and we have about 5% of our attorneys in that role. They are focused on maintaining and developing the most important relationships. The second tier is a blend of bringing in

work and having billable hours requirements. Finally, there are workers who are highly intelligent, highly capable, but not as interested in going out to the community to bring in work and are focused on billable hours.

Many firms have wasted time and energy trying to drive BD out of a partner who is better suited to helping drive growth through delivering exceptional client work. However, Wallace recognizes that value-creation flexibility allows for individuals to focus either on business origination or business delivery. Partners can choose how they want to have an impact.

Aligning an incentive system to these discrete skillsets plays an important role in successful business development strategies. Although there are some guidelines that make incentive structures more valuable, understanding your own culture is critical. The incentive system you choose should reflect your people's talents, organizational structure, and firm goals.

Too frequently, firms choose a broad and simplistic model because measurement is achievable, and it feels "fair" to everyone in the organization. If leadership is communicating the goals of the organization, the incentive system should be easily understood by employees. An overly specific or overly broad system increases confusion, creates gamesmanship, and reduces employee understanding of firm-wide goals. The incentives system a firm creates is an opportunity to cement the goals of the organization in a financial way.

Many organizations have a menu of benefits that allow employees to choose specific options. Health savings accounts, vacation, remote work flexibility, and other options allow employees to optimize on the benefits that are most motivating to them. Why is incentive compensation excluded from this structure? Why do companies have huge variation in salaries but insist upon an incentive plan to equally cover thousands of employees? After talking to dozens of leaders from expert services firms, we believe that, going forward, firms should focus on intrinsic motivation and try to create a more bespoke incentive compensation plan for employees. This will be ushered in as technologies create better visibility into growth drivers and less friction between human resources and the delivery side of expert services companies.

CHAPTER

16

Discipline 5: Listen

We can't tell you the number of times we have witnessed practice leads sit down with potential buyers and begin by talking about their own firm's experience and capabilities.

> In addition to audit and tax, we are able to help you with payroll and bookkeeping, fractional CFO services, M&A, compensation, and cybersecurity assurance. We've done this work in the automotive, manufacturing, agriculture, healthcare, consumer products, and financial services industries . . .

But if you are talking, you're not listening, and if you are not listening, you have no idea where your client needs help.

Chris Fosdick, managing partner at The Cambridge Group, states this point succinctly: "The more people can think about cross-selling as a listening exercise rather than a brainstorming-what-we-could-sell exercise, the more likely it will be to bear fruit."

But We Are Different

Sandy, a chief marketing officer for a multinational firm, looks out of the window of her downtown Chicago office. She points out the bean-shaped Millennium Monument to Stephanie Cole, a managing director at PIE, and they both look down at the crowd of tourists posing for pictures. Stephanie was introduced to Sandy by one of her colleagues, who has been engaging with Stephanie to convene a group of CFOs on behalf of Sandy's company in a different practice area. Stephanie took the opportunity to stop by Sandy's office while she was in Chicago visiting another client.

Sandy twirls a pen between her fingertips as she starts off, "What you did driving relationships between our partners and CFOs in the peer group was impressive." She pauses. "My counterpart in that division can't stop talking about the work you've been doing, and I believe it. Here's the thing, though . . . our department is different."

Stephanie leans in. Whenever she is introduced to a new buyer in a firm, the conversation inevitably begins with the statement, "We're different." This is exactly what she expected, and it provides the perfect opening for Stephanie to start asking questions.

Sandy's point is well taken. Her department is different because no one practice area, no one division, no one team is the same. Stephanie, a veteran at listening closely, knows that asking the right questions to discern these differences is paramount to giving her insight into how PIE might add value to Sandy's work. If Stephanie doesn't pay close attention, the conversation will not move beyond Sandy's initial doubt.

Boston Consulting Group (BCG) partner Thierry Chassaing explains the importance of customization:

> The easiest thing to do is to sell the same thing to others, because you've done it 10 times before and you have a strong track record that you can show. Having said that, you have to be careful. We are in the semicustom business. I had experience with our client, Coca-Cola, years and years ago. I sent in a team who had done this kind of project before. I didn't pay much attention to them, and the reaction from the client was, "Thierry, this is the first time in seven years we've worked with you guys that it feels like you're applying a mechanical process, and it doesn't feel like much value added."

Stephanie is meeting with Sandy by way of a referral. Sandy's colleague has told her about Stephanie and PIE's work, which creates its own dynamics in the conversation. The referral carries an endorsement of credibility and an implied confirmation of trust, but it also can be an obstacle to having a productive conversation about how Stephanie's expertise can be customized to meet Sandy's needs. It may frame up Stephanie's work in a way that might not be applicable to Sandy's specific challenges and necessitates even closer listening and thoughtful positioning on Stephanie's part.

A referral from someone with whom you already do work, fecund with possibility, requires both listening and being mindful of how the new buyer's needs are different. When someone says, "We're different," think of it as an invitation to unpack the uniqueness of their challenges and an opportunity to apply your expertise anew in adding value for the client.

Four Guidelines for Listening

Over the past 20 years, we've developed four guidelines for listening that we bring to every client relationship.

1. **Scope deftly** – Use the scoping process as the first opportunity to listen closely and ask questions of your client. Walt Shill of ERM tells us:

   > I always make sure I scope a project in a way that I am interviewing and/or briefing stakeholders across the client. It's a change management best practice, but it also gives me a way to talk to new people about what I'm doing for the firm and to follow up with them after we have done the good work. Setting time to ask if we might do the same work for this, different, executive is easy after that.

2. **Look for intel** – Warm leads are always better than cold ones because of the way trust is transferred from one person to another. But experts limit themselves when they only ask their current buyers for others in the organization who might be interested in buying their services. That's great to do, but more often than not, when you ask, you'll get something like, "Sure. Let me think about that and get back to you." It is not that your buyer doesn't want to help you; it is that she wants to make sure she runs the risk/reward calculus first before extending herself. You are asking her to perform the most delicate of math: What is most in her self-interest?

   It is much better to use your project managers as sources of *information* about the firm and listen closely to what they share with you.

   A client in another division might have heard of you (**Awareness**), know what you do (**Understanding**), see how it might help them (**Interest**), appreciate the quality of your work (**Credibility**) and have heard you a are straight-up provider (**Trust**), and still not be able to pull the trigger on an engagement with you (**Ability and Readiness**).

   There are many reasons the opportunity to engage with a new division might not be ripe: There might be someone new in leadership, an old boss might be about to retire, everyone might be waiting for budget direction from a yet-to-to-be-named CEO, revenues might be down, the company might be reorganizing, and the list goes on. Then there are the personal considerations, "He's just treading water until retirement," or "She's been here for 18 months and is ready to show the company she can drive change."

In many ways, intelligence like this is better than referrals, because who you know in an organization is less important than who in the organization is ready to rock and roll. However, after you have this kind of deep background conversation on what is happening in a client, it is easier to say, "Could you help me think about how I might get an introduction to Sandy? I'd love to meet her."

3. **Align incentives** – Experts interviewed for this book said it was important for them to "give" something to the potential buyer. Says one Big Four partner, "I like to tell satisfied clients, 'I'd like to get the price down for you next year. If we could bundle you inside a larger set of contracts, it would qualify you for our volume discount. Would you be open to sitting down and talking through whether that would make sense for you?'" In order to determine what incentives to offer up, one must be listening.

4. **Listen for emergency needs** – Experts are there to help when their clients are up against a wall. When we hear a call for help, it means our clients are turning to their trusted networks for some quick decisions and hoping the capability is out there.

Sometimes being a smart person at the scene of an emergency is the path to great responsibility as principals look for quick help from those in the room. More than one young person has seen themselves, seemingly plucked from obscurity, tasked with projects that were way above their pay grade just because they were in the right place at the right time. Likewise, savvy expert services providers feel the magnetic pull of crisis and try to be first on the scene with a "What can we do to help?"

As Chris Fosdick of The Cambridge Group shares,

The second project that sells at a client is not sold because we went in and said, "Hey, we've got a product to sell." The second project that is sold at a client sells because they really liked working with us, liked the outcome of the first project, and we were *ready and prepared* to help on the next one.

17

Discipline 6: Tell Great Stories

Midway through the third year of the American Civil War, John Nicolay, Abraham Lincoln's personal secretary, presented the President with a stack of invitations. As Lincoln read through them, he paused on one from David Wills, an attorney in Gettysburg, Pennsylvania. Wills had raised money to dig up the 50,000 who had fallen in the Battle of Gettysburg and to rebury them in a new national cemetery. Wills had already booked former senator, governor, secretary of state, and president of Harvard, Edward Everett, as the lead speaker for dedication of the cemetery but, in a long shot, wondered if the President might stop by and say a few words.

Three weeks later, suffering from a bout of smallpox, Lincoln traveled by train to Gettysburg, mulling over the words he had prepared. Feverish and cold, his soul, too, must have ached as he contemplated a nation raw from loss and suffering. At the same time, he saw victory on the horizon and yearned to give meaning to the conflict he alone had decided to prosecute.

Witnesses say the President looked ghastly and drawn on the day of the memorial. When finally he rose to speak after Everett's two-hour oration, his head swimming from the fever, he leaned into his words,

Four score and seven years ago our fathers brought forth on this continent, a new nation, conceived in Liberty, and dedicated to the proposition that all men are created equal.

Starting out with a bang, Lincoln summoned the ghosts of the founding fathers and their high ideals. It is hard to underestimate the power of this on the 15,000 who had gathered, most of whom knew people who had been born before the founding of the nation. It was as though he was invoking a dead grandparent, the mere mention of whom would cause them to sit up straight and act out of their more noble selves.

> Now we are engaged in a great civil war, testing whether that nation, or any nation so conceived and so dedicated, can long endure.

In a sentence, he poses the question he traveled to rural Pennsylvania to ask his country: What is the meaning of this horrific tear in our national fabric? How can we reconcile ourselves to this river of spilled blood? Why have all these young men died?

> We are met on a great battle-field of that war. We have come to dedicate a portion of that field, as a final resting place for those who here gave their lives that that nation might live. It is altogether fitting and proper that we should do this.
> But, in a larger sense, we can not dedicate – we can not consecrate – we can not hallow – this ground. The brave men, living and dead, who struggled here, have consecrated it, far above our poor power to add or detract. The world will little note, nor long remember what we say here, but it can never forget what they did here. It is for us the living, rather, to be dedicated here to the unfinished work which they who fought here have thus far so nobly advanced.

And then he delivered his message, slowly intoning each word.

> It is rather for us to be here dedicated to the great task remaining before us – that from these honored dead we take increased devotion to that cause for which they gave the last full measure of devotion – that we here highly resolve that these dead shall not have died in vain – *that this nation, under God, shall have a new birth of freedom – and that government of the people, by the people, for the people, shall not perish from the earth.*

Those words, that American government should be "of the people, by the people, for the people," have lost some of their power over the years, having grown rounded in cliché. But at the time, they were radical. The animating spirit of 1776 was the call for "liberty" and freedom *from* the oppression of King George III. Lincoln, though, turns the page and says, the American ideal will not be, as it had been, a collection of a united group of states but one nation that, in its freedom, will collectively advance itself. The "of the people and by the people" was not new to his audience. What was new was that the federal government should be "for the people." For the first time in the American experience, we saw a President suggest that government could do things for its citizens, not just defend them. In these words, Lincoln lifted up the dead and gave their lives meaning, stones on which a better America might be built, when he said that government would no longer be predicated on protection but action.

We're Made to Tell Stories

"Most employees don't understand the 'why' of the organizations that they're in," shares Gonzaga professor Christopher Stevens. "The 'why' has to be communicated to them in something other than a mission statement or a vision-and-values piece. It has to be communicated in *stories*, because people remember stories and can tell them again."

Recent titles like *Wired for Story*, *Made to Stick*, and *Resonate* have popularized the idea that humans are storytellers and take in information best in story form. We, too, strive to be storytellers when we describe our work to new people we meet across our clients. We all know great storytellers when we see them – and they always do a couple of things perfectly.

They Have Something to Say, and They Say It Clearly

Peggy Noonan was one of the most gifted speechwriters to work for both Reagan and Bush. In her book, *On Speaking Well*, she writes that the key to a great speech is not oratorical flourish or tricks, but the simple act of making a cogent argument:

> Sophisticated people tend to think that speeches are magic. They are like the natives of Easter Island when they first saw a camera: All they could see was the flash, and, understanding things according to their myths and teachings, they thought the flash was the work of powerful spirits. They could not guess at the mundane reality, that it was the work of Bell and Howell.
>
> My advice to you is: Don't be sophisticated. Be commonsensical. *Speeches actually have to say things. And great speeches are great because they say great things.*

Noonan could have been talking about the Gettysburg Address – which, while short, said something big – that from now on the federal government would do things on behalf of its citizenry, like Social Security and building roads.

It turns out that ideas matter.

Our ability to navigate the Diamond of Opportunity within a client – attracting work with those we do not know and doing work we have not previously done with them – is a function of having something to say. As Noonan argues, logic trumps technique.

Say you have an engagement with the chief safety officer of Ultra Foods writing safety manuals based on your 20 years of experience as a regulator for OSHA. You might wake up in the middle of the night and think, "I should pitch the chief human resources officer (CHRO) at Ultra on revising all job descriptions to include safety language."

You decide to lob an email off to the CHRO.

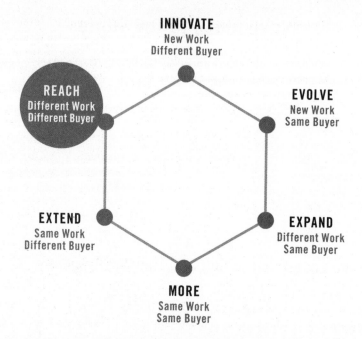

In this instance, you're trying to REACH – to develop trust with someone you don't yet know and develop credibility around a type of work you haven't previously done with this client. Your email may read something like:

Hi Ellen,

I am writing because I think I can help you strengthen the job descriptions you use from a safety perspective and reduce Ultra's exposure to safety-driven lawsuits.

For the past three years I have been working with Tim O'Brien, Ultra's chief safety officer, to rewrite the company's safety manuals used in training for every new employee. Since the inception of this project, OSHA-generated sanctions on Ultra have dropped by 16% and, more importantly, accident-free workdays in the various plants have increased by 31%.

Prior to working with Ultra, I spent 20 years serving as OSHA's chief regulator focused on agriculture. In 2000, I led the team that rewrote the standards governing this sector and served as general counsel to OSHA for five years.

In the course of my recent work with Tim, I have had a chance to look at a number of Ultra's job descriptions, which were last revised 10 years ago before you took over HR for the company. I've identified a number of simple fixes that could strengthen the job descriptions and better protect the company from unfounded safety complaints and/or litigation.

I imagine this being a small project. I think I could finish a re-draft of the safety language on Ultra's 1,300 job descriptions in less than a month.

I am currently working on site in Springdale. Would you be open to me stopping by your office next week to discuss the three specific vulnerabilities I see in the current library of job descriptions?

Assuming you are okay with this, I will work with Joan in your office to set time.

Best,

George

This note helps start building your trust and credibility by making a number of clear points:

- You are a credible source because you work closely with Ellen's colleague, Tim. (Ellen should keep reading.)
- You have already done adjacent work for Ultra. (You work with Tim on safety.)
- You have done a good job. (The metrics are in and are impressive.)
- You can trust me. (You have worked for Tim for three years. He wouldn't have stuck with you if he didn't trust you. Also, you have Ultra's back. You are not pitching a new service line so much as you are making sure Ultra is not exposed.)
- You are an expert and know what you are talking about. (You worked at OSHA and drafted the standards.)
- You bring a unique perspective that others would be hard-pressed to bring. (There are lots of safety consultants, but you were the one in charge of regulating Ellen's industry.)
- You already work for Ultra and are practically an insider. (You work in the building. You know her assistant's name.)
- You know her needs. (Because you're an insider, you know she has 1,300 job descriptions. You also have a point of view about what could be improved.)
- You are willing to stop by and tell her those improvement areas for free.

If you were the CHRO of Ultra, it would be hard not to take that meeting. The premises simply drive inexorably to the conclusion.

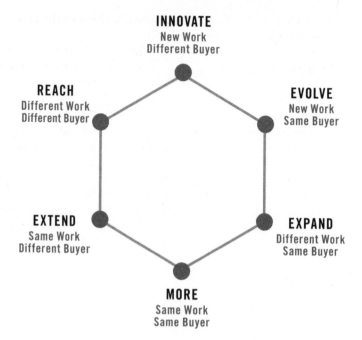

INNOVATE
New Work
Different Buyer

REACH
Different Work
Different Buyer

EVOLVE
New Work
Same Buyer

EXTEND
Same Work
Different Buyer

EXPAND
Different Work
Same Buyer

MORE
Same Work
Same Buyer

Learn to Brag a Little

Says Professor Stevens, "Firms and organizations do a really bad job of explaining to the client, 'What I just did for you added value.'" Stevens is right, but the best rainmakers know how to turn their success with a buyer into a story that can be told to others in the client company. Author and architect Art Gensler adds, "Most people find it difficult being totally honest with themselves about the value they create." We work hard to not let that be us. It is one thing to be braggadocious; it is another to honestly own the value we have created.

It is about being able to tell a story – a client had a problem, we had some experience, we helped them with the problem and now they are happy – or as CPA Michael McLaughlin writes, our job is to "help clients see their destination, how they will get there, and (our) role in the story."

But Don't Be the Hero

Stories are the bricks that build businesses. Chris Fosdick of The Cambridge Group agrees: "So much of the work I've sold has been through stories of previous successful work for clients." The key is that it must be through the prism of client success, not through the prism of consulting prowess.

Many of us probably picture ourselves as characters in an evolving narrative. When confronted with a success story, it's natural to insert ourselves into the role of protagonist and imagine our own celebration at the end of a massively successful project. But as expert services providers, we are not the protagonist. We should be envisioning ourselves cheering as our clients race past the finish line. If we are ever up for an award, our best shot is the supporting actor category. In order to foster client growth opportunities, experts should be looking for ways to make the buyer look good, not themselves.

Great stories always involve a hero doing something. Stories also include a clear objective and obstacles that the hero faces as they try to achieve their goal. The story then becomes how we engaged with a real live person at the client, how they wanted something, how it was hard, and then how, in the end, she or he succeeded, with the moral of the story always being: Engage with me and I'll make you a hero, too.

18

Discipline 7: Master the Art of the Ask

Psychologists have long speculated that when you give a person something of value, they then feel motivated to do something nice in return to balance things out. In 1971, Dennis Regan was a PhD candidate in Stanford's psychology department and decided to test this hypothesis. Regan recruited 81 Stanford freshmen and paid them $1.75 to participate in an experiment on aesthetics. Each student was paired with a second person to work on the aesthetics project. The second person, however, was not one of the 81 students; unbeknownst to the student, he was a "confederate" of the experiment. A secretary invited both the student and confederate into a room, told them to wait there, and then left the room. After some time, the phone on the secretary's desk rang, the confederate answered, and in half the cases, he is nice to the caller, saying he is sorry but he doesn't work in the building and doesn't know when the secretary will be returning. With the other half, the confederate answers the phone and says, "Hey, look, there's no secretary here. . . . Hey, I don't work here, lady, for chrissake. Just call later. . .," before hanging up abruptly without saying goodbye. In a parallel test with the same two individuals, Regan sat the confederate and student in a room to fill out a questionnaire on some art reproductions he presented them. When they were done, Regan said they would need a few minutes before they could continue. Then dividing the test groups into thirds, Regan caused one of three things to happen:

1. The confederate asked to leave the room and returned with a bottle of Coke for himself and one for the test subject, saying they might as well relax.
2. The confederate asked to leave the room and returned empty handed.
3. Regan came back into the room and gave both of the subjects a Coke.

After another questionnaire about some art, he had the confederate slip a note to the test subject, asking if the student would do the confederate a favor. The confederate communicated that he was selling raffle tickets for his high school and would win $50 if he sold the most. He was wondering if the student would buy any at 25 cents. The prize was a new Corvette. Then Regan measured whether the subject bought any tickets.

The results of the experiment were surprising.

The correlation between whether the confederate was unpleasant on the phone and whether the subject bought raffle tickets was weak. In other words, regardless of whether a person finds another to be pleasant or not does not have much to do with whether they will make the decision to do a favor for them. However, the correlation between whether the confederate gave a Coke to the student and whether the subject bought raffle tickets was high, suggesting that when a person does something nice for another, it influences whether the favor is reciprocated.

This result, sometimes called "The Law of Reciprocity," is often used as a kind of manipulation. You might have heard someone say, "In order to get someone to do something for you, you have to butter them up first with a gift or compliment."

We think there is a more profound, if hidden, insight found in this research. Human beings collect data on those they do not know and quickly determine whether the person is on their side or not, whether they are a friend or foe, and then, born out a deep sense of survival, ally with friends and disengage with the rest. Receiving unexpected value from a person is a sign of a friend. Reciprocating with a gift of value is a signal that "we should be allies" if anything should happen.

If we subscribe to the consultants' "Hippocratic oath" and first add value, then asking to grow, expand, or extend our work with a client suddenly becomes much easier. By adding value in advance of a sale, we signal to the buyer that we want to be allies and move forward into the commercial night together.

Learning the Art of the Ask

We are struck with how many people struggle to ask for what they want. For example, let's say Steve is engaged with a large construction concern reviewing their subcontractor agreements on behalf of the firm's general counsel (GC). This is steady and recurring work, but Steve is mindful of their budget cycle and knows he should ask the buyer, in this case the GC, whether his company is good to go for another year. But Steve doesn't want to. There is something inside of him saying, "If it ain't broke, don't fix it." But that's the wrong instinct; it's better to check in and confirm we are in the budget for the next year. However, when it comes time to actually ask the question, many experts struggle with the same thing – making the ask out of fear for the answer. One technique to avoid seeming desperate and commercial is to frame this ask as an administrative necessity: "I met with my managing director recently and she wanted to know if you were planning on continuing to use me in this capacity. She is trying to see what resources we have for new projects and whether she needs to be hiring." This is a reasonable thing to ask of a client. We aren't prostrating ourselves on the ground, begging for the work, we're just two professionals communicating about resource allocation. Likewise, when asking to do MORE work, it often makes sense to leverage a senior partner on the project to do the ask. At PIE we might say, "We had talked about doubling the size of the communities we've built for you – any thoughts on that? I'm trying to figure out who should be doing what on my team, and I want to make sure I reserve a few of our best deliverers for you if that was something you were interested in." Even more basically, it is important we learn how to ask, "Is there anything else we can do for you?" Professor Christopher Stevens of Gonzaga sat on a board where he listened to an auditor make her annual report. Stevens recalls thinking "Hey, you're in here. You've just spent four weeks learning about our business, and you're perfectly fine walking away. Why not dig in and say, 'What about this implementation you're struggling with? Is there a way we can do that? What about that cost-accounting system you just put in? Is there anything we can do to help there?'" Opportunities to do MORE work, EXPAND work, or EXTEND work abound; the problem is that many experts either don't know how or are afraid to make the ask.

The Ask *before* the Ask

Before we can get to the point where it makes sense to ask what different or new work we could be doing for a client, we must first understand the nature of what we are asking. A few things to consider follow.

Nature of the Conversation

- **Is it consequential?** When contact between people matters, it is more likely to occur. If our mother is sick with cancer, we don't care a whit about how weak the connection is with our co-worker's friend's sister-in-law who also happens to be a leading oncologist. We pick up the phone and call to get advice. Likewise, when contact means a lot to the person being asked for help, the likelihood of that contact happening goes up. Tom was a Peace Corps volunteer. He says, "It was a formative experience for me. I never refuse a call from someone who is thinking about joining the Peace Corps or who was a volunteer."

- **Is it valuable?** The likelihood of two people connecting in an organization goes up when both sides view the connection as valuable. Think of two hikers on the Appalachian Trail who never exchange words until a freak snowstorm blows in midafternoon and they are forced to hunker down and take shelter in place for the evening while the storm blows through to avoid walking off any dangerous cliffs. Then they start chatting like crows. At first, they saw no benefit in speaking with each other (and perhaps some risk of getting locked into an endless and pointless conversation). Then the circumstances changed and, fearing for their survival, they initiate contact because they are suddenly desperate for any shred of information or insight. Likewise, the higher the quality of exchange between two people, the greater the likelihood of future exchange.

The Takeaway: When we ask a buyer at a key client for MORE work or for introductions to others in the company with whom we might work, we need to remember to ask, "What's in it for them?" We know what is in it for us – higher revenues, performance bonuses, increased partner splits and a loving cup at the holiday party handed to us by the chief executive officer (CEO). But that's the wrong lens. Instead, it pays to keep in mind that our buyer is more likely to connect with others in the organization on our behalf when they see that brokering such a connection is consequential and valuable to them.

Let's look at what that might look like:

- **Good:** "Jane – In the course of our work, I've seen the opportunity to cut expenses in the call center run by your colleague by 20%. Could we book some time to discuss?"
- **Better:** "Jane – Our work together in your office has produced real efficiencies. You should talk to the head of all the branches and propose that you lead a working group to spread best practices to other offices. It seems like it would be a real feather in your cap. Let's set some time to discuss."

Nature of the Relationship

- **Do you need to level up?** Cavin Segil, one of our directors at PIE, puts it this way, "Sometimes the quickest way over is to go up." He means that while there are all sorts of reasons why our buyer in a client company might not want to refer us to her colleague in another division, including not wanting to share his or her secret sauce and an imbalance between perceived risk and reward, neither of those obstacles exist for their bosses. For this reason, experts know it is important to find a reason to meet the boss – the person who is not only responsible for the engagement we run for one of their units but who is also in charge of the performance of other parallel units. They don't think of us as our project manager's secret sauce; they think of us as *their* secret sauce, and if it is working, they are happy to spread it around liberally in all of the units.

Leveling up carries with it some risk. Our project manager will get nervous when we are talking with their boss. In fact, they can be downright unhelpful.

Cavin might say, "You think the next time I'm in town, I might sit down with your VP? I'd love to get to know how they view the project and brainstorm ways in which I might be helpful elsewhere."

"I'll see what I can do," she might say, followed by a whole lot of nothing.

The alternative is to write the boss ourselves, but that never feels good – it feels like we are disintermediating our most prized relationship at the client. Even if we don't think we are undermining their authority, our project manager might feel that way.

The way to get around this is to bring in reinforcements. We think of ourselves as our project manager's peer. That makes our boss the peer of our project manager's boss. This simple relationship geometry is the reason that expert services firms ubiquitously use the "senior partner" "project manager model." We deliver and then a "senior partner" swoops in and "checks in with the client." It might seem like burdensome and unnecessary oversight, but it is the springboard from which the EXPAND conversation takes off.

Jacob might visit the boss of Cavin's project manager and say "I'm glad the project's working for you. I hear the young man you've assigned to manage my team is a rock star. Everyone on my side says, he's all over this project. Someday over lunch, you'll have to tell me how you find people like that. Hey – while I have you, tell me how you have your unit organized. Cavin tells me that you have five other market-facing teams in different geographies . . ."

This is the senior partner's job: to check in on client satisfaction, make course correction if necessary, and ask for new business across your project leader's boss's domain.

- **Do we know whom to call?** Traffic across a network of human beings is slowed when we do not know what others in the network know. When Tom worked at Great Harvest Franchising, he found a way to improve the complex web of internal expertise in real time. Tom notes, "We published high-to-lows of bakery owners based on their relative expertise around seven different dimensions of the businesses. This increased traffic because people knew whom to contact."

- **Is it fair?** Sociologists report if one person in a community feels others are being rewarded in outsized ways and feels the community is unfair, they are less likely to reach out to others beyond their cubicles.

- **Is it reciprocal?** If you do us a solid favor, we feel like we "owe" you and look for ways to do you a solid favor to even the score. Fundraisers often use this to their advantage, sending you a "gift," with the hope that the resulting psychic imbalance will be "righted" with a donation. This is like the principle outlined in the Regan experiment at the beginning of this chapter.

- **Are the ties strong?** Deep, long-term, personal ties increase the likelihood of good ideas being passed between two people. A network characterized by close ties will have greater traffic than one characterized by weak ties. Churchgoers in a Latter Day Saints ward are more likely to exchange business referrals and recipes than an association of traffic engineers. That said, strong ties don't always add up. In founding LinkedIn, Reid Hoffman asserted that strong ties could be leveraged and that if he knew a software engineer in Charlotte and that software engineer knew an opera singer in Milan who knew a member of the Italian Parliament, then the sum of three strong ties would equal an ability to get an introduction to the member of parliament. But it's not proven to be true. We might know former Senator Max Baucus, who knows former President Barack Obama, but that doesn't mean that we are having dinner next week with Barack at Pineapple and Pearls on 8th Street in DC. Strong ties quickly become weak ties as the ripples of connection peter out the farther you get from the first main strong connection.

- **Are they equal?** In networks where all the nodes are meaningfully equal, exchange occurs more often than it does in open networks. One of the important rules at PIE is that when we are pulling together a peer group on behalf of a client, we make sure that the members of that group perceive each other as peers. The head of a $2 billion fashion house doesn't want to be in a group that includes a store manager from The Gap in Milwaukee.

The Takeaway: It pays for us to understand our buyer's *real* network and not just what the organization chart says is their network. Yes, our buyer might theoretically be able to ping a colleague we want to work with through the corporate messaging app, but that doesn't mean they will. We make a point of asking our buyers who their "friends" are in the organization. *This is their true network.* We might think they could easily introduce us to other division leads, but organization charts mask rivalries, distaste, past battles, and distance. Instead we look to find the well-worn paths and walk down those. If our objective is to meet the head of marketing analytics in the food division, but we learn that our buyer with the same responsibilities in the pet care division felt burned by a past effort to help, don't worry. We can still get there. It is just that we might have to first go through our buyer's good friend in the health and beauty division.

All of us in expert services are playing a long game where the surest referral path is the one that is easiest and most comfortable for our buyer.

Nature of the Payoff

- **Is the investment substantial?** The higher the ante, the more we use a network. Free networks are weaker than paid networks. Poker players are more likely to stay in a game characterized by a high ante and low bets than one characterized by a low ante and high bets.

- **Is it gratifying?** The shorter the payoff associated with an exchange between people, the greater the likelihood they will speak again. Behavioral sociologist George Homans writes, in describing social exchange theory, that connections between people in a network go up when they are rewarded. The more often they are rewarded, the more likely there will be future exchanges.

- **What are the value drivers?** David Allen in his wonderful book *Getting Things Done* writes about the need to periodically change our "altitude" when thinking of what we want to get done, like a jet that can as easily skim along the ground as soar to 45,000 feet.

  At the lowest altitude of getting things done, we ask ourselves "What's next?" Slightly higher is the world of to-do lists and daily agendas. At the highest level, we ask ourselves, "What do I want to do with my life?" or "What's on my bucket list?"

  It's useful for experts to fly at different altitudes as well. Day-to-day, we are buzzing project management trees. At 10,000 feet, we are asking ourselves, "What's my client trying to get done, and how could I amass a team that would be helpful?" Up where the air gets thin, rainmakers tell us they ask about the company as a whole. "How does this company create value in the marketplace? What are the strategic choices they have made? What are they not doing? What kind of disruption is coming their direction and how should they prepare or position themselves as the industry disrupter?"

  This should be the purpose of any account planning summit – not to ask, "What do we offer that we could sell to them?" – but, "Where is this company headed and how could we help them get there?"

  There is a simple aviation truth at work here: The higher we fly, the more opportunity we see.

  The Takeaway: Testing a client's incentive system for internal referral is easy: We simply ask for a referral. A failure to respond to our request or a bunch of excuses suggest that the client has nothing in place to reward employees who help the company as a whole as opposed to just hitting their marks in their own narrow domain. It means our request for help carries with it no upside for the buyer of our services from whom we are asking for help. All they can see is risk, work, and downside. We can change that dynamic, however. Rainmaking experts report that when they negotiate a contract up front, they often say to their clients, "If we can beat the performance metric by 20%, will you agree to introduce me to two of your colleagues?" effectively linking an asked "favor" with a gratifying event. Likewise, we've seen experts promise "group buying discounts" if they can get a foothold elsewhere in the organization.

If we've done our job by doing and incentivizing good work, leveraging our team, telling effective stories, being good friends to our clients and colleagues, and listening closely, then the "ask" should be easy. It starts with "How can we help?" We've already added value for our client, earning us the right to ask how we can add more value with more, different, or new work or people across the organization.

There is nuance to whom you ask, when you ask, and how you ask this question. However, as experts our *job* is to ask this question.

We have an obligation to ensure we are doing the most good on behalf of our most important clients, and it begins with this simple question.

Now, having described the disciplines of accomplished rainmakers, let's turn our attention to what this all means for the expert services industry – how we organized, the technology we use, indeed, the reason for our entire existence.

Section 6: Seeds of Change

CHAPTER
19

The Power of Peers

Errol Rice bends over his desk and stares at his facilitation map – a matrix of interview notes and the names of executives who plan to join a call. His knee bounces as he ignores people passing his closed glass door. Outside, gusts blow down from the Bridger Mountains, which are obscured by a leaden blanket of mid-January snow clouds.

It is 10 minutes before the hour, and Errol is getting ready to dial into the call he will lead on behalf of Grant Thornton's manufacturing practice. They have contracted with PIE to pull together a group of manufacturing company CFOs with whom they would like to do business. Errol's job will be to facilitate a discussion of best practices. He's spoken individually to each CFO in advance to ask them about their interests and priorities, and he'll use their questions to each other as the agenda for today's discussion.

His Carhartt jacket hangs on the hook next to his door, snow still clinging to it. Lean, with close-cropped hair and wind-burnt cheeks, Errol brings a good-natured earnestness to his work – a kind of range-riding version of Atticus Finch.

A ranch kid, Errol came to PIE after running the Montana Stockgrowers Association, where he represented an always-shifting coalition of cattle and sheep producers to foreign markets, financial markets, regulators, and Congress. It's the perfect background for wrangling executives on a call.

His mission: Make this call a useful hour for the CFOs who will join.

Outside his office, there is a buzz of behind-the-scenes action. The conference line and its multiple backup lines stand at the ready. Windy, the senior project coordinator who works with Errol on this project, is watching her monitor to see the numbers and names of participants as they dial in. Elsewhere, a team of other project coordinators sit by their phones to call executives who have indicated they will join but might have forgotten or may be running behind.

A bell rings on the conference line.

"Hi, this is Errol Rice. Who's just joined the line?"

The first to join is the host from Grant Thornton. Our host heads the manufacturing practice and looks forward to these quarterly calls, during which he gets to spend an hour talking directly with a dozen of his most important clients and potential buyers.

"Hey, Errol. Looks like we have a great agenda today. Any updates?"

"One member got called into a last-minute executive meeting, but we've actually had two other CFOs who cleared their calendars just this morning so they could join. We're looking at a great group of attendees for today."

Another entry bell sounds, and it's the Grant Thornton subject-matter expert (SME) joining a few minutes early. In the pre-interviews with the participants, CFOs told Errol they wanted to talk about cybersecurity, so our host has invited one of Grant Thornton's key experts on cybersecurity in the manufacturing practice to join the call. She won't be presenting, but will look to naturally weave in her expertise, questions, and insights into the conversation throughout the hour to add value to the members.

In the next five minutes, just as the hour hits, more than a dozen executives join the call. Errol sits up in chair, his game face on. He can feel his pulse quicken. "Those first few minutes of a PIE remind me of the opening kickoff when I played football in Denton. The adrenaline helps me focus."

It's game time.

Thank you to everyone for joining today's discussion. This is your call, and I appreciate everyone taking a little time with me beforehand to make sure your questions are informing the agenda. Before we get started, I'd like to hand things over to our host to say a few words of welcome.

As the host gets underway with his welcome remarks and SME introduction, Windy looks at the list of the executives who have joined and sees that four CFOs are running late. She worked hard with these CFOs' assistants to put this meeting on their schedules, but she knows that days have a way of getting away from the busy executives. She assigns two names each to the project coordinators on hand, who rush to their offices and start dialing.

"Hi, this is Kristin. I am calling on behalf of Errol Rice of the Grant Thornton Manufacturing CFO Exchange. I'm wondering if George is having trouble dialing into the call at this hour?"

Real-time responses to these conversations are shared with Errol over instant message so he can adjust his facilitation map accordingly. "George is running 10 minutes late." "Sally can no longer make it – she got pulled away by her CEO." "Jeannie's assistant said her flight was delayed but she's planning to dial in as soon as she lands."

Errol adjusts his headset. As the host wraps up his intro, Errol looks in the direction of one of the member CFOs to have them kick off the conversation by teeing up their question for the group.

The member begins, "Thanks, Errol. My question is simple. What is the data security process that you all are using to govern the onboarding of new equipment? Who owns that and how is it managed?"

In short order, Errol's call is off to the races. Other CFOs quickly jump in. Executives want to help each other – their peers.

"Once I tee up a question, executives respond with their experience, advice, and questions of their own," Errol reports. "My job is to remind participants of their questions, and thread a conversation that is generative and useful. Maybe pull in some quieter voices. I also look for places to pull my client into the conversation to make sure their expertise is highlighted. That usually happens about a third of the way through, or at a point when it seems like the members are a bit stumped and no one has a great silver bullet for their peers. I'll turn to the SME and say something like, 'Gloria, you are out in the marketplace; what are you seeing other companies do about this?' This is the chance for that person to step back and offer perspective, which positions him or her as a go-to on the subject."

We tell you about this process because we believe this system of gathering clients and potential clients together into virtual peer groups is one of *the single best tools to drive client engagement, because the process of engaging with peers as peers positions experts less as salespeople and more as trusted advisors.*

About this, Rob Benson of Kele Inc. says, "That's what we all want, right? That's what we all want to be – trusted advisors."

Jumping the Stack

Harry Wallace founded PIE in 2001 after rolling out of Arthur Andersen, where he served as National Managing Director of Business Development. He, too, is a student of how trust is built:

The thing that Jeff Bezos has figured out is that buyers trust relevant data, like customer reviews or algorithm-driven recommendations, more than they trust salespeople. Next, people trust their own instincts and family and friends' recommendations. After that, buyers trust peers – others who are in their same seat. They next look to experts without bias, like testing labs, Gartner, or professors who have studied their industry. Only then will they turn to experts-with-bias like consultants who have relevant experience, but who also have an agenda – to gin up new work. The least trusted sources of buyer information are salespeople who have an agenda – namely, to make quota – but don't have deep domain expertise.

TRUST CONTINUUM

The power of using peer conversations to engage with buyers and would-be buyers is that it allows a practice lead to "jump the stack" by two levels, from expert-with-bias to the powerful position of peer.

This takes a shift in thinking for some experts. Their first instinct may be to present – to talk about themselves or their capabilities in an effort to be helpful. But that is how someone with a sales agenda would act as they read from their brochure of things they could do. During our pre-briefs, PIE instead coaches clients to ask next-level questions to demonstrate knowledge and curiosity, and to tell stories about how other companies have approached similar problems to the ones an executive might be facing. Experts benefit from learning to take the "I" out of what they are doing; they are not some font, from which all knowledge flows. They are, rather, another smart person – a peer – who is wrestling with the same problems in real time.

Following Up

Errol brings the call to a close at the top of the hour. He reflects on timing, "These people are busy. They most certainly have back-to-back meetings on their calendar – or it's even more likely they're triple-booked. We have to be respectful of their time if we want them to keep coming back."

Immediately after closing out the call, he dials into a separate conference line to debrief with the Grant Thornton team.

It's like they just hosted a party and they want to make sure everyone showed up and had a good time. It's just how we are as people. The temptation for our clients is often to focus on how many people came to the party and how enthusiastic they were. They might say things like, "Great numbers," or "Too bad Wallace couldn't make it today," or "It was pretty lively. Everyone seemed engaged." It's my job to try and steer them toward the substance of what they heard. Sometimes you have a call where the members are a bit quieter and more pensive or calls with just a few members on the line but those conversations are just as likely to reveal opportunities for our clients to help.

My first question on the debrief is, "Did anything jump out at you as an obvious cry for help?" If a CFO said, "I'm pulling out my hair. I'm scared to death our CIO isn't paying attention to all this equipment we're buying and keeps saying cloud security is a higher priority," then that warrants a follow-up call. I will volunteer to reach out and set that up on behalf of the client.

The next thing I ask is if they heard a theme that makes them think about a service offering they could create. They just heard buyers articulate a bunch of pain points. I try to steer the conversation to, "How could we help?"

I'll ask if the firm has produced any thought leadership on the subject. If they have a recent whitepaper that's relevant to the topic we just discussed, I'll suggest the host send it out along with the executive summary of the call.

Finally, I ask about people's travel schedules. I know where all the member CFOs are based. If someone is going to Tucson and one of the executives on the calls works out of there, I'll ask my client if I can help arrange a meeting.

Errol is jazzed about this particular call. We call it the "PIE high" – that feeling when we complete a session and we know our hard work has paid off in bringing value to both the members and our client. It's fun to help people, even – or especially – when it's a high-wire act.

A Secret PIE Ingredient: Third-Party Follow-Up

We have seen that it can be valuable to have a third-party facilitator like PIE lead the charge on scheduling follow-up meetings between members and client SMEs, rather than putting that burden on the experts.

- **PIE is safe:** When we email the executive, we write something like,

I just wanted to follow up about one of the challenges you expressed during our session yesterday around communications with your CIO on cybersecurity. Your comments really resonated with the host from Grant Thornton. She wondered whether you would find it useful to set up a one-on-one call. She could share some strategies she's seen work with other clients.

They almost always say yes. They say yes, because we're responding to a felt need, and we're doing it a day after they expressed it. If they do say no, which happens on occasion, there is no bruising to the relationship – they're just kindly declining an intermediary.

- **PIE will do it:** Experts are busy. To-do lists are long. They need chances to engage to be pushed to their calendar.
- **PIE protects the group:** It is important that the group not be seen as a sales forum or just a chance for an expert to peddle his or her wares. By having the facilitator ask the client or would-be buyer for permission to broker a follow-up call, the integrity of the group is preserved.

Before All

At PIE we believe the cardinal commandment of expert services is, "First, add value." Experts should work hard to find a way of providing value to those they most want to serve before they ask for the favor of considering them as expert partners. When working to engage with those you most want to serve,

The order is *not*:

- Meet the person.
- Make chitchat.
- Tell them what you do.
- Ask them if there was any way you might get hired by them.
- If yes, say thanks, and invite them to a client conference hosted by your team.

It is:

- Meet the person.
- Make chitchat.
- Ask them what they do.
- Invite them to a best practice call you hold on this subject.
- Get to know them.
- Identify challenges they say they are facing.
- Identify how you are uniquely positioned to help them.
- Ask them how you can help.

This simple truth is the foundation on which the PIE process is built. Peer groups help clients give something of value to their clients or other likely buyers as a first step toward climbing the engagement ladder. The thing of value is free and convenient from a time and technology perspective. It is also a chance to touch base with people who are doing exactly what they themselves are doing in similarly sized companies and in similar reporting relationships. Executives value this opportunity.

Earning the Bigger Ask

"The most common question I get when I talk with practice leads about the PIE approach is, 'Why phone calls? Aren't dinners better?'" says Errol. His "PIE high" has mellowed and he's looking relaxed as he leans back in his chair, although he still keeps an eye on the atomic clock on his wall to make sure he's 30 seconds early to his next client call.

> The truth is dinners are better. We all know this. Having a few glasses of wine and "breaking bread" with a client or a potential client is of course the best way to mix in the sort of personal talk that builds trust. It gives practice leads a chance to make a personal connection with a client.

Dinners are also a way to dig into challenges an executive is experiencing and offer the chance to share snippets from your experience solving similar problems, which builds credibility with the client.

And who wouldn't rather share a glass of Pinot than a quick phone call?

As it turns out, lots of people. Your clients and likely buyers are busy people who have lives, and it can feel a little presumptuous to invite them to dinner when you barely know them. The value exchange is off. You are basically saying, "If I buy you a fancy dinner, will you listen to me pitch you?" The answer might be yes, but it just as easily could be, "I just got back from Asia where I ate out every night. I need to spend some time with my husband and kids."

An even bigger ask than a weeknight dinner is the big summit your firm stands up in Miami Beach every year. Anytime your ask to a client or would-be client is predicated on travel, you immediately reduce the likelihood they will accept. It is a bed away from home and involves expense, and, most importantly, time away from other things.

Remember when you were in college and had a crush on the boy or girl in your political science class? You wanted to get to know them better. You may have momentarily considered a weekend at the lake house your uncle owns nearby. But you would never invite them out for the weekend as a first date, it would be too much of an ask.

Instead, you'd probably turn to them (after swallowing your anxiety) and say something like, "This next assignment is going to be brutal. Do you want to grab coffee sometime this week and compare notes?" It's the whole reason there is that dating service advertised in every in-flight magazine called, "It's Just Lunch." Human beings engage in baby steps. They like to test the waters, trying out "just lunch" before they commit to a weekend at the lake house.

This is your job when getting to know new buyers in a firm with which you already work. Extend an invitation that gives them something they really value (e.g., a platform to ask questions of peers in real time) and strip away anything that makes it difficult to say yes (e.g., travel, expense, time, technology).

At PIE, we have had enormous success recruiting executives to one-hour, by-phone exchanges. Executives can dial in from anywhere, use their cell phones, and they don't have to go through a complicated technology, which may or may not be available to them. It's only an hour, and it's free. Most importantly, it's focused. A CFO in one of our roundtables told us, "This hour is like the best 60 minutes I get out of an entire trip when I fly to London for a three-day CFO summit."

So, to answer the question Errol gets when he is talking to practice leads, "Isn't a dinner better?" the answer is yes, but that is up a couple of notches on the stack. First, add value. That earns you the right to say to an executive, "It has been great getting to know you during our phone exchanges. I am going to be in Seattle next week and would love to put a face to a name. Can we grab dinner?"

Helping Our Clients Discover Diamonds

The PIE process helps *our* clients – expert services providers – best position themselves to scale trust and credibility to move across the entire Diamond of Opportunity with members of the peer groups they host.

- They develop *trust* with these new buyers over time by prioritizing listening and adding value before asking for work in return.
- Peer exchanges give experts a platform to demonstrate their various kinds of expertise to would-be buyers prior to an engagement, earning *credibility* for their work.
- They also indirectly begin earning *trust* and *credibility* as they hear first-hand stories during peer discussions about how our client has successfully helped others in the group. Executives begin to think, "If all my peers trust them to do great work, so should I."
- They stay proximate to members' needs through ongoing engagement, putting them in the best spot to help with any kind of work.

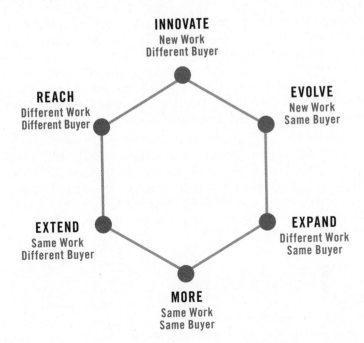

INNOVATE
New Work
Different Buyer

REACH
Different Work
Different Buyer

EVOLVE
New Work
Same Buyer

EXTEND
Same Work
Different Buyer

EXPAND
Different Work
Same Buyer

MORE
Same Work
Same Buyer

How might a PIE partner maximize their opportunities to help a client by hosting a peer exchange? Let's use an example of a public accounting firm that engages with PIE to convene a group of Fortune 250 chief tax officers (CTOs). Let's say one CTO of a large energy company has been invited. She is a current client of the accounting firm but has heretofore only purchased a small amount of state compliance work. The firm has done a good job but hasn't been able to grow the relationship. Here's the opportunity:

- The firm earns MORE of the same compliance work with the CTO by virtue of staying proximate to her needs. During the pre-interviews and quarterly sessions, the firm finds out the CTO is looking to outsource compliance work for additional states, and the firm is the first one in the door with a proposal.
- During a pre-interview for a peer exchange session, the CTO mentions she's planning an acquisition in the coming months, but for the time being the company will remain separate with its own tax team. The states the acquired company operates in are different from the ones the CTO is focused on. She sees advantages in having consistent state tax compliance work across both companies, so she puts the host firm in touch with the CTO of the soon-to-be acquired firm to encourage them to use the same provider for their state compliance as well. Thus, the firm wins EXTEND work.

- During one of the sessions, the topic is focused on international compliance, and specifically focuses on issues some CTOs and their counterparts are facing in the UK. The firm includes one of their new experts, recently hired away from the Her Majesty's Revenue and Customs (HMRC), in the discussion, and his knowledge and guidance around the UK tax system wows the members. The firm wins EXPAND work with this CTO as he looks to bring this expert in to advise his team on UK compliance matters.

- A few sessions later, the topics are focused on tax audits and controversy in the Asia Pacific region, again attended by an informative and helpful SME. After the session, the CTO pings his Asia Pacific (ASPAC) regional tax director to ask him how he likes their current advisor in the region for controversy issues. He mentions he's actually been quite frustrated lately, because he feels like his current firm is managing an ongoing audit pretty poorly in China. The CTO puts him in touch with the SME from the peer exchange, suggesting they connect about a future engagement. The ASPAC director engages the firm for REACH work.

- After about a year of hosting exchanges, the firm invites member CTOs to convene in-person for a dinner in New York. Members have become invested in this community and are eager to meet in person, so they are willing to spend extra time because they know the discussion over dinner will be valuable. Our CTO is able to attend. During dinner, the topic of robotics and the future of tax technology is paramount. The firm mentions the successes they've had so far with a number of tax departments, and how they're interested in piloting additional new technologies with firms that are interested. Having developed strong *trust* and *credibility* over the past year, the CTO opts in for this pilot program, agreeing to do EVOLVE work with the firm.

- Perhaps the type of pilot they're discussing would be impactful for the entire finance function, making the CFO the right buyer for this service. The CTO makes a warm introduction and strong recommendation that the CFO engage with INNOVATE work.

The diamond is an expert's best friend. Instead of cut, color, clarity, and carat, we're looking for our six different points of opportunity for growth: MORE, EXPAND, EXTEND, REACH, EVOLVE, and INNOVATE.

The Power of Routers

Trying to reconcile the competing interests of sales and marketing teams can be as painful as the leathery bite of a whip. It is why we call the internecine wars we see in our clients sales and marketing (S&M).

James Baldwin has a consulting practice focused on helping retailers purchase, customize, and use point-of-sale (POS) systems to drive process efficiencies and analytic visibility into supply chains. His work can yield insight, change product mixes, focus promotions, and drive revenues. He has experience with everything from emerging fresh taco brands to sewing supply chains.

We catch up with him as he is flying to Dallas to consult with a franchise client rolling out a POS system to 600 franchisees. Shares Baldwin, "The brand was struggling because they needed the franchisees to use their capital to buy the system and were struggling to articulate to the franchisee advisory board and their marketing board the return on investment for franchisees." They hired Baldwin to review the choices they had made to date, to dig into the unit economics of their stores, and to recommend what they should say as part of their planned "100% POS!" campaign.

"I'm a sole proprietor," Baldwin says. "That means, I do it all – the website, the pitch decks, the targeted outreach, the thought leadership, the speaking gigs, and somewhere in all that, the actual work for the client. It can be overwhelming."

Baldwin gets an "A" for covering the bases. He's working to build awareness and understanding, gauge interest, build trust and credibility, and stand by until his clients and would-be clients are ready and able.

He says, "I don't think about sales and marketing as separate. I think of it as the stuff I do to build my pipeline and my business."

Baldwin is not alone. Most small consulting shops are headed by people who are forced, by necessity, to be Jacks-of-all-trades. They often turn to small business gurus for help.

Michael Gerber would be one of those gurus. Michael wrote one of the most successful and influential business books for small business owners of all time, *The E-Myth* ("Over Two Million Sold!"). The book, and subsequent editions and spin-off books, are built on the power of a single phrase Michael coined: "Work on the business, not in the business." The idea is that people often go into business because they are good at something. However, to grow businesses, you need to teach others to deliver that value and instead grow muscle in areas of business development and management – what Gerber calls "working *on* the business."

An attorney we know who ran lease operations for Federated Department Stores in Cincinnati retired and then began to consult with other big-box retailers on their leases. Soon she was flying around the country, looking at locations, meeting with landlords, and negotiating leases on behalf of mid-sized retailers that hadn't yet built this capability in-house.

Two years after retiring, she has equaled her corporate income and feels good about telling her friends back at Federated that she is "keeping busy consulting."

The trouble is that she feels stuck. All of her time is spent responding to emails, setting up travel, sitting in on conference calls, and drafting contracts. She is spending 100% of the time "working in the business" and has no time to "work *on* the business" because she is too busy providing her expertise to clients. This is no way to scale.

Her background is in leasing. She's spent her entire career practicing this expertise within the cozy comfort of Federated. She never had to get a business license or do her own accounting, much less create a website, drive social media, publish, pitch clients, keep in touch with her pipeline, or any of the many other sales and marketing responsibilities that constitute "working *on* her business."

That's why consultants to small businesses often counsel their clients to outsource marketing as a way to augment their skillset.

Writing for the Small Business Administration, Anita Campbell says,

> As a small business, outsourcing allows you to get more done and trust important tasks and processes to professionals, without having to actually grow your full-time team in a significant way. It allows you to keep costs under control, increase efficiency, and focus on the parts of your business that you actually enjoy and are good at.

But what we have seen over and over again is that when expert services providers outsource marketing, it gives rise to an unintended consequence: business development gets ignored.

Says Baldwin,

I hired a marketing company to help build my firm. They did a bunch of positioning work, designed a logo, printed business cards, and launched my website. All that was good, but none of it has given me new work. It was like a sunk cost. They asked me if I was happy, and I said I thought a marketing firm was supposed to help me grow. They looked a little offended and then tried to set me up on HubSpot to push out emails and track downloads of a whitepaper they wanted me to write, which they said would be "demand gen," which was their word for giving me leads. Here's the deal, though. I tried that when I used to work at a big consulting firm, and I was not impressed with the results. It's a lot of work for me, and even though HubSpot can track every step of the way, in the end, it didn't produce results. In every case, the people who downloaded my whitepapers were not my buyers but were lower-level people. I said no to the marketing firm. They're just no help to me on actual business development.

Digging Out the Dandelion Root

Business Development and Marketing should be the twin engines propelling a takeoff in growth in the expert services industry, but instead they seem locked in a cold war with each other where no one wins.

Product firms need both marketing and sales in order to prosper:

- The job of a chief marketing officer (CMO) in a products company is to communicate to a large buying universe the benefits of their product suite. That starts by thinking about where the product is located in the wider universe of products and how their product stacks up. It involves segmenting the market into likely buying cohorts and then going back to the R&D and design shops to ensure the product looks and performs in a way that will be attractive to a buying set. The job of the CMO is to find ways to communicate those benefits to the segment whether through advertising, social media, chat boxes, endorsements, websites, collateral, channel partnerships, or earned media. Somewhere along the way, the CMO may also want to redo the firm's logo so it "speaks" to the targeted market, may look to tie the brand to a cause that resonates with the target market, and may look to host high-dollar events to engage the target market (Motorola Does MOMO!). The CMO might even be charged with the (nearly) impossible task of creating buzz and viral promotion of a new product. Finally, he or she is going to want to track and run analytics on what is working and what is not to capitalize on social media's ability to track and influence a single customer's buying journey.

- A chief sales officer (CSO), however, has an entirely different job in a product company. The CSO's job is to meet customers, either consumers, channel resellers, wholesalers, or B2B clients, and convince the buyer that their incumbent solution to a problem is not serving them well and that a switch to buying his or her product is a better decision. The CSO often runs large account groups, field sales forces, and a sales academy. The CSO might even be charged with the (nearly) impossible job of forecasting the firm's revenues down to the penny. Finally, the CSO is going to want to track and run analytics on all sales activity with a dashboard on Salesforce that alerts him or her to things like slumps on the number of outbound meetings in the western region or data indicating that salespeople recruited from engineering schools perform better after 36 months than those with an MBA and concentration in marketing.

The two disciplines often butt heads.

Sales is the point of the spear. We drive revenues. Not sure what Marketing does other than host dinners on yachts in Boston Harbor.

Marketing creates brand and product positions, which set up the preconditions under which buyers want our products. Not sure what Sales does other than expense endless dinners and take orders.

The truth is, of course, neither the chicken nor the egg came first.

The source of the problem is that expert services providers crib their go-to-market strategies from the world of product sales, a poor fit for selling expertise. Says attorney Bob Esperti, "I don't disapprove of marketing. Marketers are wonderful for products. They are not worth the price of beans when it comes to professional services." The origins lie with business schools where most marketing and sales courses focus exclusively on product case studies. Many experts base their business development strategy on what they read in the popular media about what works and what doesn't, not taking into consideration that selling an iPhone is a very different proposition than selling a cloud integration of two HR software suites. The misconception that expert services are brought to the market like products is pernicious. Getting rid of it requires us to go deep and change the way we think, like digging out a dandelion root.

Why Sales and Marketing Fails to Serve Expert Services Firms

Most expert services firms organize themselves similarly to products companies. Absent another model, they hire a CMO and charge them with brand building, events, thought leadership, analytics, websites, social media, and earned media.

They rename sales, *business development* and, understanding that experts themselves are the best suited to engage with a would-be client, push that onto the practice leads. Marketing is like artillery that softens up a help position using awareness, understanding, and the demonstration of credibility, but not trust. Unsurprisingly, we are seeing the rise of a new role: "managing director of market development." Typically, this person is a line partner who has the respect of her fellow practice leads as a rainmaker and is charged with helping drive key account planning and supporting practice leads in their business development efforts. Call them the chief growth officers. Their job is to leverage good work already performed and trust already earned to scope work.

We recently wrote a CMO of a successful consulting business, asking her if she would be willing to talk about how the firm expands their relationships with key clients. Her response speaks volumes:

> Hi, Jacob,
> In looking at the questions below, I realize that I will probably not be the right candidate to give you interesting answers. Our partners really drive sales and cross-selling. My marketing team is more front-end focused – lead generation, awareness building, thought leadership. I think I need to decline participating in this. Hope you understand and good luck.

Fair enough.

Marketing sees their work as separate and distinct from sales. In the world of expert services, business development falls to the practice leads.

This model, however, is broken. Practice leads and marketing leads come at the problem from two distinct perspectives that tend to create friction rather than sales force.

- **From the practice:** "Marketing says they do thought leadership, but how can they do that? The partners are the subject matter experts. I heard that our CMO was looking for an outsourced content development partner. That just amazes me. Our content – the substance of our expertise – is what we do, the whole reason our firm exists. How can we outsource that? All marketing is good at is 'skinning' our whitepapers so they look pretty. But they take at least four months to do that."

- **From marketing:** "The managing directors can't get out of their own way to write anything. It takes them six months and then when we get it, the prose is baroque and boring. The content is outdated by the time we get it."

- **From marketing:** "The partners don't understand how lead development works. We post content and see who is interested in it. We forward these leads to the partners, but they never follow up."

- **From the practice:** "Marketing has no idea who our buyers are. I get this sheet of names from all sorts of bizarre countries, tiny companies and business school students that they call leads. I'm not even sure they understand that we work with chief audit directors and that is who we want to talk to."

- **From marketing:** "The partners want summits, but they don't want to pay for them. When we do get budget, we will host whatever they want. However, the partners do a terrible job of recruiting participants – they are always too busy – and then we get the blame for the high cost/guest."

- **From the practice:** "Marketing does nice events, but no one ever shows up to the events but the clients I've invited. I thought their role was to get us new business. I go to these big summits, and I think to myself, this is just a gift to the people we are already working with. It's not business development."

- **From marketing:** "We're always getting hammered by leadership on ROI. They don't understand that we lay the groundwork off of which they can sell. There's no directly attributed ROI on that even if it is essential to the firm's success. It's like asking the foundation contractor on a building to take responsibility for how many leaks in the roof there are. It doesn't even make sense."

- **From the practice:** "My view is that all marketing should have an ROI tied to it. I'm tired of sponsoring golf players. I don't see how that helps our practice's P&L. For what they pay that guy, I could pay to speak at every one of our industry events for the next 10 years. Standing up in front of the relevant group of executives and talking about my recommendations is what makes the phone ring."

The Chief Listening Officer

Organizing a go-to-market effort in an expert services firm should *not* start from the list of desired outcomes:

- Cross-selling success!
- New clients!
- Practice expansion!
- New geographies!
- Non-RFPed work where we don't have to compete on hourly rates!
- Market dominance in an emerging sector! IoT! FinTech! AI!
- Growth!

Nor does it make sense to organize a firm's outreach around tasks and tactics:

- Website reboot
- Social media

- Events
- Thought leadership
- Travel and visits
- Conferences
- Social causes
- Celebrity endorsements
- RFP support
- Look, feel, and new logos and tag lines
- Account planning
- Earned media
- Market segmentation and whitespace analysis
- Loss analysis
- Field sales forces
- Training
- Analytics, data, and more analytics

Better is to ask the strategic question: *What's the objective we are trying to obtain, and how can we efficiently obtain that objective?*

Listening

Knowing what we know about how clients buy, and what we know about how clients choose to enlarge their engagement, we come back to a simple truth:

> When we ask questions around what clients are facing and what prevents them from where they want to go, we earn the right to engage with them around our experience helping others who have faced similar challenges.

If that is the objective, S&M should be an effort that:

- Enables the organization to listen to its clients in a safe forum that doesn't stink of sales or manipulation.
- Pushes this listening out to partners and doesn't rely on them to "do more," understanding that in their world, the urgency of their current clients' needs often trumps outreach.

- Ensures the firm is not listening episodically to clients but is asking questions around challenges to clients and would-be clients as often as they can.
- Ensures the listening works for the clients and would-be clients. Best would be a format that does not require travel, a heavy technological lift, or expense.
- Ensures that data is captured in a frictionless way and can be used to further inform the organization about industry trends, service lines, and opportunities.

So, do away with your CMO and your practice lead Balkanization of business development. Instead recruit a partner who knows how to listen first and scope work second as well as how to run a team. Call her the chief listening officer. Have her recruit an army of young professionals – call it the "router army" – to convene client and likely buyer peer groups around each of your practices. Start convening peer conversations regularly. Listen, engage, share stories, visit, dig into surfaced challenges, share experiences where you have helped others, and then ask, "Would it be helpful for me to sketch out how we help you with this problem?"

Routers

Routers are like synapses connecting neural networks. When a firm intentionally builds a community of clients and likely buyers, they are aggregating nodes in a network that also include all of our capabilities, all of our firm's practices spread out across geographic clusters, functional clusters, and industry clusters – and all of your partners. The trick is to connect the nodes. The higher the rate of connection, the more assists and referrals.

More than facilitation, interviewing, and follow-up, this is the work of the router army. Their job is to identify opportunities for the firm that fall outside the domain of a network's host and pick up the phone and alert a partner on the other side of the firm and offer to set up a one-on-one call.

Walt Shill knows the power of a truly gifted router. "One of the most successful account directors I have worked with started as our Salesforce administrator. She has zero technical background. She did not come up through the business and was viewed as a glorified executive assistant. But she worked for years – interacting with all our partners across the world – implementing Salesforce, getting their buy-in, getting them to use it, teaching them, and helping them with different issues. She had a friend and ended up selling a small project to a big client.

"Then people said, 'Well, okay. Let her do that on the side. It's not that big of a deal. She can do it if we have someone watch over her closely.' A year goes by and she lands four more projects. Then another one; then another one. Then she left the Salesforce team and became a very successful account director.

"There were two things that we realized. One is she did not have a single area of expertise that she was loyal to. So, she couldn't sell her own ideas. She was completely dependent on other partners coming into this account and driving it for her, which was very interesting, right. It was counterintuitive, but it worked. Her kind of creation of the range of services is one of the highest in the firm.

"The second thing is she knew every partner in the business and every one of them knew her because she had been working with them for years. She had a lot of personal capital and could pull in favors. Also, she knew who was competent and was not competent. We found that when we go out and hire account managers from other firms and bring them in, it takes them three years to be successful because people don't know them. They can't get people to come to their account. They don't know whom to call."

Esther Veenhuizen reports using her marketing team at Protiviti in a similar way. "At a conference, the marketing people should be first in line meeting people. They speak to the commercial message of the firm and broader value propositions of the services it offers. They ask questions to get a better sense of whom to respond to. Our job is to make sure the subject-matter experts and the managing directors get fully booked with meetings. Ideally, they are behind closed doors continuously taking meetings.

Rescuing Value from the Tactical Slag Heap

But what happens to all the tactical things a firm does that used to be under the CMO? Likely, they continue, but now they roll up into the chief listening officer and sit in service of the clear objective of listening to clients and likely buyers. Will there still be someone who needs to be good at standing up a summit at a golf resort in Dana Point? Yes, but now the event is not disassociated from the executives it is putatively being put on for, but instead it is being hosted to extend, deepen, and augment a preexisting group of clients and likely buyer peers.

The same is true for thought leadership. Instead of outsourcing the very wellspring of the firm's competitive advantage, namely, thought leadership, whitepapers can be written on the back of a peer group that already has momentum. Ask any marketing department's research effort what their biggest challenge is, and they will tell you, "Getting interviews with executives." Suddenly, you have existing interview relationships with executives on which your research efforts can effortlessly surf.

Salesforce? Rather than subsidizing a pointless pissing match between those who host Salesforce and those who find it not helpful but who need to be entering relationship data for the tool to be useful, you have a router army whose entire job is to both surface opportunities and follow up on them. They will use Salesforce to research who else in the firm has worked or could be working on an opportunity and so need it to be humming along full of useful data. At the same time, the tools bear gifts, because data they have input about the executives in their networks yields assists and referrals from their fellow router army members.

The Double Punchline

PIE has a $15 billion expert services client that has done exactly this, and the results have been nothing short of astounding. The firm engaged with PIE to convene 1200 clients and likely buyers in 10 different practice-lead networks focused on five different functional titles, meeting quarterly in small peer conversations.

They are not different from their competitors, organized around geographic, functional, and industry verticals. They have the same challenges sharing information across those silos. Those same problems with partners sharing credit or passing on clients to people in the firm they don't really know. Those same problems extending their credibility into clients they now serve.

Yet despite all this, they figured out a way to change the dynamic. During the years measured, the firm enjoyed 10% growth. With peer-supported executives – those in the networks – they drove 9% more growth – a pretty good punchline. It is no wonder they keep expanding the peer conversation concept to more and more verticals.

As much as we would like credit, their success was because they decided to change their culture; they decided to *listen*.

The second punchline was that by harnessing the power of listening, they did the impossible and turned around the diseconomies of scale that define business development and reign in growth in expert services firms. The more a firm grows, the less collaboration there is across both a firm and the firm we hope to serve. That clogging of communication arteries causes assistance and referrals to decline with every new dollar of revenue we collect.

By figuring out a way to systematically leverage young professionals and push opportunity to their elders and to share opportunities across the firm, this large expert services firm amplified their most precious resource – their smartest, most experienced consultants whose proven ability to help companies is the true tip of the business development spear.

CHAPTER

21

The Power of Technology

One of the two authors of this book – we won't say who (okay, it's Jacob) – has a desk littered with sticky notes of information to be entered into his CRM, half of which he can't read since the notes were written in the heat of a call with a client or scribbled in the car on the way to work.

These sticky notes make up the foundation – pebbles and sand and broken bits of stone – upon which expert services firms are built. Any one of these scribbled notes could double business with a client. The problem, of course, is knowing which one will, and the only way to know that is to follow up on the idea or the introduction.

That's where a CRM comes in. Consultants use programs like Salesforce, Azure, HubSpot, Oracle, SAP, and Bitrix24 to house and give visibility to that data.

Most ERP platforms have accounting as their DNA. What is so pregnant with possibility with CRM software is that it starts with relationships as its base. Historically, CRM software was mostly thought of as a lead tracker. You meet someone at a conference who works for a company with which you would like to work. You exchange contact information and when you are back at the office, you enter this information into the CRM database along with some follow-up notes. Perhaps it is to send a book you think they would find interesting or to set up a call. However, CRM systems today offer the promise of tracking data across your company as well as guiding you toward next steps.

At PIE, we are in the process of installing a CRM spine for our business. We customized the platform for our use – it is going to function less as a CRM for our business and more as an enterprise-resource planning tool driven from a CRM perspective. Setting aside the hard work of porting all of our legacy data over and matching the software to our process, we are excited to be creating a single bucket of notes that tracks both potential new customers and existing customers.

Still, old habits die hard and Jacob has a green sticky note in his hand as he picks up the phone to connect with a friend of a friend he met while golfing in Palm Springs this winter. We are a few weeks into using the CRM for all of our business development work and Jacob has logged his acquaintance as a contact, although he holds the sticky note that predates the software. His new friend works for a large business process outsourcing firm. Jacob knows he's not PIE's target buyer – it took him two holes to figure that much out – so the conversation sounds like this:

Can you help me understand where in the company an approach like ours might find a good reception?

His sticky-note friend of a friend responds,

Normally, I'd say our chief operating officer, Norm, but he's 65 and about to retire. From what I have seen, he doesn't have a lot of interest in new initiatives right now. So, I might send you to Steve. He is thought to be Norm's successor, but he is really a bean counter at heart and is going to be all about cost savings, which is not what you want. My best recommendation would be to go to the president of our wholly owned subsidiary, Benefice. It's run by a woman named Yesenia Garcia. She's young, has been in the job 18 months, and is eager for growth. She's ambitious and has her eyes on the top job. Seems to be trying a bunch of new things.

Boom! Now Jacob has a lead – actually, it's his second lead – and a CRM helps link the two leads together. He can do research on Yesenia Garcia and load the notes into the CRM. He can track down her executive assistant (EA) and put that in as well. He can also figure out where her office is for a potential in-person meeting. Jacob doesn't want to lose track of his first contact since he's a great golfing partner and is useful in helping him understand who's who in the company, and Jacob may want to go back to him at a later date. When Jacob has a call with Yesenia several weeks later, she likes his idea but wants to socialize it with her team. Jacob inputs more names into the CRM, all linked to each other.

Experts know this; it is how one uses a CRM in the twenty-first century.

What becomes interesting is when Jacob gets an engagement to do new work with Yesenia. As it turns out, she is indeed forward-looking and entrepreneurial, and she thinks PIE's proposal is a fit with Benefice's growth strategy. Jacob has a contract and now, with our new project management module, he can track dates and deliverables as he brings facilitators and project managers on board.

That in turn can trigger conversations with Yesenia around renewal, expansion, other services, or referrals. Now we have a machine that not only tracks our hunt for new buyers, but more importantly, reminds him to have the kinds of conversations that provide value to the clients we already have, in turn growing existing client work.

We've discussed the twin challenges and potential of scaling credibility and trust. Effective communication via CRM integration is a key component in overcoming these scaling challenges. One of the central promises of CRM is that it drives collaboration or, in the account planning or business development sense, "assist and refer" behaviors. For that to happen – for a partner in the Shanghai office to be able to build on a conversation we had in Toledo with a key stakeholder, when the partner has a chance to sit down with the CEO of the firm at our Asia Pacific (ASPAC) Summit – the information must be in the database. It's not enough to build trust and credibility on your own; you must systematically communicate across your organization. If used well, a CRM can be a powerful tool for achieving that.

The Rub

In the English game of bowls, the object is to roll a grapefruit-sized bowling ball toward a "jack" to see who can get closest. The game is played on either a flat pitch or a convex one (a variation called "crown green bowls"), and the bowling green is closely cropped. A "rub" refers to an imperfection in the grass that might cause a bowl to be knocked off its thrown trajectory. First played in the thirteenth century (but still fiercely competed today), the game was well known to Shakespeare who first used "the rub" as a metaphor in Hamlet's timeless "To be, or not to be, that is the question" soliloquy, writing, "To sleep—perchance to dream: ay, there's the rub!"

The rub on the otherwise flawless CRM green comes not from the software, but from human nature. Jacob has all those sticky notes on his desk. He inputs most of them into the software system but forgets others. It isn't that he doesn't want to or know he should; it is just that he doesn't get to it.

An enlightening aspect about CRMs is that they measure *everything*, even adoption rates:

- In firms with 10 or more employees, 91% use a CRM platform.

- Forty-seven percent of CRM projects fail.

- Eighty-three percent of senior executives say their biggest challenge is getting their staff to use the CRM.

- Less than 47% of sales reps actually use their company's CRM system.

Strategize How to Capture Data

Mark Finlan, who has worked as a principal or managing director at Bain, Censeo, and Huron leading those firms' education practices, speaks to the reality of data input at a large expert services firm:

> If you have the tools in place, but you don't have dedicated people making sure the tools are being used and the data is being disseminated and utilized properly, it's not nearly as successful as it could be. Relying on the managing directors and the senior consultants alone to do all of the activities necessary for a CRM effort to be successful – on top of their day jobs – often produces a hodgepodge of results. At places where they've invested in internal resources whose sole job is to make sure all of the partners were continuously updated on all activities on their accounts, including who was being hired, what types of things they're interested in, and were saying, "I'll put together an email for you to send this piece of IP because you mentioned they were interested in this on our account call," that is where I've seen that investment pay for itself. You cannot solely rely on the managing directors. It is a team effort and you need someone who is connecting the dots and is fully immersed in every facet of the account.

Cole Silver at Blank Rome agrees.

> If you're really way too busy, or you just hate marketing, then get help. You can ask. You can ask your assistant to do it. You can hire a virtual assistant to set up meetings. Get other people to help you. I know this one person who left a big law firm and opened up his own practice. He did not hire a paralegal, he did not hire a secretary, he hired two marketing people and they did all the work. They did speeches for him and got him connected to people. They did all the marketing. He is very successful. He practices law and does what he's good at, and these (women) do the marketing, what they're good at, and it works very well.

Ann Kieffaber, who has worked as a consultant for both IBM and Accenture, describes the differences in how she drove good data input at the respective firms:

> One key element of Customer Relationship Management (CRM) is opportunity management. You can leverage a tool, or you can manage data on a spreadsheet, but it's the process that matters and the accountability that matters. In most firms, opportunity management is driven jointly by line operations and finance. Who takes the lead and what the information is used for often influences the process that is deployed. In IBM, the process was heavily influenced by finance. They were looking for insight on bookings, therefore the strength and timing implications of the pipeline was key. How opportunities drove bookings and yielded revenue and profit was an integral part of managing the business. Historical data was used to forecast the business based on the size, timing, volume, and quality of opportunities in the pipeline.
>
> It was a similar process at Accenture, with a nuance that practice leadership used the process to drive resources to close opportunities by identifying issues in the sales process. Finance was at the table and used the data to inform forecasts, but it was an

operations-driven process. Every week, my practice leaders, my operations manager and I would meet. Every opportunity was in the system – the value of the opportunity, the responsible practice lead, the expected date of closure, the last steps that were taken, and next steps were all kept up to date. Every week we would do a rundown for an hour of all the opportunities that were in the system and do real-time updates to it. Leadership discussed what resources were needed to close key deals. This created an accountability – not to finance but to the practice and the firm. Right after the call with my team, I would be held accountable on a call with the industry team. As you can imagine, I knew inside and out what those opportunities were in that month, in that quarter, and for the year.

As Kieffaber describes, both Accenture and IBM used processes to double down on asking the managing directors to own their P&L. Regardless of who drives the process, the data, the process discipline, and the decisions that are made based on the data drive the strength and value of CRM processes like opportunity management. Rainmakers are unanimous in the view that we have to have a strategy for capturing the data or we are flying blind.

The Future

There are two major barriers to effective CRM use in the expert services industry. First, its architecture is based on a sales funnel, which is not a great fit with how experts cultivate potential buyers. Second, it doesn't work if we don't use it, which, according to the data, we don't. Let's stipulate that both issues have been fixed:

Architecture: Experts ignore all the "stage gate" features of the software, understanding that a good conversation with a possible buyer (perhaps in another division of our client) and a chance to add value to them is money in the bank. We may or may not call on this buyer in the future, but we do not classify it as a Stage 1 sales call that didn't result in an engagement and is now in the "no longer pursuing" graveyard.

Adoption: Experts develop a system that overcomes our natural resistance to being data entry clerks. We have an assistant that sits in on all calls and takes notes. We call our assistant from the road and tell him about the meeting. You use voice-to-text to create written notes and figure out a Zapier-driven way to feed those voice-to-text notes into the CRM.

Assuming, then, that our CRM works well for us and is being ubiquitously used, we get to a next-level question, which proves to be quite interesting: What could a CRM do that would help drive assist-and-refer behavior across firms? What does the future hold for expert services industry enablement software?

There are five large developments that will make CRM more useful to the expert services industry:

1. **Better entry** – Voice-to-text data collection is a big step in the right direction, but robotic-process automation-fueled note taking would be even better. When a call goes on our calendar, a CRM could detect that and check if the person being called is already known to our firm. If she or he is, the CRM should be able to add a link to the calendar hold that would port right to the person's activity log so that we can do away with looking the person up.

   If the person is not known to the firm, a CRM should be able to create a new profile and populate that object with easy-to-look-up data like company size, LinkedIn profiles, our firm's history of working with the client, and the person's place in the organization.

2. **Better signals** – If we get on a call with a client or would-be second buyer in the client, it would be good to know that yesterday the client's stock tanked, that they just announced massive layoffs, or that the CEO just got canned. Call it big data – driven relevant information.

   Microsoft has a commanding market share with Office 365, but their market share is considerably less with Azure and Dynamics 365, Microsoft's CRM platform. Chris Roy, a senior director and customer acquisition lead for corporate accounts at Microsoft, is part of the team that is charged with growing Azure and Dynamics 365 across existing Office 365 accounts. Chris wakes up every day and asks himself, "If they are using Word, Excel, and Outlook, why are they using Salesforce?

   Roy explains how Microsoft thinks of itself as "customer zero" when it comes to their CRM; they certainly work to expand Dynamics 365 in the marketplace, but they also use it to give them strong visibility on how it works or could work. Chris says Microsoft is using in-house data to generate "daily recommenders," which they send to their digital sellers, thinking of them as inside sales reps. Our digital sellers work with our partner resellers, the over 300,000 firms that drive, by Roy's estimate, the largest amount of Microsoft's sales.

   Roy extrapolates on the future of better signals:

   We're fortunate to have the access to almost 500 million professionals through LinkedIn. There's a ton of data and insights that are gained from that. We also have the volume of some of the most popular websites in the world and are able to get insights from individuals hitting them. We look at that information and track "signals," which we think of as an indication about potential to purchase our products. We analyze those signals and make recommendations to our sellers. On a daily basis, we're serving up a recommendation to our digital sellers based on, let's say, the whitepapers that someone downloaded or the volume of employees who are looking at certain pages off of Microsoft sites. Over time, as we get more signals that are run against specific algorithms, we produce a recommendation that informs the seller that says, "Signals are telling us that this organization is similar to other like-minded or -sized or industry-focused customers which are doing this, this, and this. Here is an indication that your customer may act in a certain way." Then we track our sellers' actions based on these recommendations. Is it a good lead? Is it a hot lead? Did they assign it to somebody else to follow up on it? Or did they look at the recommendation and say, "You know what? I've already talked to this customer on this topic, and they're not interested." Then we use all of this feedback from our sellers to improve the algorithms that enhance our technologies. Since we are customer zero, we are now adding this functionality into Dynamics 365 based on what we've actually proved within our own sales team.

This kind of prompting with just-in-time relevant information is great. Better still would be if CRM suites were able to access public information outside its four walls.

3. **Better product intel** – Nichole Jordan tells us that she is focused on making sure her firm knows what clients are interested in:

When you use technology, there are all sorts of things you can do. At Grant Thornton, we team closely with Microsoft and use their platform and have built artificial intelligence and machine learning tools so we can understand when a particular engagement has been sold within a specific industry sector or within a specific geography, and it is highly valuable. We're now able to leverage technology to surface opportunities where we have a higher likelihood of winning and a higher likelihood of bringing relevant value to a customer base. We ask, "How can we use technology to uncover similar clients or targets across the entire firm?" Maybe it's a team on the East Coast that has sold a particular engagement to help a company and that same offering would bring value across businesses in the same sector or peer group. But those businesses are based in cities across the US. How do we get this information to our teams instantaneously as opposed to waiting for everybody to get to a meeting or get on the phone or happen to catch each other at the water cooler?

4. **Better referral** – Wouldn't it be nice to have AI read notes and trigger referrals? Better yet, what if natural language recognition could listen to calls and pass on the important parts? Or a CRM could send those recommendations based on input notes? Better still would be a CRM that could listen to a conversation and send tailored recommendations based on those conversations. Those leads would be worth following, all of which would be from prequalified buyers and just in time. The leads would not be indicative data; they would be straight from the source data.

5. **Better storytelling** – The CRM we are holding out for is one that captures the kind of stories that drive engagement.

Chris Fosdick of The Cambridge Group expands:

So much of the work I've sold has been sold through anecdotal stories of work we've done. Adding those stories to a systematic database would allow everyone to have access to the breadth of stories of what we've done to help clients. It would also be a track record of our total client base based on the work that we've done. I think that could be pretty compelling. It's both the left brain and right brain pieces: You've got a great story of success to tell about an individual client, but then you've also got a broader data set that says, "Hey, when we work with people, they do well."

Gonzaga Professor Christopher Stevens agrees:

Storytelling is where small to medium-sized professional services firms can truly kick the big boy's ass: When you build that level of intimacy in an organization where everybody understands what you're doing, where there is internal story-telling that highlights high performance, then it's fairly easy for the rank-and-file consultant to say, "Oh, yeah, we provide that service. And I think that it might make sense for you."

The challenge is not to produce those stories. As we focus on delivering good work, those stories come to us naturally. The challenge is collecting, storing, and accessing those stories so we sift, sort, and condense, and pick the right one out in the middle of a call with a prospect. It beats rummaging through a pile of sticky notes.

BDaaS

We are sitting down with Murry Joslin at the San Diego Yacht Club interviewing him for this book. We order iced teas as a warm breeze kisses the shore and we see skittering sailors across the water just past the deck.

Joslin runs business development for Integreon, a large outsourced provider of legal and marketing services. We understand what he means when he says the company has an army of offshore contract specialists who serve the legal industry. What shocks us is how he describes the marketing work Integreon sells:

Largely, we're an outsourced provider of presentations. We have large financial services clients where we embed teams of one hundred who are just focused on building various kinds of PowerPoints – some focused on investors and others on business development. We have a large presence inside of a very large strategy consultancy, for example. You'd be surprised by the number of decks those people produce.

It is the numbers that surprise us. PowerPoint-as-a-Service (PPaaS) is big business, as it turns out.

In the Uber on the way to the airport, we try to unpack what we had just heard, deciding that increasingly companies are laser focused on the value they uniquely produce and outsource the rest. This is doubly true when the work they outsource is tedious. Jacob notes, "It used to be that outsourcers did specialized work, but increasingly, they just do the work that people in the company don't want to do."

That's when it hits us. PIE aggregates groups of executives with whom expert services providers want to engage. We perform business-development-as-a-service. "We're BDaaSes!"

After we stop laughing, the notion grows legs. Tom says, "Experts are good at helping clients with their expertise. They have little training, time, or appetite for the mechanics of business development. In the future, much of that work – the logging of calls, the following up on internal referrals, the convening of likely buyers – will be outsourced to firms that specialize in that work. Teams from PIE, for example, might be embedded in our biggest clients, helping them systematically drive growth."

Jacob follows up, "Some of our practice lead clients have assistants who do that work, but the next level is for a large firm to have a growth enablement army, not just following up on new logos, but working to unearth and refer opportunities with existing clients around the room. It's the missing link."

Compensation Clarity

Walt Shill said when he was at Accenture, he leaned heavily on the idea of "gainsharing." He is referring to the compensation model in which the expert gets a cut of the value produced, rather than a fat retainer that must be paid regardless of the results of their work.

Gainsharing works best when an expert is working to drive efficiencies and cut costs in a company. It works less well when the services being provided are driving new business growth, since success is a function of many actions.

Yes, we might have introduced a key executive to a client, but who are we to say that it was our work that produced the win? Certainly, the client's marketing department had a role. There was the whitepaper the practice pushed out a year ago, and, as it turns out, one of our client's account managers met the executive at a conference and made a really good impression, or so she says.

At the same time, the promise of gainshare is cloaked in information asymmetry. An expert has to trust that their client will accurately and consistently report wins. This reporting (or lack thereof) is where technology should grow to disrupt how we bill clients.

We've noted the importance of robust incentive systems that make sure everyone who contributes to the generation of new revenues is fairly compensated, that is, systems that drive internal alignment with a collective goal of growing the business. However, there is an even bigger misalignment in the expert services industry – the gap between cost for expert services and results. Incentives should align with the success of the client but rarely do. If a firm has the client's best interests at heart, it only makes sense that the firm gets paid for value creation, not "sales" behavior.

This is not a new idea. Savvy actors have long participated in the "ups." At the height of his career, Jim Carrey made $20 million for his star turn in *The Cable Guy*, nearly half of the $47 million budget for the movie produced by Judd Apatow and directed by Ben Stiller. But when producer Bruce Berman signed Carrey for *Yes Man*, the actor traded up-front cash for a percentage of the film's profits. He worked for nothing during the filming, but after all the grosses were in, pocketed $35 million or 36.2% of the film's net.

But as with the film industry, the difficulty for the expert services industry comes with transparency and accountability of success.

This is the real promise for technology. It is not that experts will automate repetitive tasks, but that technology will provide both expert firms and our clients greater visibility into what we are doing together. This clarity will in turn pave the way for a more satisfying model of compensation for us and for our clients.

22

The Power of Experience and Insight

Tomal Ashan lives in a comfortable sixth-floor flat with his wife and two sons in the Dhanmondi neighborhood of Dhaka, Bangladesh. "We have four bedrooms, and I have turned one into an office."

Tomal's a freelancer, one of half a million in this sprawling capital city of 21 million people. Focused on technology enablement, he is an expert services provider.

His window looks out on a construction site. A new six-story apartment building is growing in front of him, one cinderblock at a time. Below, the street is a boiling river of SUVs, cycle rickshaws, and men loading flats of eggs on bike trucks. Inside Tomal's office, though, all is quiet and calm. We can feel how apart he is from the hubbub swirling below. He says, "From my office, I'm connected with the US, Europe, the Philippines, Pakistan, India. It doesn't matter where I am."

Tomal comes from a good family. "My grandfather started an import business in the hardware sector after working as a fruit and vegetable contractor in Assam, India for a US army base. "I grew up in a large house he built on this location." When he died, we tore it down and built this apartment building."

Tomal's easy smile and careful attention to each word masks his ambition. "I lost my father when I was five and have always been the one to care for my mother."

First was education. He graduated from the University of Dhaka with an undergraduate degree. Then he went on for his MBA.

I was going to go to Southeast Oklahoma State University, all the paperwork was in, but I wanted my brother to go to the US. So, I needed to stay in Dhaka to care for my mother. When she got cancer, that's when I turned to Upwork.

Headquartered in Mountain View, California, Upwork is an online market-place of freelance talent from around the world, boasting $300 million in freelance revenues across 70 categories of services. Firms like General Electric, Airbnb, and Microsoft post projects and full-time contract work on the site, and freelancers like Tomal apply for the gigs.

"From this desk, I worked for Field Nation, which does point-of-sale installations for retail chains," Tomal says as he adjusts his headset. "I managed the installation of cash registers, cameras, and traffic counters in a thousand McDonald's. I did the same for Steak 'n Shake, Duane Reade, and Toys "R" Us. I interviewed local installers, managed client satisfaction, and organized customer support."

Part of the global gig economy, Tomal likes his work. "I am grateful that I can do work I find challenging and where I interact with intelligent people. Freelancing gives me a chance to explore my ideas, prove my worth, and practice my intelligence. It also gives me a chance to work with leaders and entrepreneurs.

We can hear his wife, Shirin, in the background and ask about her.

Both of my grandfathers rode to their weddings on an elephant. My father went in a car, but because Shirin lived in Kandapara, which was then an island, I went by boat. I think I am taking the family backwards!

He and Shirin have a partnership. "We both cook and care for the boys. My specialty is the Bangladeshi version of Chinese food with chicken and vegetables."

Outside his window a RAV4 beeps its horn impatiently in front of the Rahomania Pharmacy.

One of the things I really like about freelancing is the time I spend with my family. It's very crowded in Dhaka. We have 175,000 people living in a square mile. It takes 25 minutes to travel a kilometer by bicycle. It would be very hard to go to an office here. This way, I spend all day with my family and work simultaneously.

Tomal seems satisfied. "I get work with people all over the world. I get to learn from them, and every assignment is different, which makes life interesting. Whenever a job comes in, I apply, and when I do, I change who I am to fit the client's needs. I am a shapeshifter, morphing all the time."

Going Deep

In 2018 we published *How Clients Buy* to understand how new work is won in the context of expert services. *How Clients Buy* showed us just how hard it is to make the stars align to be able to help someone new – someone who doesn't know us and doesn't know our work. We feel good about that book. But we also realize that once we land a new logo, we're left with an even bigger – perhaps more important – question. We know how much we all rely on existing client relationships – on farming – to see continued growth in our companies. We realized what we really want to know is, "What is the secret to *growing* our work – to being even *more* helpful to those we're already helping?"

If our goal as experts is to be the most helpful, we need to look to where we can have the greatest impact and that often means starting with our current clients whom we know best.

We maximize our ability to help by being a good friend, doing good work, listening, knowing ourselves, knowing our clients, and showing up for them again and again just like Tomal does for his clients. In this way we make an impact on the world around us.

It's a practice that is constantly evolving. We change and adapt, our clients change and adapt, and our clients' needs change and adapt as the world around us shifts. That's the beauty of it. All of us are shapeshifters. Our job is to keep coming back, to continue to listen, to continue to deliver good work, to continue to help, and to continue to ask where and how we can add value.

Solving Problems

Solving thorny challenges is satisfying – as much for Tomal as it is for the Bain strategy consultant advising a $5 billion company on possible acquisitions. As human beings, we are creative animals, and we like figuring out better ways to accomplish goals and make things happen. We are happiest when we have a job, and as experts, the job we like best is helping companies overcome their challenges.

For people who like to solve challenges, we are in the right place. More than ever, the world needs our help as we face a raft of challenges: economic disparity, finite natural resources, south-to-north migration, climate volatility, and cross-border hostilities. Yet at the same time, the seeds of promise are all around us. Global GDP growth fuels new opportunity. Literacy rates are at historic highs as are levels of education. Technology continues to shock, awe, and transform.

As experts, we play a central role in building the bridge from the world's challenges to a land full of solutions, one stone at a time. This is good, not just because it is satisfying and useful, but because it gives rise to a better place for our children to inherit.

A Smaller World

At PIE, our mission is to "connect powerful minds, making the world smarter and smaller."

For us, "smarter" means something very specific. It's when a self-driving car consultant in Santa Clara consults with a tractor manufacturer in India on the future of auto-driven farm machinery. It's when a dam engineer in Liverpool is on a conference call with a general contractor in Peru who needs her very specific advice. It is when an Abu Dhabi sovereign wealth fund manager calls a tax expert in Amsterdam, because he is uniquely prepared to address the fund's challenges.

But how does the work we do as experts make the world "smaller"?

Experts shrink the world by wiring us all together.

Technology increases the size and tightens the links of what we call community. Videoconference providers port our faces around the world and allow an intimacy with colleagues two thousand miles overseas in a way that was previously unimaginable. Global marketplaces allow us to make purchases that support small business owners a continent away. Virtual means of communication – email, phone, videoconference, social media – allow us to share best practices, collaborate, and innovate across time zones.

In the twenty-first century, experts are the sinew that makes the world stronger, safer, and more stable.

Companies and organizations have work to complete, challenges to solve, and potential to realize. They turn to the world of expert services providers to help them solve those problems with immediacy and accuracy. This allows experts to specialize – to become the leading expert in hedging supply-chain currency-exchange-rate risk, in unilateral mandatory disclosure requirement compliance, or in cybersecurity for IoT in commercial properties – and to market that expertise to a wide number of firms that need that help.

We make the world smarter and smaller by helping those we are most pre-pared to serve. This combination of needed help and willing helpers fuels the rein-forcing dynamic of collaboration, innovation, shared prosperity, strong ties, and peace:

- **Collaboration:** When experts and clients come together, each bring their own experience and insights. It is almost always wrong-headed to think the expert has all the answers. A better paradigm is to see the client as the one with deep understanding of the forces at play in their company. The expert has deep experience on the forces at play that *give rise to* the challenge, and a library of best practices to tackle it. Together, in collaboration, clients and experts work to right-size a solution for the company. Each is vital to the process, and together they are stronger.

  Says Tomal, "I love learning from my colleagues and the satisfaction that comes with helping people. Putting our minds together, with our different experiences and backgrounds, we are able to do better work. I worked for Wayfair for three years. I had a contract with them as part of their supplier outreach program. On their behalf, I recruited a lot of people from around the world for their phone call team, including people from Greece, India, Pakistan, and Jamaica. When you have a team of 10 people – the best minds in their countries – you get an interesting blend of perspectives and end up doing better work."

- **Innovation:** From this mixing of experiences comes new insight – epiphanies born of client and expert putting their heads together and generating answers that each might not have been able to create on their own.

    "We accomplish more when we are learning from each other, both learning about each other's cultures and blending our different ideas," says Tomal.

- **Shared prosperity:** This creates value that is enriching to the client and to the expert.

We do this work because it puts food on our table, but we are learning and adapting. India used to be a good place for call centers, but they learned and added more skills, and now all the call centers are in the Philippines. India is now good for IT. They are climbing up the food chain. In Bangladesh, we are learning as well.

- **Strong ties:** Shared prosperity strengthens the ties between people, regardless of background.

I am a Muslim and so, ordinarily, you might not think that I would want to work with a Jew. Lebanon might be a good example of how Muslims and Jews do not work well together, for example. But in my work, I have a Jewish client named Sig from Canada. He and I get along very well. When people work together, we forget our backgrounds, our race, our ethnicity because we are trying to accomplish something together.

- **Peace:** Finally, these forces make for a more peaceful world. When we are dependent on our neighbor to harvest the corn while we travel to a funeral, we are less likely to complain about unmended fences. Even more powerfully, when we raise a barn together, we put down our pitchforks. Political conflict does not exist when people work together as co-collaborators.

    Says Tomal, "None of us who work together have any conflict even though we are very different. The conflict between nations lies within the politicians."

We are growing toward a better world – one where the promise of something larger than the community, tribal, ideological, or national identities that divide us exists. It is a world where origin is respected but where there are ties that bind us together across those differences. This will be a world that is smarter and smaller, yes, but one in which peace becomes the rule and not the exception.

We're excited to be part of creating that world. We know you are as well.

So, let us learn, create, and share. We have work to do!

Further Reading

"2018 Sales Operations Optimization Study." *CSO Insights*, The Research Division of Miller Heiman Group, 2018, www.csoinsights.com/wp-content/uploads/sites/5/2018/08/2018-Sales-Operations-Optimization-Study.pdf. Accessed April 1, 2020.

Allen, David. *Getting Things Done*. Penguin Books, 2001.

"Barbara Minto: 'MECE: I Invented It, So I Get to Say How to Pronounce It.'" McKinsey & Company, 2020, www.mckinsey.com/alumni/news-and-insights/global-news/alumni-news/barbara-minto-mece-i-invented-it-so-i-get-to-say-how-to-pronounce-it. Accessed June 7, 2020.

Buckingham, Marcus. *StandOut 2.0: Assess Your Strengths. Find Your Edge. Win at Work*. Harvard Business Review Press, 2015.

Campbell, Anita. "10 Small Business Functions That Can Be Easily Outsourced." *U.S. Small Business Administration*, November 19, 2019, www.sba.gov/blog/10-small-business-functions-can-be-easily-outsourced.

Emerson, Richard M. "Social Exchange Theory." *Annual Review of Sociology* 2, no. 1 (1976): 335–362. www.annualreviews.org/doi/10.1146/annurev.so.02.080176.002003.

Ensor, Phil. "The Functional Silo Syndrome." *AmE Target* (1988, Spring): 16.

Gensler, Arthur, and Michael Lindenmayer. *Art's Principles: 50 Years of Hard-Learned Lessons in Building a World-Class Professional Services Firm*. Wilson Lafferty, 2015.

Gerber, Michael. *Why Most Small Businesses Don't Work and What to Do About It*. Harper Collins, 2004.

Gormley, John. "Pilots Aim to Show They're Ready for Post-Panamax Era." *Professional Mariner*, April 2, 2014. www.professionalmariner.com/April-2014/Post-Panamax-era/index.php?cparticle=2&siarticle=1.

Harding, Ford. *Cross-Selling Success: A Rainmaker's Guide to Professional Account Development*. Adams Media Corporation, 2002.

Krigsman, Michael. "CRM Failure Rates: 2001–2009." *TechRepublic*, August 3, 2009. www.techrepublic.com/blog/tech-decision-maker/crm-failure-rates-2001-2009.

McLaughlin, Michael. *Winning the Professional Services Sale.* Hoboken, NJ: Wiley, 2009.

Noonan, Peggy. *From On Speaking Well.* HarperCollins Publishers, 1998.

Pink, Daniel H. *To Sell Is Human: The Surprising Truth about Moving Others.* Penguin, 2013.

Quattrone, G. A., and Jones, E. E. "The Perception of Variability within In-groups and Out-groups: Implications for the Law of Small Numbers." *Journal of Personality and Social Psychology* 38, no. 1 (1980): 141–152. *Adapted with permission.* https://doi.org/10.1037/0022-3514.38.1.141.

Regan, Dennis T. "Effects of a Favor and Liking on Compliance." *Journal of Experimental Social Psychology* 7, no. 6 (1971): 627–639. www.communicationcache.com/uploads/1/0/8/8/10887248/effects_of_a_favor_and_liking_on_compliance.pdf, 10.1016/0022-1031(71)90025-4.

Ringelmann, Max. "Recherches sur les moteurs animés: Travail de l'homme (Research on animate sources of power: The work of man)." *Annales de l'Institut National Agronomique* 2, no. 12 (1913): 2–40.

"The Rise and Rise of Accenture." *The Economist*, March 12, 2020. www.economist.com/business/2020/03/12/the-rise-and-rise-of-accenture.

Schiffman, Stephen. *Upselling Techniques.* Adams Media, an Imprint of Simon & Schuster, 2005.

Sims, David. "CRM Adoption 'Biggest Problem' in 83 Percent of Cases, Wigan Gets CRM Treatment, CDC and Savills Asia Pacific, PacificNet Q3 Results, UltraSoft Wins UK CRM Award." *First Coffee, November* 30, 2007. blog.tmcnet.com/telecom-crm/2007/11/30/crm-adoption-biggest-problem-in-83-percent-of-cases-wigan-gets-crm-tre.asp.

Smilansky, Oren. "Tips for Maximizing CRM Investments." *CRM Magazine*, April 28, 2017. www.destinationcrm.com/Articles/Editorial/Magazine-Features/Tips-for-Maximizing-CRM-Investments-117856.aspx.

Twain, Mark. *Life on the Mississippi.* New York: Penguin Random House, 1985.

Wachowski, Andy, Larry Wachowski, Keanu Reeves, Laurence Fishburne, and Carrie-Anne Moss. *The Matrix.* Burbank, CA: Warner Home Video, 1999.

Wallace, W. A. "Fortnightly Review: Managing In-Flight Emergencies." *BMJ* 311, no. 7001 (August 5, 1995): 374–375. www.ncbi.nlm.nih.gov/pmc/articles/PMC2550436/?page=1www.ncbi.nlm.nih.gov/pmc/articles/PMC2626355/#B1, 10.1136/bmj.311.7001.374.

Acknowledgments

We would like to thank the entire team at PIE. We are lucky to be part of a team that is dedicated, smart, and effective in all that we do. No one who writes a book believes they did it alone. A thousand hallway conversations and off-handed insights informed what we have written. We are the people we surround ourselves with. We are so fortunate to be in a community of smart people who make us, by mere association, smarter.

So, let us name them: Aimee Chang, Alanna Rhinard, Alice Buckley, Andi Baldwin, Andy Weas, Ashley Meyer, Caitlin Marassi, Carlie Auger, Cavin Segil, Christina Salerno, Dana Roach, Emily Graden-Rainey, Emily LeVeaux, Erika Flowers, Errol Rice, Jake Klompien, Jess Milakovich, John Nord, Josh Iverson, Julia Yanker, Kristin Horgan, Leah Kreitinger, Madeleine Smerin, Martin Smith, Matt Ulrich, McKayla Murphy, Melinda Murphy, Meredith Schon, Mikayla Comes, Morgan Klaas, Nicole Wolfgram, Paul Quigley, Rachel Schmidt, Robert Samson, Renee Storm, Sage Cowles, Stephanie Cole, Susan Miller, Susie Krueger, Taylor Weyers, Windy Esperti, Yetta Stein. Thank you.

A special thank-you to four of them, Erika Flowers, Dana Roach, Andi Baldwin, and Alice Buckley, our in-house team of readers and editors. We gave you a manuscript and you gave us back a book. Each of these individuals are special in their own way. The team lead, Erika, is a Dartmouth grad and qualified to represent the United States at the FIS Cross-Country Skiing World Cup this year. She also runs for The North Face. Dana is a Dartmouth-trained MFA who can spin gold from our words of straw. She is currently working on her first novel. Andi is our house grammarian who sits on PIE's management team and has been instrumental in our company's success. Alice, who came to us by way of Yale, is currently running for the Montana State House of Representatives. These women – each strong, independent, brave, and talented in her own way – fought their way through our leaden prose and alchemized our vision into something compelling and useful. Each of you is mighty. No words can express our thanks.

We are also deeply indebted to Dave Bayless. He was one of our primary readers, but more, he has been a patron saint to all we do at PIE. Our part-time fractional CFO, Dave, is so much more. A classically trained banker and investor, he pushes us to participate in the world of ideas, making us better, and for that we are forever grateful.

Thank you, Sridhar Gurram, for to alerting us to the fact that the matrix we had come up with about how expert services providers extend their reach inside their clients has its roots in the model pioneered by Igor Assoff in 1958 and later expanded and deepened by the team at Bain.

Thank you to all who agreed to be interviewed for this book and thank you to the PIE interview team, led by Jacob; that includes Emily LeVeaux, Paul Quigley, Matt Ulrich, Caitlin Marassi, and Jess Milakovich. A shout-out as well to readers who made sure we stood on the shoulders of those who have written on this subject before, Caitlin Marassi, Carlie Auger, Josh Iverson, Dana Roach, and Jess Milakovich.

Tom would like to thank Matt Ulrich for keeping his energy and focus up during this project – always reminding him of how much expert services providers need what is to be found in these pages.

Jacob would like to thank Andi Baldwin for her friendship, writing support, and for turning our ski run metaphor into something useful – the Diamond of Opportunity.

We both would like to give a shout-out to our editorial team at Wiley – the incomparable Richard Narramore, Mike Campbell, and Kelly Talbot. You saw the vision for this book early and were ardent champions of the project throughout. Thank you.

And thank you to our agent, Sheree Bykofsky, an acclaimed author in her own right. Sheree advocated for us when others would have passed on the project, she recommended readers and, when we needed it most, took the side of our publisher, and gave us a swift kick in the pants. You are the best.

Thanks to Dr. Harry Wallace, a professor of psychology at Trinity University, for his insight into how trust is handed off from one person to another and to Tom's co-author of *How Clients Buy*, Doug Fletcher. Doug continues to be a friend and an advocate for this project. Look for his upcoming book, *How to Win Clients When You Don't Know Where to Start* (Wiley, 2021).

Finally, we want to thank our spouses. Traveling around the world, offering our expertise, we wouldn't be able to do what we do without the understanding, love, and support of those we married. Marriage is a partnership in all manner large and small – children, finances, and whose parents' house to go to at Thanksgiving. But we are among the fortunate who married not just their ideal partners, but their best friends. Mary and Amy make us laugh, they challenge us, and cause us to be better people. We are both so lucky and grateful.

About the Authors

Tom McMakin is CEO of Profitable Ideas Exchange (PIE), a leading consultancy focused on helping expert services firms with business development by building peer communities of likely buyers. Over the last 20 years, Tom's company has conducted 10,000 best practices interviews with senior executives at 350 companies in the Fortune 500. Tom is the co-author of the bestselling *How Clients Buy: A Practical Guide to Business Development for Consulting and Professional Services* (Wiley, 2018). He is also the author of *Bread and Butter* (St. Martin's Press, 2001), in which he described his work at Great Harvest Bread Co. and how he and his team created a nationally recognized corporate learning community and culture of best practices using collaborative networks. He has been featured on the pages of *Inc.* magazine, *Fast Company, Money, Entrepreneur, Success,* the *Economist, Newsweek,* the *Washington Post, USA Today, Christian Science Monitor,* the *New York Times,* the *Wall Street Journal,* and is often on the road speaking before consulting and professional services firms. Before joining PIE, McMakin was a co-founder and managing director with Orchard Holdings Group, a private equity firm as well as an operating affiliate at McCown DeLeeuw and TSG Consumer, two billion-dollar consumer-focused buyout groups. Prior to this, he served as the Chief Operating Officer of Great Harvest Bread Co., a multi-unit operator of bread stores. He is a graduate of Oberlin College and a former Peace Corps Volunteer in Cameroon. Tom and his family live in Bozeman, Montana. Tom can be reached at tmcmakin@profitableideas.com or through the PIE website, www.profitableideas.com.

Jacob Parks is the COO of Profitable Ideas Exchange (PIE), having led growth and operations in the company for 17 years. Jacob headed the research team on *How Clients Buy,* interviewing over 100 rainmakers at expert services companies, including consultants at Accenture, McKinsey, Baker Tilly, Deloitte, Goldman Sachs, and KPMG. Jacob moderates a peer group of middle market consulting firm CMOs, including CLJ, AT Kearney, Segal and Simpson Thatcher. Additionally, he has facilitated executive roundtable discussions on behalf of CFOs and COOs representing the largest companies across the globe. Jacob has taught as an adjunct professor of business at the Jake Jabs School of Entrepreneurship at Montana State University, where he did his undergraduate work. He is currently pursuing a Master of Business Administration at Gonzaga School of Business. Jacob has published research in academic journals on the topic of driving successful innovation in large corporations. Jacob serves on the board of the Spokane Community Colleges Foundation. He and his wife live in Spokane, Washington. Jacob can be reached at jmparks@ profitableideas.com or through the PIE website, www.profitableideas.com.

Index

80/20 principle (Pareto Principle), 21

A
Ability/readiness, 167
Accenture, 56, 115, 121, 210–211
  gainsharing, 215–216
  procurement practice, 162
  skillset, impact, 1
Account planning
  emphasis, 25
  process, steps, 114
AD Creative, PIE project, 131
Add-on opportunities, harvesting, 22
Add-on work, earning, 8
Adjacencies, inequality, 116
Advisory Board, The, 18
Agility, boutique firm advantage, 89
Allen, David, 182
Allen, Paul, 122
Ancillary services, limiting, 116
Arthur Andersen, 92–93, 189
Art of the Ask. *See* Ask
Art's Principles (Gensler), 123
Ask
  conversation, examination, 178–179
  earning, 193–194
  mastery, 176, 177–178
  payoff, characteristic, 182–183
  preparation, 178–183
  relationship, characteristic,
    179–181

Awareness, 48, 167
  building, 198
  client awareness, 47
Azure, 207, 212

B
Back-office centralization, 1
Bain, 132, 210
Baldwin, Andi, 43
Bauerle and Company (Wipfli acqui-
    sition), 93
Benchmark companies, 49
Benefice, 208
Benson, Rob, 50, 69, 117
Best practices, harvesting, 154
Big firm opportunities, 89–90
  advantages, 90
Blank Rome, 20, 210
Boss (colleague type), 154–155
Boss, work (winning), 50
Boston Consulting Group (BCG), 66,
    95, 136, 140, 156
  customization, importance, 166
Bottom-of-the-funnel measurements,
    161
Boutique firm opportunities, 88–89
  advantages, 89
Bragging, 174
Brainstorming, 1, 23, 36, 76
  client brainstorming, 144–145
  employee usage, 114

Brainstorming (*Continued*)
  exercise, 165
  ideas, suggestions, 117
  opportunities, 98
  perspectives, 180
  strategy discussions, 128
Brand
  awareness, 132, 133
  building, 122
  personal brand, 97–98
  prison, avoidance, 99–100
  struggles, 197
Bridges, term (usage), 142
Brochures, avoidance, 102–103
Bryant, Peter, 22
Buckingham, Marcus, 87
Buckley, Alice, 140, 143
Budget
  cycles
    attention, 106
    initiation, 117
  strategy/priorities expression, 64
Burch, Bill, 22, 143
Bureaucratic function, 75
Business
  creation, 133
  development/delivery, organization
    process, 163–164
  models, knowledge, 54
  relationships, formation, 70
  units, client opportunities, 114
  working, 198
Business development
  achievement, clues, 10
  cold business development,
    expense, 22–23
  CRM, usage, 208
  driving, expert services firms
    (role), 43
  expert services firms, assis-
    tance, 9–10
  perspective, 24–25
  practice leads, impact, 201

  skills, importance, 163
  support, 9
  work product, relationship, 122
Business-development-as-a-service
  (BDaaS), 214–215
Buxton, Diana, 59–60, 70
  expert service network, 61
  network, 60
Buyers
  abilities, 65
  assistance, 31
  budget proposal, brainstorming, 23
  capabilities, offering, 12
  exit, actions, 108
  expert adjustments, 109
  in-person meeting, 108
  internal services pitch, 25
  MORE work, request, 179
  new buyers, relationships (estab-
    lishment), 28
  peer group discussions, aggre-
    gation, 132
  potential, 142–143
  priorities, questioning/listening,
    108–109
  questioning/listening, 103
  referrals, rarity, 62
  services, offering, 44
  strategic intent, understanding, 126
  trust, 30, 189–190
    transfer, difficulty, 50
  trusted expert engagement, 68
  value, addition, 109
Buying power, impact, 74

C
Cambridge Group, The, 69, 116,
  162, 165
  project sale, reason, 168
  storytelling, 174–175, 214
Campbell, Anita, 198
Capability network, 61
  opportunity network, interaction, 62

Capability reach, expansion, 115–117
Capstone Event Group, 19
Career-day strategy, resource usage, 133–134
Carmody, Cora, 155
Case studies, elements, 135–136
Caterpillar, 121
Censeo, 210
Challenges
    connections, 10
    identification, 192, 205
    overcoming/solving, 135–136, 219–220
Change management, usage (value), 104–105
Chassaing, Thierry, 66–67, 95, 136, 156
    customization, importance, 166
Chief listening officer, 202–203
Chief marketing officer (CMO), role, 199
Chief sales officer (CSO), role, 200
Circle of friends, growth, 141–145
Citibank, 98
Clareo, 22
Client account leads (CALs), 53
    reaching, 115
Client firms, reorganizations, 91
Client relationships, 103
    building, importance, 105
    expansion
        challenge, 51
        importance, 44
    growth, 26
        obstacles, 53
Clients
    action, readiness, 45
    assistance, 192
    awareness/understanding, 47
    best practices, offering, 153
    big firm growth, difficulty, 89–90
    brainstorming, 144–145
    "breaking bread," 193
    budget

process, opportunity, 117
    strategy/priorities expression, 64
capabilities, addition, 28
colleagues, introduction, 151–153
conversation, elevation, 128
CRM system, integration, 107
diamond clients, capture, 121
diamond discovery, assistance, 194–196
engagement, 142–143
    ability, 45
expert services knowledge, 101
expert services provider engagement, elements, 44–45
farming
    difficulty, 44
    impact, 23–24
friendships, 149
goals, setting, 127
good friend, 140–141
interest, 47, 49
    proof, 50
kickoff meeting, 127
new projects, resources/ bandwidth, 51
new work, 53
    challenges, 65, 70, 82
organization, awareness (absence), 48
priorities
    alignment, 160–161
    employee priorities, alignment, 163–164
projects, number (expansion), 67
respect, 153
serving, opportunities, 114
storytelling, lagniappe (impact), 125
target audience, knowledge, 32
trust, 47
trusted advisors, role, 11
value
    addition, 62
    creation, balance, 161–162

Clients (*Continued*)
  work, increase, 21
  wow process, 126–128
Clifford, Sarah, 131
Clio partner, 116
Clio platform, switch, 146
Cognizant, 59
  capability network, 61
  network, 70
    characterization, 60
  opportunity network, 60
Cold business development,
    expense, 22–23
Cole, Stephanie, 70
Collaboration credit, 161
Collaboration, importance, 221–222
Colleagues
  buyer identification, 144
  capabilities, knowledge
    (importance), 95
  client examples, 97–98
  good friend, 139–140
  interaction, 173
  introduction, 151–153
    challenge, 66
    hesitancy, 69
  knowledge, absence, 69
  leveraging, 151
  relationships
    building, 69–70, 95
    control, loss, 70
    investment, 139
  trust, building, 95
  visiting types, 154–156
Commissionable activities,
    159–160
Communication, emphasis, 64
Community, links (tightening), 220
Companies
  long-term success, impact, 109
  politics, 64
Comparative shopping method, 7
Compensation package, clarity, 94

Competence (demonstration), question
    quality (impact), 143
Competitive advantage, sources, 54
Complexity
  communication, 130
  creation, 59
  growth, 10
  incentive, 55
  roadblocks, 52
Concentration risk, 65
Consultants, credit-taking, 143–144
Consulting
  conversation, 43–44
  customer experience summit, 32
  engagement, value creation, 106
  organizations, product/service
    definition (absence), 87–88
  practice, setup (decision), 9
Contract, re-up/expansion, 122
Conversation
  elevation, 128
  examination, 178–179
Cooley, 53
Corporations, brand umbrella, 27
Cox, Trey, 20, 151
Credibility, 167
  ability, 80
  belief, 44
  building, 114, 173, 198
  cultivation/development, 157,
    172, 196
  decrease, 130
  delivery, 8
  earning, 47, 194
  increase, 116–117
  scaling, 79–82, 134, 140, 154, 209
  transfer, difficulty, 50
Cross-border work, 8
Cross-selling, 12, 201
  difficulty, 69–70
  effectiveness, 53
  opportunity, 27
  process, 13

Cross-Selling Success (Harding), 82, 138, 142
Culture
  assessment, 94
  boutique firm advantage, 89
Curiosity, importance, 142–143
Customer relationship management (CRM), note-taking (importance), 145
Customer relationship management system (CRMS), impact, 90
Customer relations management (CRM)
  barriers, 211–214
  impact, 77
  integration, 107
  measurement capability, 209
  opportunity management, importance, 210–211
  software
    stage gate features, 211
    usage, 207
  spine, installation, 208
  usage, 207–209
  usefulness, developments, 212–214
Customers
  meeting, CSO role, 200
  sales process, 22
Customization, importance, 166

D
Daljord, Øystein, 158–159, 163
Data
  buyer trust, 189–190
  capture process, strategization, 210–211
Delivery, importance, 123
Deloitte, 18, 22, 107
  projects, work (relationship), 24
Demand generation, 199
Diamond account planning, 111
  opportunities, 112–114

Diamond clients, capture, 121
DiamondCluster, 138
Diamond of Opportunity, 10, 26, 131
  appearance, 28
  EVOLVE appearance, 36
  EXPAND appearance, 31
  EXTEND appearance, 32
  growth
    chasing, 80
    opportunities, identification, 149
  Innovate appearance, 38
  jump, 155
  MORE appearance, 29
  MORE work, 54
  navigation, 171
  perspective, changes, 99
  question, 88
  REACH appearance, 34
  work, new expert introduction, 68
Diamonds, client discovery (assistance), 194–196
Diseconomies of scale, 74–75, 121
Diversity and inclusion (D&I)
  candidates, recruitment, 29
  human resources pitch, 133
Double counting, 160
Double punchline, 206
DXL Group, 69
Dynamics 365, 212

E
Earnings projections, reverse engineering, 111
ECFx, 22
Economies of scale, 72–73
  existence, question, 73
Email
  chain, following, 147–148
  introductions, 152
  REACH email, 172–173
  response, time consumption, 198
Embark, 122
Emergency needs, listening, 168

Employee priorities, client priorities (alignment), 163–164

E-Myth, The (Gerber), 198

Endorsing quotes, inclusion, 136

Engel, Greg, 97

Ensor, Phil, 63–64

Enterprise resource planning (ERP) systems, usage, 91

Enterprise Risk Management (ERM), 68

Environmental Resources Management (ERM), 11, 55, 97, 104, 124, 161
  project scope, 167

Ernst & Young (EY), 103, 110, 114, 140
  clarity, creation, 149

Esperti, Bob, 200

EVOLVE (Diamond of Opportunity component), 28, 35–37
  avoidance, 88
  inclusion, 115
  organically grown firms, success, 93
  process, 67
  relationship, evolution, 96

Excel-driven comparative shopping method, 7

Excellent work (Level II), 123–124

Executive leadership team (ELT) leaders, 59–60

EXPAND (Diamond of Opportunity component), 27, 28, 30–31
  conversation, 180
  ease, 98
  opportunities, 88
  organically grown firms, success, 93
  relationship expansion, 96
  work, 123, 134, 144
    opportunities, 178

Experience-based experts, proliferation, 59

Experience, power, 217

Expertise
  client purchase process, 7–8
  demonstration, 194
  providing, 9–10
  selling, 6

Experts
  goals (achievements), structures/ strategies (usage), 113–114
  introducing, 67–68
  jobs, types, 154–155
  partner referral, risk, 55–56
  self-talk, problems, 54
  trust, development, 106

Expert services
  assistance, sales/marketing failure (reasons), 200–202
  companies, business development (perspective), 24–25
  credence good, 12
  differences, 7–8
  economies of scale, existence (question), 73
  firms, professional hiring approaches, 94
  geography/industry/functional capabilities, 53
  industry
    CRM developments, impact, 212–214
    diseconomies of scale, 74–75
    scale advantage, 73
  measurement alternative, 158–159
  network, 61
  outsource marketing, 198
  practitioners, self-promotion/calls (balance), 83–84
  selling aversion, correlation, 1
  senior partner, involvement, 180

Expert services providers
  ability/readiness, 51
  capabilities, knowledge, 48
  client awareness/understanding, 44, 48
  client engagement (preconditions), 44–47
  client interest, 49

credibility, 49
incentivization, 104
market strategies, source, 200
partner shift, 117
trust, 50–51
EXTEND (Diamond of Opportunity component), 28, 31–33
ease, 98
geographies, 92
opportunities, 88
relationship extension, 96
work, 80, 108, 134
extension, 67–68
opportunities, 178
winning, 195
Extension agent, 77–78

F
Farming
client closeness, 23–24
difficulty, 44
impact, 25
intensiveness, reduction, 24–25
opportunities alert, 23
ROI, hunting ROI (contrast), 22–23
Farming disciplines
ask, mastery, 176
good friend, 138
good work, 121
incent good work, 157
listening, 165
storytelling, 169
team, leveraging, 150
Feedback, 6, 148
initiation, 128
providing, 129–130
Field Nation, 218
Finance operating model, addition (problem), 104
Finders, 18–19, 142
Finlan, Mark, 116, 132, 210
Firms
big firm opportunities, 89–90

boutique firm opportunities, 88–89
capabilities, knowledge (importance), 95
niche, defining, 98–99
revenues, generation, 97
size, impact, 88–90
First milestone meeting, 127
Fletcher, Doug, 6
Follow-up
importance, 147–148, 190–191
third-party follow-up, 191–192
Formalized training, absence, 54
Fosdick, Chris, 69, 116, 162, 165
project sale, reason, 168
storytelling, 174–175, 214
Friction, creation, 201–202
Friends
circle of friends growth, 141–145
making, role, 142
maximization, 219
"Functional Silo Syndrome, The," 63–64

G
Gainsharing, 215–216
Garcia, Yesenia, 208–209
Gensler, Art, 123, 140, 174
Geographies, opportunities, 114
Gerber, Michael, 198
Getting Things Done (Allen), 182
Getting to Equity program, 20
"Getting to know you" video interviews, 36
Gibson, Dunn & Crutcher, 20
Global reach, big firm advantage, 90
Global work, localized expertise (impact), 90
Goalposts, movement (problem), 157
Good friend (farming discipline), 138
follow-up, importance, 147–148
hard questions, asking, 148–149
helpfulness, importance, 145
note-taking, importance, 145

Good work (farming discipline), 121.
    See also Incent good work
    case study, 134–137
    delivery, strength, 132
    expectation setting, 132–134
    incent good work, 157
    ingredients, 131–137
    Level I, 123
Goodyear Tire and Rubber, 63–64
Google Alerts, usage, 107
Grant Thornton, 100, 188, 213
    team, debriefing, 190–191
Great Harvest Franchising, 180
Green, Bill, 56, 121–122
Grinders, 18–19, 142
Growth
    mergers and acquisitions
        growth, 93
    opportunities, identification, 149
    organic growth, 92–93
    strategy, 92–93
Guernsey, Kenneth, 53

H
Hannafey, Cindy, 97
Hard information, usage (advantage),
    102
Harding, Ford, 82, 138, 142
Hard questions, asking, 148–149
HBR Consulting, 124
Heroes
    role, avoidance, 174–175
Heroes, remembrance, 143–144
Homans, George, 182
Honesty, importance, 145
Horne, Ashley, 20
How Clients Buy (McMakin/Fletcher),
    6, 7, 9, 219
    clients, landing success
        (elements), 44
HRIS solutions, 34
HubSpot, 199, 207
Huron, 116, 210

I
IBM, 113, 155, 210–211
Ideas, importance, 171
Implicit trust, 46, 81
Implied trust, advantage, 102
Incent good work, 157
    alignment, improvement, 161–162
    bottom-of-the-funnel
        measurements, 161
    collaboration credit, 161
    commissionable activities, 159–160
    double counting, 160
    top-of-the-funnel metrics, 161
Incentives
    alignment, 168
    problems, 55
    systems, robustness (importance),
        216
Incentive system, repair, 157
Incumbent relationship, breakthrough
        (difficulty), 50
Individual outcomes, importance
        (understanding), 106
Industries
    opportunities, 114
    trends, search, 110
Influencer, potential, 142–143
Information
    asymmetries, 11
    sharing, challenges, 206
Innovate (Diamond of Opportunity
        component), 28, 37–39
    avoidance, 88
    geographies, 92
    inclusion, 115
    PIE skills, innovation, 96
    process, 67
    REACH, contrast, 95
    work, 123
Innovation, importance, 222
In-person introductions, 153
Insider status, leveraging, 102
Insight, power, 217

Integreon, 214–215
Intelligence, search, 167–168
intentional training, avoidance, 20
Interpersonal dynamics, 64
Introductions, types, 151–153

J
Jacobs Engineering, 155
Jones, Ned, 150–151
Jordan, Nichole, 100, 213
Joslin, Murry, 214–215
Just-in-time information, providing, 27

K
Kanter, Harvey, 69
Kele Inc., 50, 69, 117
Key account managers, 53
Key relationship partners, 53
Kickoff meeting, 127
Kieffaber, Ann, 155, 210
Knowledge, challenge, 43
"Know Your Strengths"
        (Buckingham), 87
KPMG, 97, 101, 109, 160
Krueger, Susie, 26–27
    EVOLVE appearance, 36–37
    EXPAND appearance, 31
    EXTEND appearance, 32–33
    Innovate appearance, 38–39
    MORE appearance, 30
    REACH appearance, 34–35
    work, expansion (opportunities), 96

L
Lagniappe (Level III), 124–125
    usage, 128
    value, 154
Lateral hire, PIE problems, 94
Law of Reciprocity, 177
Leadership
    dashboard/direction, 160
Leadership client tour, 154
Leadership Womble program, 20

Lead partners, 53
LeSage, Jeff, 109, 160
Level I (good work), 123
Level II (excellent work), 123–124
Level III (Lagniappe), 124–125
Leveling up, 117, 146
    risk, 180
Level IV (The Pivot), 126
Lincoln, Abraham (Gettysburg
        address), 169–170
LinkedIn, importance, 149
Listening, 165, 203–204
    bragging, 174
    chief listening officer, 202–203
    decision, 206
    effectiveness, 103–104
    exercise, 165
    guidelines, 167–168
    importance, 54
Loss analysis, conducting, 107
Lubowe, Dave, 103, 110, 114, 140

M
Maersk, 72–73
Market
    characteristics, knowledge, 54
    effort, organization, 202
    insight, 132, 133
Marketing
    analytics, firm-wide scrutiny, 48
    leads, impact, 201
    sales/marketing, failure (reasons),
        200–202
Marks, hitting, 127
Matthews, Sarah, 147
MAXIMUS, 53
McCarty, Steve, 97
McGrath, Rita, 139
McLaughlin, Michael, 143, 174
Measurements, alternatives, 158–159
Mercer, Charlie, 17
Mergers and acquisitions, 114
    growth, 93

Mergers and acquisitions, impact, 52–53

Metrics
defining, 129
scoping, 134

Minders, 18–19

Minto, Barbara, 46

Mirro, Chris, 53

MORE (Diamond of Opportunity component), 27–30
appearance, 29–30
contract growth, 96
earning, 195
opportunities, 88
Salesforce work, investment, 131
work, 54, 123, 125
opportunities, 178

Mutually exclusive collectively exhaustive (MECE), 45–46

N

Networks
interaction, 58–59
nodes, equivalence, 181
opportunity network, 60
serving, challenge, 57
weakness, 182

New talent (colleague type), 156

New work, 53
bringing, 21
challenges, 56, 65, 70, 82
winning, 6

Niche, defining, 98–99

Non-RFP work, source, 23

Noonan, Peggy, 171

Nord, John, 24

Note-taking, importance, 145

O

Office 365, 212

On Speaking Well (Noonan), 171

Operating model, perspective, 91

Opinion, valuation/usefulness, 145

Opportunity management, importance, 210–211

Opportunity network, 60
capability network, interaction, 62

Organic growth, 92–93

Organizations
challenge, 52
matrix/structure, impact, 91–92
practice leads, knowledge (absence), 52–53
transformation project, 132

Organon (Aristotle), 46

Other-centered focus, 117

Outcomes, measurement, 158

Outgroup homogeneity bias, 150–151

Outsource marketing, expert service provision, 198

P

Palmer, Mike, 138

Pareto Principle, 21

Parson Brinckerhoff, 82

Partners
business partners, awareness (importance), 205
CFOs, relationship (example), 166
interaction, quality (variation), 56
opportunities, 21
referral, risk, 55–56
shift, 117, 146

Partnership Executive Program (PEP), 155

Patience, importance, 147

Payoff, characteristics, 182–183

Peace, 221, 222

Peer (colleague type), 155–156

Peers
conversations, usage, 190
exchange session, example, 195
exchanges, value, 194
group conversations, facilitation, 75
meeting, 187–189

performance, 162
power, 187
Perficient, 129
Perkins Coie, 122, 140, 163
Personal brand, 97–98
Personal ties, strength (importance),
181
Phone
exchanges, 194
introductions, 152–153
Pink, Daniel, 1632
Pivot, The (Level IV), 126
Playbook, personalization, 109
Political dynamics, understanding, 106
Politics, 64
Post-Panamex ships, 72
Power-law relationship, 22
Practice leads
communication, 194
driving, incentive systems
(failure), 55
impact, 201
PricewaterhouseCoopers (PwC),
Robotic Process Automation
investment, 88
Prieto, Bob, 82
Problem, solutions, 219–220
statement, 135
Product
communication, CMO role, 199
definition, absence, 87–88
delivery, ensuring, 131
firms, marketing/sales roles,
199–200
intel, improvement, 213
Professional services, new work
(winning), 6
Profitable Ideas Exchange (PIE), 6
founding, 189
PIE high, 191
PIE Pack, 156
research projects, 34
skills, leveraging, 906

usage, 8
usefulness, 9
Project
credit, zero-sum game, 62
manager, relationship, 146
risk, 132
scope, 167
Prospect (contact), senior consultants
(time expenditure), 55
Prosperity, sharing, 222
Protiviti, 205
Provider, partner shift, 117, 146
Public policy, coverage, 17

Q
Quality of earnings (Q-of-E) calls, 29
Quality of work, problems, 129
Quality, variation, 56
Quattrone, George, 150–151
Questions
effectiveness, 149
hard questions, asking, 148–149
quality, 143

R
REACH (Diamond of Opportunity
component), 28, 33–35, 172
capability reach, expansion, 115–117
geographies, 92
Innovate, contrast, 95
new buyer contact, 96
organically grown firms, success, 93
work, 196
Reciprocity
identification, 180–181
law, 177
Referrals
buyer internalization, 62
improvement, 213
myth, 62–64
partner referral risk, 55–56
production, 133–134
Regan, Dennis, 176–177

Relationship
 bruising, absence, 191
 characteristic, 179–181
 development, 132, 133
Reorganizations, impact, 91
Request for proposal (RFP)
 non-RFP work, source, 23
 preparation, 107
 pre-RFP collaboration, 23
Return on investment (ROI), 133
 claim, inclusion, 136
 performance, record, 9
Revenues, projections, 111
Ringlemann Effect, 78
Ringlemann, Max, 77–78
Risk
 concentration risk, 65
 partner referral risk, 55–56
 perception, 63
 reduction, farming (impact), 25
Robert E. Nolan & Company, 142
Robotic Process Automation (RPA),
  144, 160, 212
 harnessing, 73
 PwC investment, 88
Rock star (colleague type), 154, 180
Routers, power, 197, 204–205
Roy, Chris, 212–213

S
Sales
 definition, 11
 force, creation, 201–202
 funnel, 211
 manipulation, avoidance, 6
Sales and marketing (S&M)
 effort, 203–204
 failure, reasons, 200–202
Salesforce, 204, 207
 installation/usage, 129, 131
Salespeople, negative association, 11
SAP Hana, installation/integration, 38
SAP SuccessFactors, 132

Sarbanes Oxley compliance work, 38
Scale
 advantage, 73
 buying power, impact, 74
 challenge, 71
 diseconomies of scale, 74–75, 121
 economies of scale, 72–73
 technology, impact, 73
 time (high-dollar work), 73–74
Scope creep, 125
 allowance, 116
Scoping, care, 167
Segil, Cavin, 179–180
Self-knowledge, 87, 100, 116
 time, investment, 139–140
Self-talk, problems, 54
Selling
 language, differences, 44
 services, 155
Services. See Expert services
 ancillary services, limiting, 116
 definition, absence, 87–88
 employee delivery, 75
 leveraging, complexity, 114
 matrix, opportunities, 114
 offering, interest, 44
 service lines, usage, 92
 usage, 136–137
Seven2, 131
SHELIE, 126–128
Shill, Walt, 1, 11, 55, 68, 97, 104–105
 collaboration penalty, 161
 gainsharing, 215–216
 project scope, 167
 router, 204
 team delivery, quality, 124
Silos
 breakout, 69
 information sharing, challenges, 206
 term, usage, 63–64
Silver, Cole, 20, 210
Size, impact, 88–90
Small Business Administration, 198

Smith, Laura, 113
Social exchange theory, 182
Social interaction, importance, 141
Social loafing principle, 78
Social media, investment, 133–134
Soft information, usage (advantage), 102
Solan, Jim, 154–155
Spears, Stephen, 132
Speeches, content, 171
Sponsored peer-exchange discus-
        sions, usage, 44
Spot bonus, impact, 62
Statements of work (SOWs)
    basis, 125
    examination, 127
    expansion, 23
    metrics, scoping, 134
State Street Bank and Trust, 121
Stevens, Christopher, 23, 54, 69, 171,
        174, 178
    storytelling, importance, 214
Stockamp & Associates, 18
Storytelling, 169
    boutique firm advantage, 89
    bragging, 174
    drive, 171
    importance, 214
    improvement, 213–214
    lagniappe, impact, 125
Structure, organizational impact, 91–92
Subject-experts, meeting
        (requirement), 160
Subject matter expert (SME), meeting,
        38, 188, 196
Success, metrics, 162
Sullivan, Dennis, 142
Sunderman, Matt, 124
Sunk costs, 199
Supply chain
    currency-exchange-rate risk,
        hedging, 220
    optimization, 1
Syllogism, example, 45

T
Team
    composition, 94–97
    excellent work, delivery
        (knowledge), 124
    leading, 32
    leveraging, 150
    members, addition (impact), 96–97
    pack, perspective, 156
Technology
    attention/understanding, 106–107
    big firm advantage, 90
    ecosystem, integration, 107
    enablement, EXPAND, 131
    impact, 220
    power, 207, 219
Third-party follow-up, 191–192
Thomson Reuters, 26–39, 68, 96
    Krueger partnership, growth
        (acceleration), 96–97
    professionals, collection, 27–29
Timmermans, Kris, 99, 115, 162
Top-of-the-funnel metrics, 161
To Sell Is Human (Pink), 163
Trust, 30, 167
    ability, 80
    building, 6, 114, 173, 189–190, 198
    casualty, 157
    client trust, 45, 47, 50–51
    continuum, 190
    cultivation/development, 157,
        172, 194, 196
        social interaction, usage, 141
    delivery, 8
    disappearance, 130
    earning, 194
    expert development, 106
    implicit trust, 46, 81
    implied trust, advantage, 102
    investment, 140
    leveraging, 96
    scaling, 79–81, 140, 209
    transfer, difficulty, 50

Trusted expert, buyer engagement, 68
Trusted relationship, creation, 108
Twain, Mark, 124

U
UHY, 97
Ulrich, Mark, 76–77
Understanding, 48, 167
  building, 198
  client understanding, 47
Upsell, process, 13
Upwork, 218

V
Value
  addition, importance, 192–193
  creation, balance, 161–162
  delivery, 26
  drivers, identification, 182
  rescue, 205–206
VanDyken, Carrie, 100
Veenhuizen, Esther, 205
Vertical silos, 63–64
Vetting, importance, 94
Videoconference introductions,
    152–153
Virtual peer-exchange group,
    building, 36
Voice-to-text data collection,
    usage, 212

W
Wallace, Scott, 11, 122, 140,
    163, 189–190
Weas, Andy, 129–131

Williams, Will, 101
Wilson Allen, 68
Wilson, Bruce, 68
Wins, enthusiasm, 127
Wipfli, 93
Womble Bond Dickinson, 20
Work. *See* Good work; Incent good
    work; New work
  bid, strategic input (occurrence),
    126
  capability, 35
  client knowledge, 27
  control, 122–123
  expansion, opportunities, 96
  extension (EXTEND), 67–68
  global work, localized expertise
    (impact), 90
  growth, 8–9, 219
  intensity, 76–77
  internal history, 27
  mediocrity, 1221
  product, business development
    (relationship), 122
  quality
    client knowledge, 50
    knowledge, 30
  reaching (REACH), 68
  testing, 116
Workplace happiness, importance, 94
World, smarter/smaller goal,
    220–222
Wow
  deconstruction, 123–126
  process, 126–128
  service, usage, 136–137